A TRAILS BOOKS GUIDE

BIKING WISCONSIN

50 GREAT ROAD AND TRAIL RIDES

STEVE JOHNSON

©2004 Steve Johnson

Library of Congress Control Number: 2003099013
ISBN: 1-931599-34-3

Editor: Stan Stoga
Photos: The following courtesy of the Wisconsin Department of Tourism: pages 1, 4, 88, 96,
R. J. and Linda Miller; 22, 44, 62, 72, 104, Gary Knowles; 66, Donald S. Abrams; 28,
Doug Alft; 80, Jim Bach; 68, Suzette Buhr; 2, John Cronin; 8, 50, Don Davenport; 12,
Bonnie Gruber; 24, Philip G. Olson; 3, Robert Queen; 58, Phil Van Valkenberg.
All others by Steve Johnson.
Cover Designer: Kathie Campbell
Cover Photo: R. J. and Linda Miller

Printed in the United States of America.

09 08 07 06 05 04   6 5 4 3 2 1

Trails Books, a division of Trails Media Group, Inc.
P.O. Box 317   •   Black Earth, WI 53515
(800) 236-8088   •   e-mail: books@wistrails.com
www.trailsbooks.com

This book is dedicated to the memory of Greg Marr.

You touched us all, and in the quietness of our outdoors—the dip of
a paddle, the whisper of a ski, the stroke of a pedal—we'll stop and listen, and
always remember.

CONTENTS

PREFACE

And the end of all our exploring will be to arrive where we started
and know the place for the first time.

—T. S. Eliot

I'm sitting on the porch watching the evening sky blush with orange-red hues only a summer sunset can compose. My bike is leaning gently against the nearby railing. Out of habit—or simply because I can't stop doing it—my gaze drifts over the bike's smooth curves and strong lines. I flew with her free spirit over many miles this summer, and we've become the best of friends. I smile and ponder the many miles we spent together over the summer.

I think I was somewhere near Mount Horeb when I was taken for a ride. My bike was leading me into a dense wood on a road so smooth it didn't seem real. We floated along the pavement like a cool fall breeze whispering through the trees. Right then and there I thought I had found the best ride in Wisconsin. Well, I lost track of the number of times over the past season when I declared I had found my favorite ride. How hard can it be, I thought. Surely those trips through the state's deep North Woods could not be bested. How about the many rides on Rustic Roads that cruised through fragrant forests one minute, rich farmland the next. And what to make of all those incredible roller-coaster rides in the magical Coulee Country?

This debate followed me around almost as soon as I began scouting the state for this book. It gave me a chance to see—to touch—parts of Wisconsin I'd never been to. My roots run deep in the northwest lakes and forests; other regions I had visited only briefly or through maps and photos. Picking one favorite was too much for me. But I did find many places that gave me a boundless enthusiasm for the state's biking opportunities.

Cyclists of all types and skill levels need look no further than Wisconsin to find their own two-wheeled Eden. This is a state with a special blend of unspoiled scenery and friendly towns. Here you can pedal a Great Lakes shore-to-shore tour, cruise big-city trails sans traffic, roll through hill and dale in farm country, or attempt to tame hills so steep you might question your choice of sports. Wisconsin is rich in historical firsts, as well, and is home to many towns with extended titles. Baraboo is the hometown of the Ringling Brothers Circus. The nation's first kindergarten—a circus of its own—was established in Watertown. Sheboygan is the bratwurst capital of the world. Chippewa Falls is the proud producer of over 250,000 barrels of Leinenkugel's beer annually. Wisconsin is also home to the first ice cream sundae and is the number-one cheese producer in the country.

There are apple orchards, fields of corn and wheat, over a thousand miles of shoreline akin to an ocean's, and even a few remote stands of noble, old-growth forest. Best of all, cyclists can raise a glass (of milk) to the dairy farmers of the olden days. Thanks to them, and the need to get their goods to market each day, a reliable system of roads was built—roads that happen to be perfect for bikes. These are narrow, quiet, byways with little vehicle traffic, winding through Wisconsin's most beautiful locales. I like to say they built these roads *on* the land, following its direction, not that of a blueprint. Hills weren't flattened, curves weren't straightened, and I've never ridden such silky-smooth tarmac. This is truly a bike-friendly state, even in big cities like Milwaukee, Madison, or Green Bay. In those towns you can find long miles of off-road bike paths, in addition to fun rides on city streets, all the while being in close proximity to diversions like historic sites, parks, and ice cream shops. Scattered throughout the state is a large selection of rail trails, nice and flat and just right for an easy cruise or an extended trip. Wisconsin is the nation's leader in rail trails, with over 1,100 miles of former railroad beds converted to bike trails to choose from. But my favorites are the roads. Pick almost any road—it will most likely be made to order for a perfect day of riding.

But where to go for that ride? If you are new to an area, how do you find out about the trails that others consider the most rideable and scenic? If you're a long-time local, how do you avoid the customary pilgrimage to the same tired routes week after week? If only there were a way to find new and challenging terrain in areas that are bike-friendly. Or to find terrain on which you can just roll along and enjoy the sights when you're not in the mood for a lengthy and taxing trek.

Welcome to *Biking Wisconsin*. This book presents 50 rides ranging from easy spins on flat rail trails to cruises on smooth, curvy forest roads to brutally steep hill climbs that make your legs beg for mercy. My selection of rides followed a wayward path, like a hunting dog's footprints on a layer of newly fallen snow. This book will take you on a tour of the entire state, starting from the bluffs of Maiden Rock along the Mississippi River. We'll travel through the forestland and visit the splendid sights of Door County. Then it's southbound along Lake Michigan to Milwaukee. We'll explore rolling farmland, stop in Little Switzerland, and finish off with several gorgeous tours in western Wisconsin's Coulee Country.

Ride descriptions in *Biking Wisconsin* are written in an easy-to-read narrative format, which provides brief information on distance, surface conditions, level of difficulty, trailhead location, and other vital statistics. A description of the full ride, including what to expect along the way, should help you select which rides are best for you before starting out. Remember, landmarks and sights I encountered during my trips might have changed, or be gone altogether, when you ride here. Always refer to a good map.

I relied heavily on the excellent map set provided by the Wisconsin Department of Transportation and the Bicycle Federation of Wisconsin. Get a set today. Many park-brochure maps work well, as do some USGS topographic maps. Use the one that works best for you, but be sure to include some form of map in your on-ride gear, especially on the more remote rides where help may be a long time coming.

That said, I hope you enjoy reading and using this book as much as I had writing it. I'm glad I had the opportunity to share my experiences with you. Grab your bike, choose a route, and hit the road.

I'm going to celebrate the completion of this project by going for a ride. No worries about mileage and terrain, history and trailheads. I'm just going to ride. Hope to see you out there.

THANK YOU

Those two words fall far short of expressing the sincere gratitude I have for all the people who helped see this project through. I would be a wretched mess without the support of many people over the last year and a half.

Many thanks to state park and state forest staff all over Wisconsin for hints on where to ride and for providing a good piece of ground to sleep on. Bike shops throughout the state generously helped scope out the best routes and sometimes even gave away a secret loop. Phil Van Valkenberg, Wisconsin's big hitter for the sport, and the late Greg Marr, to whom this book is dedicated, offered their favorite rides and provided inspiration.

Special thanks go to the helpful tourist information staff in Three Lakes for guiding me through the woods. Thanks to the friendly parking lot attendant in Milwaukee for directions to the Oak Leaf Trail. And I can still taste that delectable strawberry smoothie at the trailside café in New Glarus.

Much appreciation goes to Stan Stoga, Mike Martin, Erika Reise, and the rest at Trails Books for their enthusiasm and patience.

To my young son, Jack, thanks for running into my office, crawling over maps, pulling papers off the desk, and hitting the *off* button on the computer (man, am I glad I saved that stuff). Thanks for lifting my spirits with your jolly, unfettered giggles and telling me all about your day in that small-fry gibberish I love so much.

My wife, Michelle, deserves sainthood for infinite patience and support in the midst of many days away from home and a backlog of chores. I enjoyed too many gorgeous views and quiet sunsets without you. Next time I hope you'll come with me. We've got a groovy kind of love.

Before we get into the rides themselves, here's a little background information about Wisconsin and some tips about the diverse conditions it can throw at bicyclists. I hope the information will deepen your appreciation of this richly endowed state and of the rides you'll find yourself enjoying throughout its length and breadth.

ABOUT WISCONSIN

Wisconsin is named after the Wisconsin River; the river's name was derived from an Ojibwe term thought to mean "gathering of the waters" or "place of the beaver." But people seem to be most familiar with the state's nickname, the Badger State. Funny thing is, the badgers in question refer not to the four-legged kind, but to the miners who burrowed into the hills in search of lead in the early 1800s. And Wisconsin's famous moniker, America's Dairyland, is well deserved: more than two billion pounds of cheese and 11 metric tons of milk are produced here every year.

The Handiwork of Glaciers

Because the rides in this book will create an intimate bond between you and the Wisconsin terrain, let's take a minute to see how some of those twists and turns and hills and valleys got that way. Besides, when you're laboring up a steep hill, you can alleviate some of the pain by realizing that you may well be on a pile of debris that glaciers created tens of thousands of years ago.

Although they worked awfully slow, Wisconsin's crew of glaciers left us with spectacular surroundings for riding a bicycle. Creeping across the state, turning tail and retreating, then taking another run at it, these massive ice sheets left behind eskers, moraines, kettles, and frost pockets that dot much of the state today. The last great movement of ice, the 400-foot-thick Wisconsin Glacier, covered about half the state but skipped the southwest corner. Now known as the Driftless Area (and Coulee Country), the region's steep hills and winding valleys are a dream come true for two-wheeled excursions. Some areas of the state had much closer contact with the ice; head to the south-central and southeast sections to find undulating, fertile farmland and the striking Kettle Moraine, which boasts rugged glacial terrain famous the world over.

While glaciers indeed put a stamp of dramatic scenery on some areas, their efforts are also testament to Wisconsin's geologic diversity. The Superior Upland makes up much of the north, heavy on glacial terrain with prominent moraines, hundreds of lakes, and rounded hills. The northern reaches are also thick with forestland, displayed with much grandeur in places like the Chequamegon and Nicolet National Forests. Timm's Hill, the highest point in the state at 1,952 feet, is in this region. Altitude sickness probably won't get to you, but Wisconsin's hills will still test your limits.

The Till Plains area, south and west of the Superior Upland, is largely level to gently rolling, with some flat plains that were covered long, long ago by Lake Wisconsin. An exception to the plains landscape is the scenic Dells Gorge of the Wisconsin River.

Southwest Wisconsin boasts the Driftless Area. Glacial deposits are largely absent here, and the results are deep valleys, upwards of 600 feet, and rugged beauty. This is truly one of the state's most breathtaking areas. It's gorgeous to look at, to be sure, and riding a bike up and down these steep valley roads will have you begging for more oxygen.

Most of the eastern half of Wisconsin lies in the Eastern Great Lakes Lowlands. This area's lightly rolling plains are stocked with first-rate soils that make this the best agricultural land in the state. Of special note in the region are the scenic Kettle Moraine and the state forest of the same name, a dramatic collection of glacial topography not to be missed.

Water Everywhere

Wisconsin is loaded with a healthy supply of fresh water—both the placid and flowing kinds. Inland lakes number between 10,000 and 15,000, depending on whom you ask, and that's not counting the countless little ponds and wetlands. Many of these lakes are the products of glaciers, and often their waters are see-all-the-way-to-the-bottom clear. A majority of our lakes are up north, and two of the biggest are Lake Winnebago and Lake Petenwell. Of course, the granddaddy of them all is Lake Superior, but the term *lake* is hardly a suitable title. Call it an inland sea—the largest of its kind on the planet—and it's colder and deeper and meaner than all the rest.

Rolling through idyllic Wisconsin countryside.

Bikers bird-watching at the Trempealeau National Wildlife Refuge north of Trempealeau.

Don't forget about the rivers—big ones and little ones, deep ones and shallow ones. Wisconsin's major watersheds are generally defined by the south-flowing Wisconsin River, which directs the state's largest rivers east and west. The Menominee, Peshtigo, Wolf, and Fox Rivers flow east and northeast into Lake Michigan, while to the west the Chippewa, Flambeau, Black, Wisconsin, Namekagon, and St. Croix Rivers make their way to the Mississippi.

It's So Green

We are fortunate here in Wisconsin to have regular rainfall that gives rise to an ample supply of foliage. Although today there is an appallingly low percentage of the majestic pine forests that once covered the state, pockets of old-growth hold on, much of it on protected land; the Chequamegon National Forest, for example, makes up some of the 43 percent of Wisconsin that is forested land area. The northern part of the state is particularly abundant with pine, birch, and poplar trees. Menominee County, home to the Menominee nation, contains significant old-growth forest. The area is known worldwide for its enlightened logging practices.

Dense blankets of ferns and other groundcover, along with second-story undergrowth, add to the richness of the North Woods. Large-scale pulpwood and lumber operations make use of this area, but it is also prime recreational land, attracting mountain bikers, hikers, cross-country skiers, snowmobilers, and hunters. Farther south, broadleaf deciduous forests of maple, oak, hickory, basswood, and other varieties are more common, but much of the original landscape has been cleared for agriculture. Mixed with this farmland are rolling prairies with myriad varieties of wildflowers (the wood violet is the state flower) and a number of areas enjoying restoration to their native state from days gone by.

Wildlife

Wisconsin's ample supply of flora provides ideal room and board for all kinds of creatures. These include the noble bald eagle, black bear, white-tailed deer, and timber wolf. Deer are prevalent and commonly seen statewide—look for them on rides along quiet back roads. Eagles can be seen along river bluffs and lakeshores, especially during winter. Several species of hawks and owls also grace the skies. Bears are seldom sighted and wolves even less. Spotting either (from a safe distance) is a real treat; consider yourself very fortunate if you do.

In addition to these, you might also spot beavers, woodchucks, foxes, lynx, coyotes, pine martens, mink, and river otters. And don't forget the badger, our state animal and adopted mascot of the University of Wisconsin–Madison. Closer to the ground are leopard frogs, toads, salamanders, snakes, squirrels, and chipmunks. Our hardwood forests are favorite haunts of ruffed grouse and wild turkey. Numerous songbirds are found throughout the state: chickadees, orioles, grosbeaks, wrens, swallows, and more. Look in wetlands for ducks, swans, geese, herons, and the figurehead of the North, the beloved loon. In the lakes and streams are some big and formidable fish, the most famous being the stalwart muskellunge, which can easily tip the scales at 40 pounds. Other denizens of the deep include walleye, trout, sunfish, perch, bass, and dozens of members of the minnow family.

The People

Long before the introduction of European culture into the area that later became Wisconsin, prehistoric Indians arrived and prospered here. The first were mound builders, living along the bluffs of Lake Michigan and on the inland prairies. Later, new groups established themselves throughout the area. The Chippewa claimed much of the northern forestland, while the Menominee generally stayed east, with the Winnebago and Sioux to the south.

Beginning in the early nineteenth century, Wisconsin's population was transformed into a rich ethnic stew by the influx of immigrants from many parts of the world. At first, the ingredients included a large helping of Norwegians, Swedes, and Germans, with a good measure of Poles, Irish, Italians, and African-Americans. More recently, Hispanic-Americans, especially those of Mexican heritage, and Hmong from Laos have contributed to the state's ethnic diversity. Many of the early immigrants made their way here to work in big cities like Milwaukee, to farm the rich land, or work in the logging industry. Although times have changed, their modern counterparts still come for the jobs, of course. But they also are attracted by Wisconsin's reputation for tolerance, for welcoming outsiders and making them feel at home.

Along with their work ethic, many newcomers brought with them an affinity for nature, a trait that shows in our present-day craving for outdoor adventure. Wisconsinites are a hardy breed, and Wisconsin's outdoors are the stuff of legend. Camping, canoeing, hunting and fishing, and boating are all popular pursuits before the snow flies. There isn't much of a drop-off in outdoor activity when winter arrives, either. Downhill and cross-country skiing, snowmobiling, ice fishing, and sledding are some of the mainstays of our free time in the colder months. Whatever the season, Wisconsin's spirit is alive in its people and its small towns. Friendly waves and smiles are the norm, and there is always an interesting tale to hear at the local family-owned restaurant or tavern.

BIKING IN WISCONSIN

How Long Is the Season?

The answer to that depends on your dedication (or sanity). Wisconsin's weather spans a wide range of extremes. The weather can be unbearably hot or cold enough to freeze your thoughts. Generally, the best riding time is May through October. Spring breathes new life into the land and is a refreshingly unpredictable time to ride. The weather can be in the 60s one day and leave frost on your handlebars the next. Some springs, roads are sloppy from the melting winter mess and seem to take forever to get clean and dry enough for safe and pleasant biking.

In the summer, average high temperatures hover around 80. Many days, however, are laced with stifling humidity, days when your strength drips off the end of your nose, streams down your legs in salty rivulets, and drops onto the road in a puddle of withering confidence. But a little suffering makes you a better rider, right? Even so, hydrate often to ward off heat stroke—drink *before* you're thirsty. When the temperature climbs into the 90s, and especially when it cracks the hundred-degree mark (a rare but not unheard-of occurrence), stop and rest. If you're lucky enough to be near one of Wisconsin's thousands of lakes, take advantage of its cool, clear waters.

Fall is tough to beat for ideal biking conditions. Daytime highs drop to the 60s and even 50s, conditions are usually dry, and the bugs leave with the summer crowds. The forests come alive in fiery autumn dress around mid-September and fly their brilliant colors into late October. Every trip out feels like riding through a postcard. It's a magical time indeed, especially in the northern part of the state.

When winter hits, most of us tuck the bike away and move on to alternate athletic endeavors. Some brave souls just keep on riding. Snow has been known to linger into May, and some years will surprise us with a big storm in late October. They say the average temperature for January is around 17 degrees, but it can stray well off that number—usually downward. Don't be surprised to see the mercury plummet to 40 below zero, and bitter wind chills can make it feel like 50, 60, even 80 below! On those days, stay inside with a good book and a warm fire. But proper equipment, like wider tires, fenders, and lots of warm clothes, can add a couple more months to your pedaling season.

What Can You Expect?

Along with a fidgety thermometer, Wisconsin also supplies cyclists with an assortment of terrain to suit any riding occasion. Many of the routes begin innocently enough on easy flats, then challenge riders with roller-coaster hills or precipitous climbs. Rolling hills and steep, wooded bluffs turn the southwest Coulee Country into a magical land you'll never forget. Heading east, we are treated to challenging rides amid dramatic glacier-carved hills and dales, along with leisurely cruises through idyllic farmland. Riding up north means curvy, quiet roads through noble forests—sometimes flat, sometimes hilly, but always fun. Many of our state parks offer top-notch paved trails and unspoiled scenery. Big cities like Milwaukee and Madison boast many miles of bike paths and on-street routes. Try the 96-mile Oak Leaf Trail in Milwaukee for a marathon tour through historic neighborhoods and shoreline cruising along Lake Michigan.

Wisconsin is truly a diverse place, and that makes for great biking. There are many outstanding areas to ride; included in this book are some of the best. So go

One of the great things about biking—any number can play.

Family fun on the Elroy-Sparta State Trail.

forth and explore—ride along mighty Lake Superior or quiet woodland ponds; visit charming small towns or the bustle of a big city; roam farmland regions or remote wilderness. Wisconsin is best viewed on two wheels.

Preparing to Ride

Certain details of your preparations for an easy spin on a flat forest road will be considerably different than those for an extended tour in steep bluff country. On some of your rides, the terrain can change drastically from one mile to the next. It is important to be ready for those changes before you set out. Put in plenty of miles to achieve a respectable fitness base ahead of time, and know your limits. Don't try for a hundred-mile day with 10,000 feet of climbing if you don't like hills and only recently took your bike out of the garage.

Be sure your trusty steed is in fine shape as well. Short of a complete overhaul, be certain to clean your rims, brakes, shifters, derailleurs, and chain (basically all parts that move) to ensure they are functioning properly and are free of defects. Get into this habit on at least every other ride. Your bike will thank you, and you'll ride faster and happier.

A helmet is essential for safe riding, no matter what some stubborn critics might say. Modern helmets are light and comfortable, and they can save your life and prevent serious injuries. Don't ride without one. Cycling gloves are another indispensable piece of safety equipment. They can save hands from cuts and abrasions during falls, and they dramatically improve grip and comfort on the handlebars. A cycling-specific jersey and shorts will make your day (and your butt) more comfortable.

Always pack or carry at least one full water bottle. On longer rides, don't leave the house without two or three bottles or one of the larger hydration packs, or plan your ride so it passes someplace where potable water is available. A snack such as fruit or energy bars can keep those huge quads cranking for extra hours and prevent the dreaded "bonk," the sudden loss of energy when your body runs out of fuel. Believe me, this is an experience to

be avoided. Dress for the weather; pack a jacket that repels both wind and water in case the skies turn ugly. Don't forget sunglasses and sunscreen (use the sweatproof stuff that won't run into your eyes and mouth).

A basic tool kit or multitool can save you from a long walk home. A tire pump and tube-patch kit are vital and can make the difference between a five-minute pit stop and a disaster. Carry a set of Allen wrenches (or a multitool) for tightening or adjusting parts or repairing midride breakdowns. While I generally carry just the minimum, some folks aren't comfortable unless they bring all their tools. They carry extra weight but are rarely left stranded by mechanical failures.

BIKE-BUYING TIPS

Follow these basic pointers before riding off on a shiny new bike. Get a bike that's right for your type of riding, and make sure it fits you properly. Courtesy of personal trainer Vicki Pierson, here are some quick tips:

Types of Bikes

Road Bikes. They used to be known as 10-speeds; now, road bikes range from 12- to 21-speed. Within this category of bikes are touring, racing, and sport bikes.

Touring Bike. This bike is not built for speed; rather, it's designed to provide comfort for the long haul. A touring bike is an excellent choice for long-distance riding. The drop handlebars provide comfort and good control and allow for multiple hand positions. Twenty-one speeds will take you over any type of incline you'll encounter, and cantilever brakes can stop you even when you're heavily loaded down.

Racing Bike. This bike is built for speed, sporting an aerodynamic, thin, and ultralight frame. A short wheelbase allows the bike to respond to the slightest movements; 12 or 18 gears will get you to, and keep you at, top speed. If you're into winning races, this is the bike for you.

Sport Bike. This bike falls between the touring and racing bikes—not as light as a racing bike but more responsive than the touring bike. The sport bike's drop handlebars provide comfort and control, and the aerodynamic design allows for faster speeds. If you're into taking rides of 10 or more miles while turning up the intensity by adding some speed, this bike can take you there.

The Perfect Fit

Once you know which type of bike you want, make sure the bike you select fits you properly. There are essentially two ways to get a good fit. If you want a *perfect* fit, for about $50 you can have a quality bicycle shop calculate your bike size using a computerized program called the *Fit Kit.* The bike shop staff measures the length of your legs, torso, and arms, then gives you a printout of your measurements and information on which frame height and length best suit your body.

The second-best way to get a good bike fit is to follow these guidelines:

Frame Height. Straddle the bike. You should have one to two inches of clearance between the top bar of the bike and your crotch, three to four inches if you're going to be riding on off-road terrain. If you want to be a little more exact, measure your inseam, straddle the bike, pick it up until the top bar touches your crotch, then measure the distance between the bottom of the tires and the ground.

Frame Length. When you sit on the bike, be sure you can comfortably reach the handlebars. If they are too far away, you won't have adequate control; if they're too close, you'll be uncomfortable and tire easily.

Seat and Handlebar Adjustment. A quality bike shop will make the necessary adjustments for you to fine-tune the fit of the bike. A critical adjustment is seat height. Your knee should have a 25- to 30-degree bend when the ball of your foot is on the pedal at its lowest position. The handlebars should be one inch lower than, or the same height as, the seat. Check to be sure you can comfortably reach the brakes and that the width of the handlebars is approximately the width of your shoulders.

Take a Test Ride. Just like purchasing a car, this is where the rubber meets the road. You should feel comfortable and in control. Your elbows should be relaxed with a slight bend, and squeezing the brake levers should be easy. Slide your rear back off the saddle, stand up on the pedals, flex and round your back, and move your hands to various positions on the handlebars to ensure you can move around on the bike easily while it's in motion.

Accessories

Once you select a bike, you'll want to get some accessories to go with it. Most important is a helmet. You may also want to consider a tire pump, tube-repair kit, pressure gauge, seat pack, water bottle and cage, and a lock. The bicycle shop can help you select and install these on your bike. Depending on how much you spend on your bike, you may be able to convince the salesperson to throw in some of the accessories at no charge.

BIKE SAFETY TIPS

Here are 10 bicycle safety tips from the National Highway Traffic Safety Administration.

1. **Wear your helmet.**
   Never ride without one. Better a broken helmet than a broken head.

2. **Make sure your bike is adjusted properly.**
   Be sure your bike fits you and all of its parts are working the way they should.

3. **Check brakes before riding.**
   Your bike's speed is controlled with its brakes. Make sure they are adjusted and working properly. If a pad is worn, replace it.

4. **See and be seen.**
   Wear clothes that make you more visible—bright colors in daytime and reflective ones at night.

5. **Avoid riding at night.**
   It's dangerous, but many bike commuters ride during dark hours. Equip your bike with front and rear lights if you ride when light is scarce.

6. **Stay alert.**
   Watch for anything in the road that might lead to a crash or make you swerve into traffic.

7. **Go with the flow of traffic.**
   Ride on the right side of the road, in the same direction as other vehicles. Stay as far to the right as safely possible, but allow some room to maneuver, too.

8. **Check for traffic.**
   Always be aware of what's around you. Look ahead, make eye contact with drivers, ride defensively.

9. **Obey traffic laws.**
   Cyclists must follow the same rules as motorists. Obey road signs, especially stop signs, signal your move, and yield to pedestrians.

10. **Wheels should be securely attached.**
    Most late-model bicycles have quick-release levers on wheels for easy on and off. But if you forget to tighten the lever, your wheel might go rolling away without you. Double-check before you leave.

RIDE 1
Fair Maiden

Pepin County

Only a few miles after beginning this ride, we cross into Pepin County, one of the state's most historic and striking areas. Named after the 28-mile-long, 3-mile-wide Lake Pepin on its western border, the county has received rave reviews for over a hundred years from the likes of William Cullen Bryant and Mark Twain. More recently, an editor of the *New York Times* wrote, "This back country has an untouched quality, as if dreaming of early pioneer days, when the wilderness came down to the edge of the fields." The steep hills and valleys that line this western Wisconsin corner are especially wild in Pepin County, with only two small villages along the Mississippi River, Stockholm and Pepin, and not many more as we travel inland. The dramatic river vistas give way to pastoral farmland with old-world churches and hundred-year-old round barns.

Of special historical note is the reconstruction of the 1863 log house where author Laura Ingalls Wilder was born. Pepin County is also the setting for Wilder's celebrated *Little House in the Big Woods*, an account of growing up in the area. The Laura Ingalls Wilder Museum is in the town of Pepin, and there is even a festival each September.

From rugged, river bluffs to quiet, rolling farmland, Pepin County offers plenty of opportunity for outdoor recreation. Cycling, of course, is unforgettable in this scenic country, along with hiking, snowshoeing and skiing, canoeing and kayaking, and hunting and fishing. Rounding it all off is a wide selection of hometown cafés, restaurants, and taverns with fine eats and drinks. Take a look at www.explorewisconsin.com for detailed information.

Location: County highways and bluff roads in and above Maiden Rock and State Highway 35.
Distance: 19.5-mile loop
Pedaling time: 2–2.25 hours.

Surface: Paved roads.
Terrain: Rolling throughout, with two monstrous climbs in the coulees.
Sweat factor: High.
Trailhead: The junction of County S and State Highway 35 in Maiden Rock.

Sometimes, it's the little guys you have to look out for. Such is the case with Maiden Rock, a quiet town in the shadows of 400-foot-high bluffs on the shores of Lake Pepin. About 130 people call this burg home, but a perpetual parade of summer travelers keeps the town on its toes. Events like Summerfest in June and the April and October motorcycle tours draw big crowds, and most every weekend in summer and fall is bustling. Halfway up one of the nearby valleys is a u-pick berry farm, and an apple orchard is perched atop a neighboring bluff. For cyclists, the area is tough to beat for flat-out gorgeous countryside. Narrow, winding valley roads lead to long, steep climbs that give way to wide-open, ridge-top riding. This particular route starts with a cruise along the Great River Road, then explores a secluded valley road before a mile-long climb takes us to the tops of these bluffs. Lots more ups and downs are the order of the day on this ride.

Before we leave Maiden Rock, it's worth noting the story behind its intriguing name. According to Dakota legend, a young woman named We-no-nah was distraught over being forced by her father, a tribal chief, into a marriage with a brave she didn't love. She was so opposed to her father's plans, and to be absolutely sure the union would not take place, she jumped from atop a nearby 400-foot-high bluff. Maiden Rock was named in honor of the tragic event.

From the heart of town, we follow Highway 35, the Great River Road, south along Lake Pepin. We are treated straight away to gorgeous views of high bluffs next to the road on the left and of the lake and Minnesota's rugged border to the west. There is a nice hill that glides down to a left turn at County AA at 1.5 miles. This is a beautiful ride through lowland woods along Pine Creek. If you're lucky enough to begin your ride early in the morning, you'll be in the midst of steep bluffs rising skyward and veils of fog drifting about in early morning sun. It feels as if we're riding on some forgotten path from days long gone by.

We pass Rustic Road 51, (a gravel road also known as 20th Street) at 2.1 miles, and our ride rapidly becomes a bit more challenging as the road curves south and becomes County E. It slopes upward here, curving into a heavily wooded coulee, and continues to climb for an entire mile. It's a tough grind all the way to the top, but the scenery is exquisite and helps take your mind off the hurt in your legs.

At the top of the ridge, the road continues south past cornfields and farms, and at 4.7 miles, Maiden Rock Apple orchard appears. This young orchard prides itself on producing high-quality, environmentally friendly apples. Stop in for a taste, along with apple cider and pies, caramel apples, pumpkins, hayrides, and picnics. Lots of homemade food and gifts—of apple origin and more—can be bought at the orchard's charming country store down the road in Stockholm, The Good Apple (www.thegoodapple.com).

One mile later we take a hard left and begin a long descent. This hill is steeper than the first one and nearly as long, so use caution and control your speed—50 mph is easily attainable. Not only that, but there is a stop sign at the bottom at the junction with County J (6.3 miles).

A right turn here leads down to the Mississippi River and Highway 35 at the town of Stockholm. We'll go left and immediately begin to climb again. Here is another uphill mile that tests your legs (and spirit). Back on the top of the bluff, we follow County J along a rolling, curvy road accented with breathtaking views. Several tidy farmsteads add flavor to the scene on the way to 11.5 miles and the tiny town of Lund, where we turn left on County CC and ride due north. The road is still full of rolling hills, but now it goes in a straight line, passing an old Swedish Methodist church and cemetery at 13.1 miles. County CC eventually curves west and takes us to County S at 17.4 miles. We continue west on County S for a mile and a quarter, then lean downhill and drop down into a coulee for a long descent back into Maiden Rock. This is another hill with a steep descent, so use caution and stay in control to the end of this challenging 19.5-mile loop back at Maiden Rock.

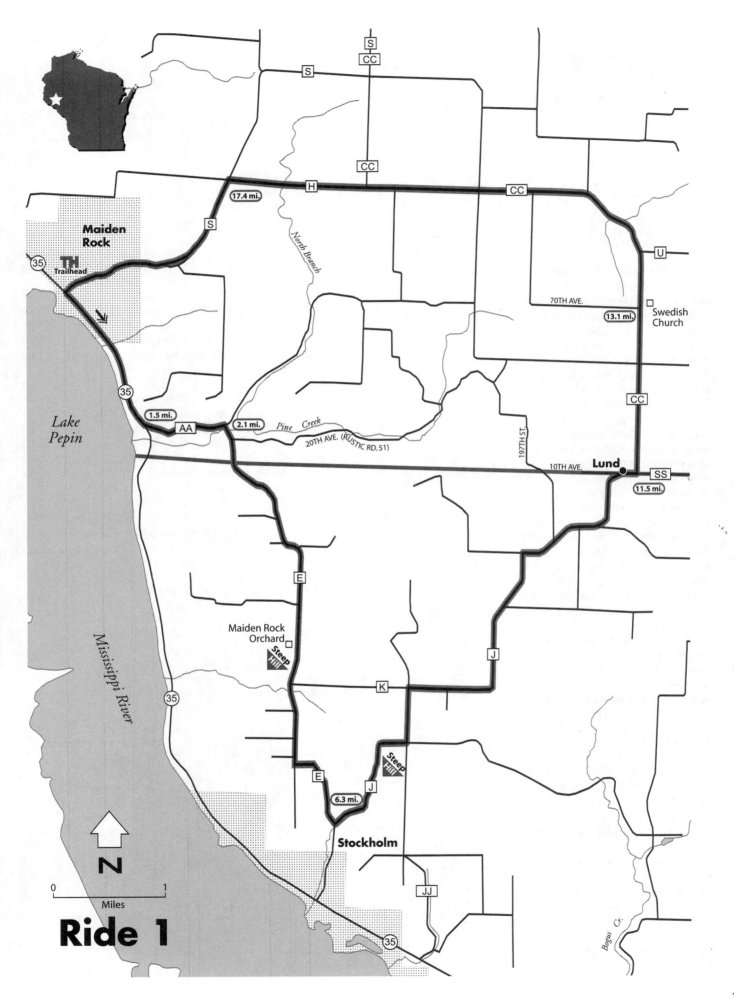

Maiden Rock

TH
Trailhead

35

Lake
Pepin

35

Mississippi River

Maiden Rock
Orchard

Steep
Hill

Steep
Hill

Stockholm

N

0   1
Miles

Ride 1

S
CC

S
CC

S

CC

H

17.4 mi.

S

CC

U

70TH AVE.

13.1 mi.

Swedish
Church

North Branch

Pine Creek

1.5 mi.

AA

2.1 mi.

20TH AVE. (RUSTIC RD. 51)

197TH ST.

CC

10TH AVE.

Lund

SS

11.5 mi.

E

J

K

E

J

6.3 mi.

JJ

Bogus Cr.

35

RIDE 2
Alma Out and Back

Location: County and back roads southeast of Alma.
Distance: 20 miles out and back.
Pedaling time: 2–2.25 hours.
Surface: Paved roads, with one section of gravel.
Terrain: Rolling, with two huge climbs.
Sweat factor: Moderate +.
Trailhead: Lock and Dam 4 parking area on State Highway 35 in Alma.

A Revered Refuge

Just offshore from Alma is the Upper Mississippi River National Wildlife and Fish Refuge, the longest wildlife refuge in the lower 48 states. Extending from the mouth of the Chippewa River north of Alma nearly all the way to Rock Island, Illinois, the refuge was established in 1924 to protect essential bottomland habitat for fish and migratory birds, along with a wide variety of additional species of animals and plants. The importance of this protection increases annually with a steady decline in habitat throughout the Midwest. Over half of Wisconsin's wetlands have been lost, streams are being rerouted to accommodate development, and rare bottomland forests are barely surviving. The refuge displays the rewards that a healthy river valley offers: bald eagles, ducks and geese, swans, sturgeon, and much more.

The refuge is very attractive to human visitors as well. Over three million of them visit each year and pitch in about a *billion* recreational dollars to the area, due in large part to the aforementioned wildlife populations and natural scenic grandeur. Residents from a much earlier time also recognized the richness of this area, and the valley exhibits much historical evidence of ancient Indian tribes and villages, battlegrounds, trading posts, forts, and the first routes of early European explorers.

Although a visit to the refuge and adjacent lands today reveals towns and cities in place of Indian villages and long-distance highways following age-old trade and travel routes, there is still much wildness in the area.

This out-and-back ride near the Mississippi River climbs a couple of huge hills and travels along rolling ridgetop for a quick but challenging trek. Our beginning point, Alma, has lots to offer for such a little town. Ever since 1848, when two Swiss men arrived in the area to cut wood for fuel for the steamboats, the Mississippi has been a big part of the town's personality.

Alma offers several options for food and lodging and is loaded with century-old buildings, like the Gallery House Bed & Breakfast. In fact, most of the town is on the National Register of Historic Places. On the ride, it will be difficult to resist stopping frequently to admire the spectacular views of the river valley below.

This ride leaves Alma at Lock and Dam 4 on the Mississippi River. This is a great place to get up-close views of barges and other boat traffic navigating the nearly 75-year-old lock and dam. It's fascinating to watch a big barge squeeze its bulk into the locks, squirt out the other side, and motor on downriver.

To begin the ride, follow State Highway 35 through Alma's quiet downtown area to the junction with County E at 0.3 mile. The lofty smokestacks of the Dairyland Electric Cooperative stand near the banks of the Mississippi just south of town. After only a short flat surface, County E starts to climb, gently at first, then steeper and longer and tougher all the way to 2.2 miles. Imposing bluffs tower above the road

on the way up, so close you can almost feel them crowding in. We slowly pass Buena Vista City Park, a gift to the city by long-time residents, just below the crest of the hill. The park affords great views of the river valley below and is a fine place to unwind after a ride.

The road levels at the top, and we'll cruise along mostly flat terrain for a couple more miles to a right turn at Blank Hill Road at mile 4.4. This is an enjoyable traffic-free stretch over fun rollers to start. Then we cruise through a cornfield tunnel to 6.8 miles, where the road turns to gravel. Road riding in the dirt is not the most pleasant experience, but this section is very rideable. Ultra-skinny tires will have a difficult time navigating this part of the ride, so come prepared. The gravel drags on for what seems like forever, but it's only 2 miles.

At around mile 8, we start a downhill stretch. Get ready to fly because this is a *2-mile* descent, with some pitches steep enough to send you and your bike into the 40 mph range. We blur past thick woods with beautiful views to the north of high bluffs and expansive farm fields of the Waumandee Valley. Use great caution as we near the bottom; there is a stop sign at the junction with State Highway 88 at mile 10. The squiggly Waumandee Valley is just past the highway, lazing its way toward a rendezvous with the Mississippi. This is our turnaround point, as well. A short break is in order before we take on the huge hill we just came down on.

Overall, the ensuing climb back up isn't as difficult as others in the area. Still, 2 miles of uphill is a bit of a challenge. Back at the top of the ridge, we simply follow our tracks back to Alma. Before descending the final hill, we are treated to gorgeous views of the river valley; then we sail down toward Alma. This is a huge hill, and its speed limit is only 25 mph. We can easily exceed that, but we've got to pull on the reins enough to avoid careening into town or missing the turn and riding into the river. We follow County E through town again to Highway 35 and the trailhead near the river.

The Great River Road (Highway 35) and railroad tracks running through downtown Alma.

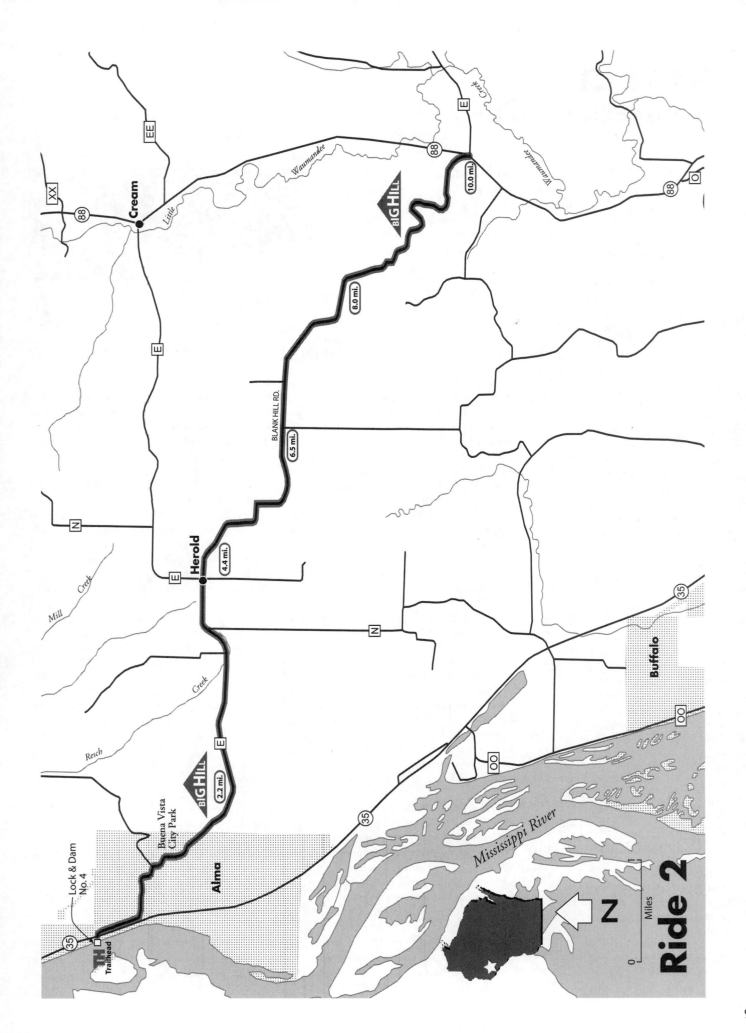

Cream

88
EE
XX
88

Little
Waumandee

88
E

Creek
Waumandee

E
88
O

BIG HILL
10.0 mi.

8.0 mi.

E

BLANK HILL RD.
6.5 mi.

N

Herold
E
4.4 mi.

N

35
Buffalo

Mill
Creek

Creek

OO
OO

35

Resch
E

BIG HILL
2.2 mi.

Buena Vista
City Park

Alma

Mississippi River

Lock & Dam
No. 4

35
TH
Trailhead

N
Miles
0

Ride 2

RIDE 3
Rustic Red Cedar

Location: Southwest of Menomonie on a state trail and country back roads.
Distance: 16.2-mile loop.
Pedaling time: 1.5–1.75 hours.
Surface: Paved roads and packed gravel trail.
Terrain: Flat on trail, rolling on roads with two big climbs.
Sweat factor: Overall, moderate +; low on trail.
Trailhead: The Depot Visitor Center and Red Cedar State Trail access on State Highway 29 west of Menomonie.

The start of the Red Cedar State Trail near Menomonie.

This is a fun trip that combines easy cruising on a scenic state trail with hilly riding on bucolic back roads, including a couple of challenging climbs to keep you honest. Starting and finishing near a fun college town, the route follows a historic rail line, then detours onto one of the state's finest Rustic Roads. We ride through peaceful countryside, hilly and wooded, and tendrils from the main road unfold to hidden valleys and open ridges. Let it fly down the hill halfway through for high-speed thrills, and visit a primeval hideaway tucked in a pocket of the river's limestone banks. After the ride, the shops and cafés of Menomonie (it's home to the campus of the University of Wisconsin–Stout) offer great eats and après-ride activities.

The original railroad freight depot in Menomonie on State Highway 29 has been converted to the Depot Visitor Center, with historical displays and loads of information inside on area attractions, including the highlight of this ride: the Red Cedar State Trail. Trail passes at $3 a day can be purchased here, or at the self-register kiosk outside. An excellent trail map is posted on the kiosk and is printed on the trail brochure. Right next door to the depot is Trailside Sports, which offers bike rentals and guided canoe trips, as well as other outdoor recreational opportunities.

The Red Cedar Trail will have to wait until a bit later. First, we ride west on Highway 29 0.3 mile to County P. Only a short way along is a left at the junction with Rustic Road 89 (also aptly named Paradise Valley Road), which parallels the Red Cedar to our port side. There is a nice little climb to start, taking us to a quiet ridgetop and fields of corn. At 2.2 miles, we reach Devils Punch Bowl, a scientific study area managed by the Wisconsin Farmland Conservancy. Pull your bike over and take a walk down the footpath into the woods. In short order, a fascinating sight is unveiled through the trees: a natural-rock amphitheater ensconced in a jungle of greenery, with a lazy waterfall dribbling into a stream that wanders down to the river. Several distinct natural communities can be seen here, and some rocks from the streambed and adjoining cliffs have been dated to 500 million years ago.

Back on the bike, we pass a few more idyllic farmsteads and river homes, then coast into the tiny town of Irvington at 3.2 miles. Here, at the access point at County D, we hop on the Red Cedar Trail and follow it south.

Great river views greet us straight away, and the smooth, crushed-gravel surface is easy riding, even for skinny tires. We'll roll through some wooded areas, then through open wetlands. It's quiet out here on weekdays, but be prepared to share the wealth on weekends, especially in summer. At 5 miles, a small parking lot appears on our right.

We exit the trail here and continue our trip west on the adjacent road, good old Rustic Road 89, for a short distance. A big hill rises up from the river valley, and at the top we continue straight west on 370th Avenue. (R-89 continues left here to Downsville, home to the Empire in Pine Museum, which has displays and images representing the area's timber-producing past.) The road loops north on a long, gradual climb, then sweeps back south to meet 350th Street. At 7.4 miles, just when the pavement gets really smooth, the road drops out of sight down a monster of a hill. Get ready for a 45 mph descent! Scenic, rolling countryside is the order of the day as we coast all the way to 310th Avenue and take a left along wide-open fields—corn on one side, soybeans on the other. At 9.5 miles, we turn left on 390th Street, riding on a short, flat stretch, then up a short hill, then up again on a longer, more painful hill. Our reward is an even longer descent back to 370th Avenue. We turn right here, heading back toward Menomonie.

The junction with County D arrives at 13 miles. Here we turn right and return to the Red Cedar Trail at the same point we used earlier, this time heading north. This trail originated as the Red Cedar Junction Line in the 1800s to serve the Knapp and Stout Lumber Company, the largest in the world at the time. The company store for their lumber operations still stands on Main Street in Downsville. Abandoned in 1973, the trail was acquired by the Wisconsin Department of Natural Resources, which maintains and operates the trail today.

At 14.8 miles there is an inviting picnic site perched on the riverbank. We cross an authentic railroad-trestle as we near the trailhead and visitor center at 16.2 miles. Riverside Park is a relaxing place to unwind after your ride and is right next door to the trailhead. Fun cafés and shops are just down the road in Menomonie.

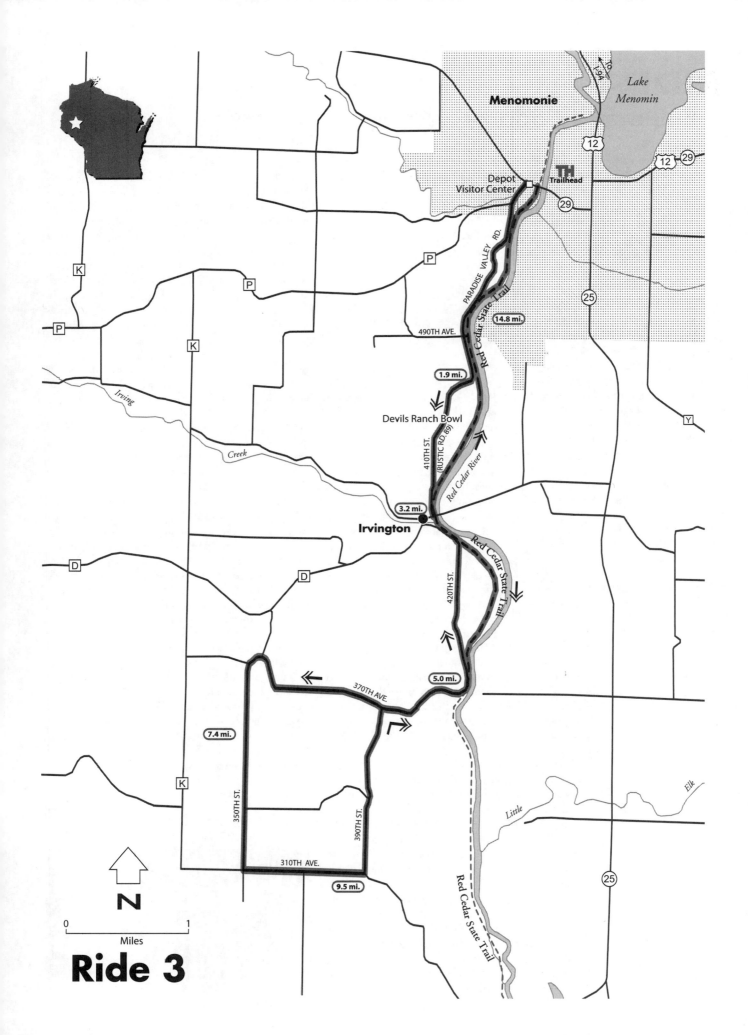

Lake
Menomin

Menomonie

Depot
Visitor Center

TH
Trailhead

PARADISE VALLEY RD.

Red Cedar State Trail

14.8 mi.

490TH AVE.

1.9 mi.

Devils Ranch Bowl

410TH ST.
(RUSTIC RD. 89)

Red Cedar River

3.2 mi.

Irvington

Red Cedar State Trail

420TH ST.

5.0 mi.

370TH AVE.

7.4 mi.

350TH ST.

390TH ST.

310TH AVE.

9.5 mi.

Little

Elk

Red Cedar State Trail

N

0   1
Miles

Ride 3

RIDE 4
Chippewa Country

Location: South of Eau Claire and I-94, on county roads and a state trail.
Distance: 16-mile loop.
Pedaling time: 1.5–1.75 hours.

Surface: Paved roads and paved bike trail.
Terrain: Flat on trail, rolling on roads.
Sweat factor: Moderate.
Trailhead: Start at the access for the Chippewa River State Trail on Jopke Road and State Highway 37, a quarter mile south of I-94.

The Historic Chippewa Valley

In the early 1800s, the Chippewa Valley buzzed with the booming lumber industry. Eau Claire alone had 11 active mills and was a center of activity. Many grand buildings and stately homes were built, and today scores of these are included on the National Register of Historic Places—there are over a dozen in the downtown area alone. The Historic Downtown Walking (or biking) Tour is a great way to see these survivors from days gone by. The Paul Bunyan Logging Camp is a collection of buildings that recalls the area's timber boom. Carson Park boasts the Chippewa Valley Railroad, a fun train for the kids, and the Chippewa Valley Museum, another excellent choice for going back in time. Details on things to do and see in the area are available at www.eau claire-info.com and www.chippewa valley.net

The 23-mile Chippewa River State Trail offers cyclists smooth, paved riding along remote stretches of the river, with access to more miles on the Red Cedar State Trail at the south end and Eau Claire's City Trail on the north side. This ride takes its lead from the Red Cedar loop and combines quiet country roads with a short trip on the trail. There are only two real hills on the loop; the rest of the terrain is gently rolling and then flat on the trail. The roads are mostly traffic-free and take us through a mix of farmland, wetland, woods, and riverside. Easy access to the City Trail provides an opportunity to explore some of Eau Claire's sights.

Parking for the Chippewa River State Trail, a section of the abandoned Milwaukee Road line, is available at the end of Jopke Road. Self-register at the kiosk ($3 for a daily pass) and save your trail pass for later because we won't be joining the trail until the last portion of the ride.

Ride down Jopke Road to Highway 37 and turn right. Watch for traffic and follow the sign for County B. This is a left turn with a pretty good hill to take us up and away from the river. There is a good shoulder here and a quiet stretch of tall pines. We twist and turn for a bit, and soon the road surface turns a rusty color as it rolls up and down a couple of hills to the junction with County II at 2.6 miles. We ride right on by, taking in the fine views to the east.

A steady climb brings us to County Z on the right; past that, look for the scenic wetland, followed by wavy fields of wheat and corn. After a short stair-step turn south, we continue on County B to the junction with County HH at 6 miles. It's a right turn here on a smooth road with more fine views of the rolling countryside all around. We'll follow HH to 7.4 miles and the junction with Highway 37. Here we carefully take a left, staying alert for traffic. Less than 1 mile later, we turn right off the highway on to Betz Road, a skinny thoroughfare with an excellent surface. We ride on gently rolling and wooded terrain at first, then pass by farmland.

At 9.1 miles, there is a T intersection at Langdell Road. Turn left and ride 1 mile to County Z. Now we turn right, heading north through open countryside. At 11.6 miles, County Z takes a right turn, but we keep cruising straight north to a nice long descent back toward the Chippewa on what is now Jene Road. The road curves to the right as it passes some lowland farm property; we then turn left onto Cemetery Road at 12.7 miles.

Immediately after passing the cemetery on the left, we meet the paved Chippewa River State Trail, which is on the rail bed of the former Chippewa Valley line. Lumber was in great demand in the 1880s, and access to markets for both lumber and wheat was crucial. River transportation soon became inadequate, and a more efficient means of transportation, the railroad, arrived in Eau Claire in 1870. Built in 1882, the Chippewa line ran from Eau Claire to Red Wing, Minnesota, giving rise to many small settlements along the way. As rail traffic gradually declined, the line was finally abandoned in 1980 and became part of the Rails-to-Trails network, much to the delight of cyclists, hikers, and in-line skaters.

This junction is our cue to turn right on the trail and start back toward Eau Claire, with superb views of the river for the duration of the ride. (If you're so inclined, take a left here and follow the trail west all the way past Meridean to the Red Cedar State Trail.) Continuing east on our main route, we pass underneath State Highway 85 at mile 14, hugging the river. Our loop ends back at the trailhead at Jopke Road, for a total of 16 miles. If you want a few more delightful miles to top off the day, keep on riding to sample the City Trail in Eau Claire. A historical marker on this trail notes the Road of War, the name given to this section of the Chippewa Valley that served as a neutral territory between the warring Dakota to the south and Ojibwe to the north. The area was established by the United States in 1825 to suppress Indian hostility, but it often proved ineffective in stopping the bloodshed.

Taking a break on the Chippewa River Trail.

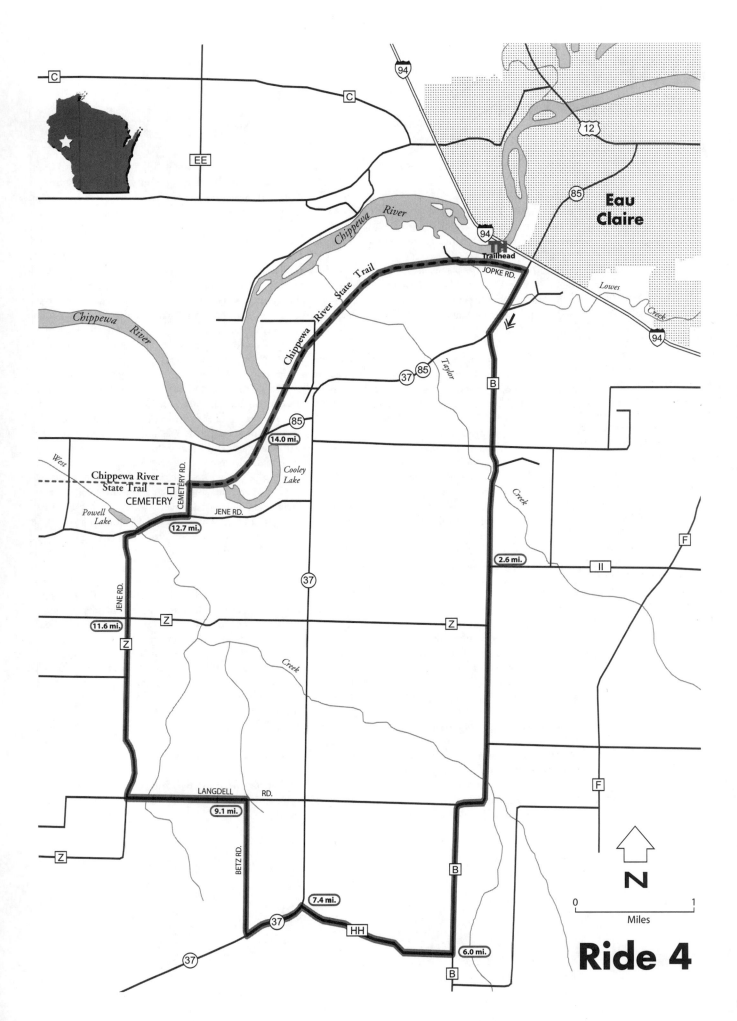

C

C

EE

12

94

85

Eau Claire

Chippewa River

Trailhead

JOPKE RD.

Lowes Creek

94

Chippewa River State Trail

Chippewa River

37 85

Taylor

B

85

14.0 mi.

Chippewa River State Trail

CEMETERY

CEMETERY RD.

West

Cooley Lake

Creek

Powell Lake

JENE RD.

12.7 mi.

JENE RD.

F

2.6 mi.

II

37

11.6 mi.

Z

Z

Z

Creek

F

LANGDELL RD.

9.1 mi.

N

BETZ RD.

Z

0   1

Miles

37

B

7.4 mi.

37

HH

6.0 mi.

Ride 4

37

B

RIDE 5
Amish Delights

Location: Southeast of Eau Claire, between Augusta and Fairchild.
Distance: 26-mile loop.
Pedaling time: 2.25–2.75 hours.
Surface: Paved roads.
Terrain: Flat to rolling, with a couple of bigger hills.
Sweat factor: Moderate.
Trailhead: The mileage begins at the junction of U.S. Highway 12 and County G on the west side of Augusta. A nice trailhead with parking is available at the Wood Shed antiques store on Main Street (back lot), which will be the staring point of the ride.

This tour is a relaxing ride through simpler times. The route is named for the stagecoaches that used to travel this route and the many Amish horse-drawn buggies that follow it today. It follows rolling, quiet roads through picturesque Amish farmland. You'll probably see more horse-drawn buggies here than cars—that's surely a sign of a great biking day. Amish farmsteads, one-room schoolhouses, and sawmills are on the way, and Amish goods are available as well, like tasty foodstuffs and hand-crafted furniture. The Amish are a friendly lot, and the hearty waves from proud folk in buggies or out in fields make this an especially enjoyable trip. Terrain is relatively easy with the exception of a few moderate hills. Augusta and Fairchild offer old-time stores for shopping and plenty of restaurants for fueling up before and after the ride. Check www.chippewavalley.net for lots of area information.

At its junction with U.S. Highway 12, we'll roll south on County G, shortly leaving the town proper and curving into rolling farmland of wheat and corn. A somewhat long climb comes along at 2.5 miles, and after that we reach the top of a ridge with some amazing views of the countryside and bluff tops to the west. Amish farms begin to appear in this area, and we're likely to see a black horse-drawn buggy with a bearded gent in a black hat at the reins. (Pedaling a nonmotorized vehicle in such parts will provide you with a special appreciation for such self-reliant folk.) But, before we go any farther, be forewarned to watch for horse droppings in the road—the downside of a bike trip through the area.

We pass more Amish farms, with fields speckled with conical haystacks and nary a single mechanical im-plement to be found. At 4 miles, County G takes a hard right and then continues south; we go straight ahead here and then curve due east on Livermore Road. There is a nice downhill right off the bat, followed by a good climb past Gregor Road at mile 5. After a couple of short curves, we cruise down a nice long hill, cross Diamond Valley Creek, and arrive at the junction with County M at 6 miles.

Continue straight on Brunzil Road, which makes a big ascent to start, then takes a long curve past a large pasture with cows and horses milling about. Keep an eye on the sky, as well, for up there are raptors the likes of eagles and hawks. At 7.5 miles we reach a four-way stop at Hay Creek Road. Straight ahead we go, onto County RR, following the handy green-and-white bike-route signs posted throughout this ride. Now, it seems as if we're in an entirely different part of the state; thick stands of pine line the road, and the farmland all but disappears. A deciduous forest begins to appear after a bit, and at just over 10 miles, farmland again dominates the scenery, along with bluffs scattered in the distance.

At 12.6 miles, we reach Highway 12, where we will turn right and ride toward Fairchild. There will be more traffic here, but the shoulder is wide. Another 1.4 miles bring us into the sleepy town of Fairchild. The CO-OP Shopping Center on Front Street is loaded with antiques and other old-time sundries and is a fun place to relax. The Buffalo River State Trail parking area is also an excellent place for a rest stop or for ending the ride and skipping the round-trip mileage. If you're up for a longer adventure, the 36-mile Buffalo River trail follows a gravel surface of the former Chicago & North Western railroad through pastures, woodland, and wetlands.

We begin the return trip by retracing our tracks back up Highway 12 and west on County RR. At Hay Creek Road and 20.5 miles, we turn right this time and stay on RR as it runs in a northwesterly direction. At the junction with County M, turn right. The remaining miles of the ride are relatively flat, and 24.8 miles bring us to Highway 12 again, where we turn left. Less than a mile later, we're at The Wood Shed in Augusta. This isn't exactly the place where we began, but its location in the middle of town is a convenient spot to end our 26-mile tour. Stop in the store to shop for authentic Amish goods.

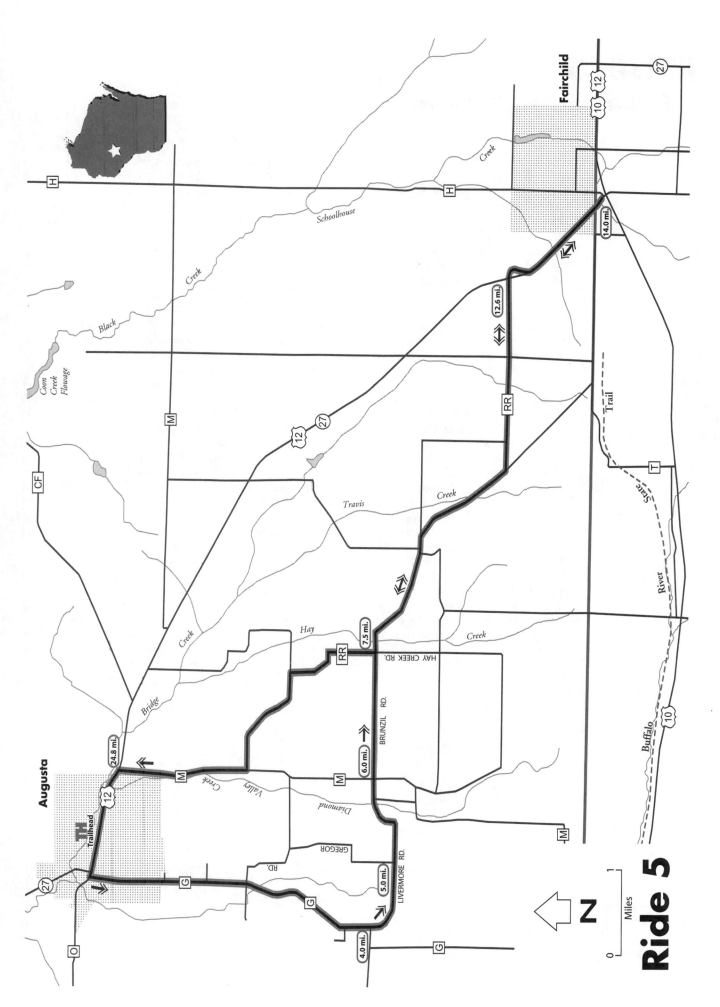

Fairchild

Augusta

Trailhead

14.0 mi.

12.6 mi.

7.5 mi.

6.0 mi.

5.0 mi.

4.0 mi.

24.8 mi.

HAY CREEK RD.

BRUNZIL RD.

LIVERMORE RD.

GREGOR RD.

Schoolhouse

Black Creek

Coon Creek Flowage

Travis Creek

Hay Creek

Diamond Valley Creek

Bridge Creek

Buffalo River

State Trail

Ride 5

N

Miles

0   1

15

RIDE 6
Turtle Beats the Hare

Location: Turtle Lake and neighboring country roads.
Distance: 9.3-mile loop.
Pedaling time: 50–60 minutes.
Surface: Paved roads.
Terrain: Gently rolling.
Sweat factor: Low.
Trailhead: Start from the Dairy Queen on U.S. Highway 8 in Turtle Lake, a quarter mile west of the junction with U.S. Highway 63, across from the Saint Croix Casino.

This relaxing ride wanders through picturesque farmland and forested marshes. Look for an aged, abandoned church, a mysterious giant boulder in a hilltop field, and wildlife aplenty near the shores of Skinaway Lake. The terrain rolls gently throughout the ride, with good surface conditions from start to finish. The last couple of miles are on hard-packed gravel and are especially scenic. The town of Turtle Lake offers an assortment of options for food and rest and postride activities, like the go-cart track on the west end of town or the Saint Croix Casino.

This ride can start virtually anywhere in Turtle Lake, but let's head out from the Dairy Queen, where we can partake of some postride goodies. Head east on U.S. Highway 8, then turn left—cautiously—onto U.S. Highway 63. A couple hundred yards north on Highway 63 is a right turn onto 13th 1/2 Avenue. We'll pass Tom Hartzel Memorial Field, a great small-town ballpark complete with billboard signs on the outfield fence, and turn north again on 1st 1/2 Street, traveling on a flat, narrow road through open farmland and cornfields. We roll past a tree farm as the road curves back east on 14th Avenue, which leads to 2nd Street at 2.2 miles and a left turn.

This stretch of 2nd Street allows great views of the farm country and eventually Upper Turtle Lake to the east. In the distance, dozens of silos stand tall, staking their claim on fields colored green and gold. At the crest of a small rise, Lakeview Cemetery keeps silent watch over the farmsteads. The neighboring hundred-year-old Perley Church, now abandoned and slowly being claimed by age and encroaching foliage, sits silent in a yard across the road. A steady descent delivers us in a northwesterly direction back to Highway 63. Here we'll carefully cross the highway and turn a couple of pedal strokes south to 16th Avenue.

There, at mile 4.7, we'll swing right and find ourselves heading west on Rustic Road 67. Rolling past thick stands of birch and poplar and an occasional dollop of marshland, the road casually rises to Barron County's western edge, where we turn due south on County Line Road (follow the Rustic Road sign) at mile 6. Along the way you might notice a giant boulder pointing skyward from a hilltop field. You may imagine some celebrated historical significance attached to this stone, but alas, it's but a sturdy decoration placed there by the landowner. Still pretty neat, though.

We'll coast downhill and cross Beaver Brook at 7.5 miles; here the pavement ends, giving way to hard-packed gravel. Abruptly the road enters a heavily wooded forest, largely populated with oak and birch, with rolling hummocks and dozens of smaller habitats among the woods and marsh. This is a fun, rolling ride that curves through the woods and along wetland areas at the fringes of Skinaway and Elbow Lakes. Keep your eyes peeled for wildlife near the water—maybe a family of turtles sunning on a log, a motionless heron patiently waiting to stab a fish, a brood of mallards lazing about the bay. One last curve to the right and the Turtle Lake water tower comes into view. From here it's just another quarter mile back to town. Cross Highway 8 carefully and head for that strategically selected trailhead—the DQ!

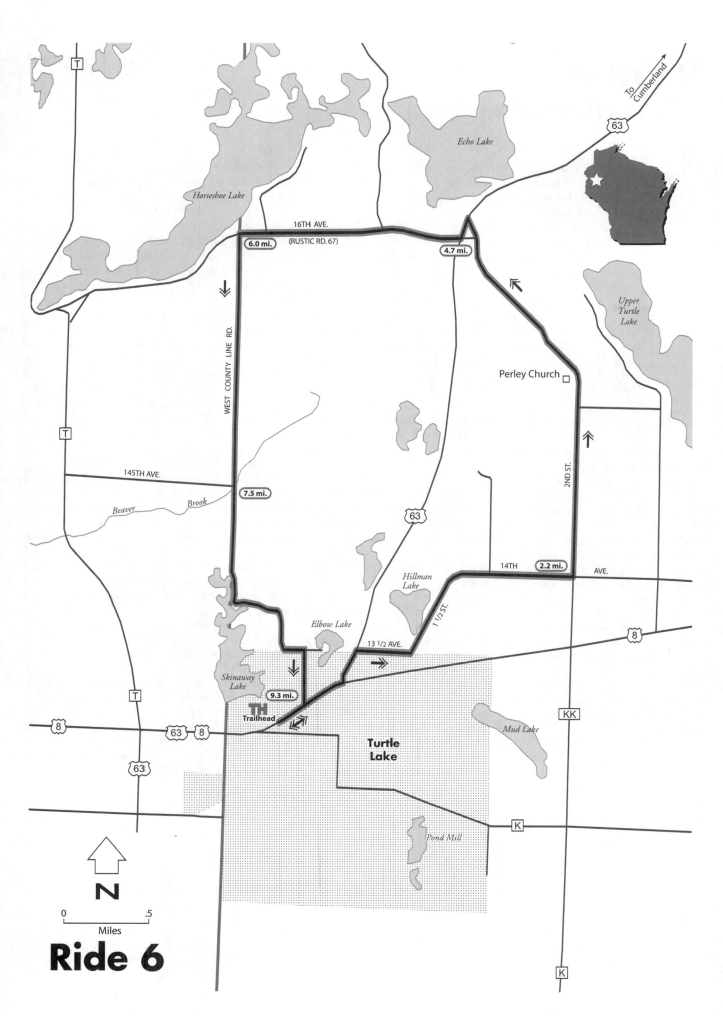

To Cumberland

63

Echo Lake

Horseshoe Lake

16TH AVE.

6.0 mi. (RUSTIC RD. 67) 4.7 mi.

Upper Turtle Lake

WEST COUNTY LINE RD.

Perley Church

2ND ST.

T

145TH AVE.

7.5 mi.

Beaver Brook

63

Hillman Lake

14TH 2.2 mi. AVE.

1 1/2 ST.

8

Elbow Lake

13 1/2 AVE.

Skinaway Lake

9.3 mi.

KK

Mud Lake

TH
Trailhead

T

8 63 8

Turtle Lake

63

K

Pond Mill

N
0   .5
Miles

Ride 6

K

17

RIDE 7
Blue Hills Buffet

Location: County roads in the hills west of Bruce.
Distance: 27.7-mile loop.
Pedaling time: 2.25–2.75 hours.
Surface: Paved roads.
Terrain: Mix of flat and hilly.
Sweat factor: Moderate.
Trailhead: Start at junction of U.S. Highway 8 and State Highway 40 at the west end of Bruce.

Ice Age Trail

Just northwest of Weyerhaeuser, a small segment of the Ice Age National Scenic Trail runs through the Blue Hills. Despite the designation of "national," this remarkable trail is wholly contained within Wisconsin. When completed, it will stretch for a thousand miles across 30 counties as it follows the moraines created by the retreat of the last Wisconsin glacier. The trail will snake eastward from the Saint Croix River in Polk County to about the middle of the state, then turn south and make its way close to the Illinois border; it will then wind back north and stretch all the way to Door County. About 60 percent of the planned trail is complete, with many short and some long segments now in use.

This medium-length ride gives us a taste of both easy flatland riding and more difficult hills in the bluffs west of Bruce in Rusk County. The Blue Hills, called "Paja Toyela" by the Woodland Sioux tribe who once made this their home, are considered to be one of the oldest mountain ranges in the country. Appropriately enough, the Ice Age National Scenic Trail winds through the area. The hills' present form is the result of millions of years of erosion and other geologic phenomena. Roads are excellent on this route, and peace and quiet are the order of the day.

We'll leave on this trip from the junction of U.S. Highway 8 and State Highway 40 at the west end of Bruce. We ride north on Highway 40 for a half mile to County O, then turn left, following the sign for the Blue Hills Trails and Christie Mountain. We're on an open road through flat farmland, but the ancient Blue Hills, rising 500 feet up from our current elevation, are right up ahead. After a series of stair-step climbs and a long descent, we cross Devils Creek at 4.2 miles. At mile 5, County O zigs and zags north and west again. This stretch passes through farms and pastures mottled with stands of birch and maple and passes an alpaca farm on the fringes of the hills. Sumac, blackberry bushes, and other squat shrubbery cover the lower slopes.

We cross Devils Creek again and the road to the Blue Hills Trails, where mountain bikers, hikers, and horseback riders can explore densely wooded trails, discover hidden waterfalls, and follow white-tail deer past clear mountain lakes. Just beyond the trails road at 8.1 miles, we begin a long climb. Hills once blue are now the dark green of spruce and hemlock. Halfway up is the Christie Mountain Ski Area, a time-honored winter playground that boasts 21 lighted runs and 5 tubing runs. Once over the top, we ride over a succession of ups and downs—a continual test of our endurance. At the junction with County F at mile 11.4, we turn left and roll along again for a while. Thick woods are the current scenery on this part of the loop. At 13 miles, the road curves left and begins a 2-plus-mile descent. Whoopee! It's not very steep, but it just keeps going down, so we have a nice long coast all the way into the sleepy town of Weyerhaeuser at 17.5 miles. This is one of the many small communities that sprouted with the logging-industry boom in the late 1880s.

Highway 8 arrives at mile 18, and this is a left turn for us. There is a convenience store here if you'd like a break. The shoulder on Highway 8 is small, but traffic is generally light, unless it's a summer weekend with the parade of RVs and fishing boats. Just a mile down the road, we hang a left on Norwegian Road, a really smooth number traveling through swampy areas and lowland pasture. It's just us and a few cows on this stretch. Nice and quiet. The junction with Tyman Road arrives at 21.5 miles; we turn right here through more lowlands on easy rolling hills.

We return to the junction with County O at 26 miles and a right here takes us back to Highway 40 at mile 27. Another right takes us back to the trailhead for a total of 27.7 miles.

Several hometown cafés and restaurants in Bruce and nearby Ladysmith serve up yummy vittles after the ride. Check out the Back Door Café or Cazzoli's Pizza in Ladysmith or the Chippewa Trails Café in Bruce. Extend your stay and float the gentle currents of the Chippewa River, or take an exciting whitewater trip on the Flambeau River, only a short drive from Bruce.

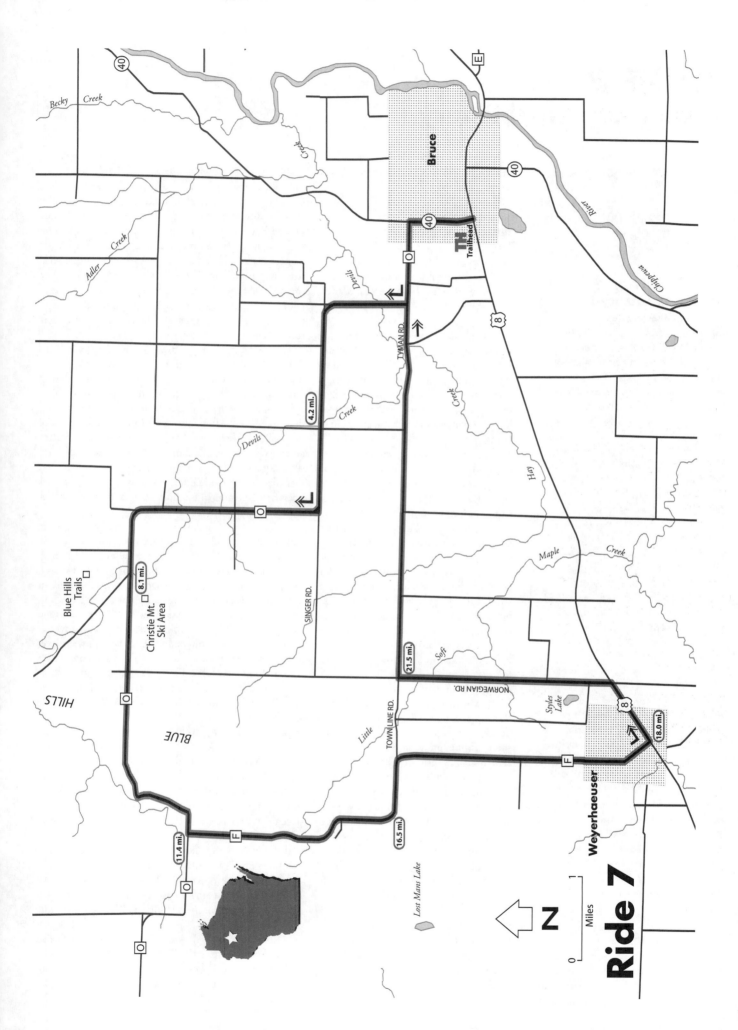

Ride **7**

N

Miles
0 1

Becky Creek
40

Adler Creek

Creek

Devils Creek

4.2 mi.

Devils Creek

8.1 mi.

Blue Hills Trails

Christie Mt. Ski Area

BLUE

HILLS

O

11.4 mi.

O

Singer Rd.

Lost Mans Lake

16.5 mi.

Little

Town Line Rd.

21.5 mi.

Soft Creek

Norwegian Rd.

Styles Lake

Maple Creek

Hay Creek

Tyman Rd.

O

40

Bruce

TH
Trailhead

8

E

Chippewa River

F

Weyerhaeuser

8

18.0 mi.

F

RIDE 8
Danbury Ramblebury

Location: Danbury and environs south to the village of Yellow Lake, in Burnett County.
Distance: 15.5-mile loop.
Pedaling time: 1.25–1.5 hours.
Surface: Paved roads.
Terrain: Flat to rolling.
Sweat factor: Moderate.
Trailhead: The junction of State Highway 77 and County F, on the west edge of Danbury.

A Positive Step Backward

Thanks to some clear-headed thinking in the early 1970s, the state of Wisconsin took steps to stop time on nearly 500 miles of scenic country roads. Today more than 90 of these designated Rustic Roads offer hikers, bikers, and motorists glimpses into the past. Dirt, gravel, or paved, these quiet byways travel through areas of rugged terrain, native foliage and wildlife, or open farmland. The roads have a maximum speed of 45 mph, but they're most fun at bike speed. Look for the distinct brown and yellow signs. Additional roads are added on a regular basis. A free guide to all the roads in the system is available from the Wisconsin Department of Tourism, (800) 432-9747 or www.travelwisconsin.com.

Also nearby is the Crex Meadows Wildlife Area, a 30,000-acre state management project that has restored the land to its original condition of a brush prairie-wetland complex. This area was drastically altered by settlers in the late 1800s. Habitat-restoration efforts began shortly after the state purchased the area in 1946. The wildlife response to prairie and wetlands restoration has been dramatic. The abundance and diversity of wildlife has made Crex a wildlife showplace, part of a national network of wildlife-viewing areas. Over 120,000 people visit Crex each year.

This ride is a variety pack of terrain and scenery. A stretch of Rustic Road arrives shortly after the start, then we travel through rolling woodland, open fields, a small lake community, and through a thick forest loaded with wildlife. A historical park halfway through offers an interesting spot for a break. A couple of hills are respectable enough to require some extra effort, and with an almost total lack of traffic, encountering a vehicle is a rare event. Peace and quiet are constant companions on this country ride.

Danbury is located in Burnett County, which is packed with spectacular wilderness scenery and opportunities for your favorite outdoor activity. Over 500 lakes and dozens of creeks and rivers were left behind from Glacial Lake Grantsburg, a huge lake that disappeared after covering the area thousands of years ago. That means out-of-this-world fishing and perfect habitat for waterfowl, beaver, otter, deer, bear, and more. The county's western boundary is the Saint Croix River, which, along with the Namekagon River, makes up the Saint Croix National Scenic Riverway—over 150 miles of some of the prettiest wild and scenic shoreline in the nation. The rivers course through 150,000 acres of dense forest and 50,000 acres of restored wetlands, bogs, and prairie. In addition to over 250 species of birds and dozens of mammals, the woods offer hundreds of miles of recreation trails for skiing, snowmobiling, hiking, bicycling, and horseback riding.

South from Danbury on County F, the first stretch of this route takes us through wooded farmland and offers a taste of the variety to come farther down the road. The terrain is mellow and easy-going, except for a minor undulation or two. Before reaching mile 2, we turn left on Glendenning Road, aka Rustic Road 79. This is a short and flat cruise on flawless pavement and, as with all of its bucolic brethren, offers a healthy shot of scenery. Dense oak hardwood forest shades the road and arches into a canopy overhead. Soon we cross a little bridge that affords further intoxicating views of Round Lake to the north, then pass the Gandy Dancer Recreational Trail before arriving at the junction with Highway 35 at the 3.2-mile mark. The Gandy Dancer is a 98-mile trail set down on an old railroad bed stretching from Saint Croix Falls north to Superior. The southern half sports a crushed-limestone surface ideal for biking and hiking. The northern segment travels through more remote lands and is shared by ATVs and other off-road machines.

We turn right on Highway 35 and do so with caution and in single file to avoid mishaps with rapidly moving traffic. Steer clear of the shoulder, which consists of loose, tire-swallowing gravel. But the trip on this road is a short one, less than a half mile, to a right turn on Hayden Lake Road. After another half mile, the junction of Hayden Lake Road and French Road means a left turn and the completion of 4.2 miles. We now head due south, spinning along more rolling hills past quiet woods and marshland. The road climbs up from the woods to pass open farmland and, at 7.5 miles, enters the tiny community of Yellow Lake and County U.

We'll take a right there, ride by a charming little church, and, just like that, we're past Yellow Lake. Now the route drops through a narrow valley and begins a longer, flat stretch adjacent to fields of corn and wheat, further evidence of the varied landscape on this ride. In only a short distance, we've seen open fields, marshes, and dense, rolling forestland. And now a fort! At the 9-mile mark is the Forts Folle Avoine Historical Park, a reconstructed, early 1800s fur-trading post and Ojibwe village. Stop in to view exhibits from the fur trade and Native American archaeology. The park offers living-history tours and a museum; it's open Memorial Day to Labor Day, Wednesday through Sunday, (715) 866-8890.

The road drops in elevation as it nears a bridge crossing the Yellow River. An immediate right on East Bass Lake Road takes us back in a northerly direction through a heavily wooded area. This is a great spot to catch a glimpse of wildlife, as was the case today when a gang of eight deer sauntered across the road. When mile 10 rolls over, your tires will sing on new, velvety pavement, and with nary a car in sight, that is a sweet melody indeed. At 12.7 miles, we reach the junction with County F and head east again, riding along the Danbury State Wildlife Area, a joint project between Danbury and the Wisconsin DNR. After just a mile, the road curves left, passing the Rustic Road 79 turnoff, and retraces our tracks back to Highway 77 to complete this 15.5-mile loop.

To reward yourself, you might want to visit one of the local watering holes in Danbury, like the Last Cast or Anglers, or try your luck at the Hole in the Wall Casino. Better yet, enjoy an ice cream treat or a sandwich at the Log Cabin Store.

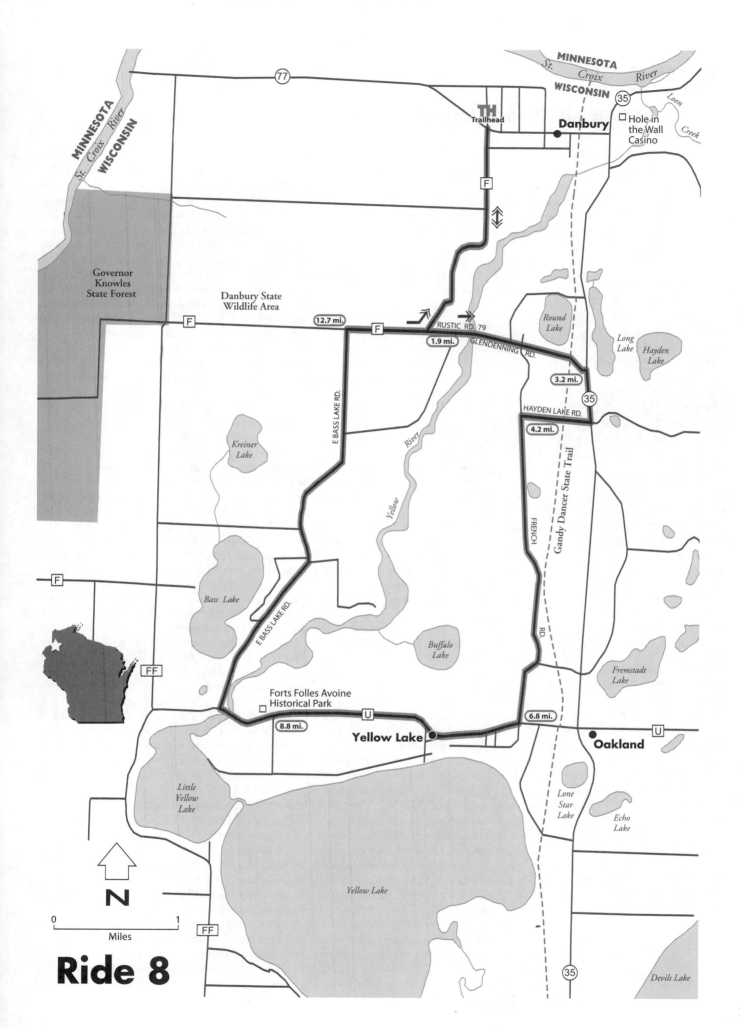

MINNESOTA
St. Croix River

MINNESOTA
WISCONSIN

77

TH
Trailhead

Danbury

Hole in
the Wall
Casino

35

Loon Creek

F

Governor
Knowles
State Forest

Danbury State
Wildlife Area

F

12.7 mi.

F

1.9 mi.

RUSTIC RD. 79

GLENDENNING RD.

Round
Lake

Long
Lake

Hayden
Lake

3.2 mi.

35

HAYDEN LAKE RD.

4.2 mi.

E BASS LAKE RD.

Kreiner
Lake

Yellow River

FRENCH RD.

Gandy Dancer State Trail

F

Bass Lake

E BASS LAKE RD.

Buffalo
Lake

Fremstadt
Lake

FF

Forts Folles Avoine
Historical Park

U

8.8 mi.

Yellow Lake

6.8 mi.

Oakland

U

Little
Yellow
Lake

Lone
Star
Lake

Echo
Lake

N

0   Miles   1

Yellow Lake

FF

35

Devils Lake

Ride 8

21

RIDE 9
Osaugie and Gitchi Gummi

Location: Osaugie Bike Trail from Superior and along the shores of Wisconsin Point.
Distance: 9.6 miles one way.
Pedaling time: 45 minutes to 1 hour.
Surface: Combination of paved trail and road.
Terrain: Flat.
Sweat factor: Low.
Trailhead: In Harbor View Park on U.S. Highway 2/53 and Belknap Street in Superior.

SS Meteor Maritime Museum on Barker's Island.

Any time spent close to Lake Superior is good time, and if it's spent on a bike, well, that's a real treat. The Osaugie Trail and adjoining roads allow an up-close encounter with the big lake, Gitchi Gummi, and its neighboring bays. We ride through maritime and local history on this paved, flat trail, then a short spin on quiet roads leads to the very shores of the largest freshwater lake in the world. Duck into one of the numerous access points for sweeping views and choice picnic sites, or trek out to the lighthouse to really feel the lake's mood. Allow extra time to play on Wisconsin Point.

We start our ride on the Osaugie Trail from Harbor View Park, which sits just off U.S. Highway 2/53 in Superior, 1.5 miles south of the High Bridge and Wisconsin's border with Minnesota. But even before we start, distractions at the trailhead might delay us. One is the park's newly opened Richard I. Bong World War II Heritage Center, which honors the country's leading World War II flying ace, a young man who grew up in nearby Poplar, Wisconsin. Another, only a few hundred yards down the trail, is Barker's Island and the SS Meteor Maritime Museum, which tells the fascinating story of the area's shipping history. Fewer than 50 of the cigar-shaped whalebacks were built in the early part of the last century, and the last surviving one is on display here. Down the road from the *Meteor* are Barker's Island Inn and its marina.

Finally, overlooking Lake Superior from the other side of the road is the Fairlawn Mansion, a stunning 1889 Victorian home built by lumber baron Martin Pattison. Stop in and see for yourself whether the rumors about it being haunted are true.

Oh, yes, back to our ride. After 1.5 miles, the trail jogs close to the King Midas Flour elevators. There are a couple of beat-up, gravelly sections to watch for through this section. Two miles into the ride, we arrive at the Burlington Northern ore docks. Just before the docks, we have to portage over a set of railroad tracks, then drop down to the neighboring boat landing's parking area. The trail continues on the other side of the lot, passing directly beneath the docks. Note the shrubs and small trees on top that look to be growing directly from the dock. We cross the cloudy-brown Nemadji River over a short, plank-floored bridge at 3 miles and pass the village of Allouez. Here the trail shares billing with the Tri-County Corridor Multi-Use Trail. This section receives especially heavy use in winter from snowmobiles and ATVs, so be sure to practice good share-the-trail habits when encountering other users. Another short bridge, at 4.5 miles, brings us into Itasca, at the fringes of Superior's city limits. My favorite stop in Itasca is the Choo-Choo Bar, a little pub in an old rail car that has remained largely unchanged for decades.

At 5.4 miles, we arrive at the junction with Moccasin Mike Road. The trail straight ahead turns to gravel and goes clear to Ashland, 60 miles yonder. We go left here and head toward the lake on a road that isn't in the best shape, but it's generally quiet with little traffic. One mile later, we make a left turn onto Wisconsin Point Road and, following the sign, head back to the northwest. The road along the point has seen better days and in places is downright unfriendly to a bike. Try to ignore the bumps and potholes and look for glimpses of Lake Superior over the tops of low hummocks of sand near the shore. To the left, we can look across Allouez Bay to the sights we rode past earlier in the trip. Numerous access points along the road lead down to the water's edge.

We are riding on one of the longest freshwater sandbars in the world, a skinny, 10-mile-long finger of land between the twin ports of Duluth and Superior. The natural opening in the center splits the sandbar into two appendages, Wisconsin Point and Minnesota Point.

Near the end of the ride, the road sneaks through an especially scenic stand of old-growth red and white pine and terminates just short of 10 miles at the South Entry Channel. A perfect midride diversion is a stroll out to the South Breakwater Lighthouse for fantastic, sweeping views of the largest of the Great Lakes. Superior is also the cleanest, clearest, and coldest of them all, with enough capacity to flood all of North and South America under a foot of its icy water. At the lake's deepest point, 1,333 feet, nearly all of Chicago's Sears Tower, one of the world's tallest buildings, could be submerged. In many other areas of the lake, dozens of shipwrecks rest in frigid tombs. Some are protected in lake-bottom preserves and are visited by recreational divers.

Back in the bike saddle, we'll point our bikes in the opposite direction and retrace our tracks to the trailhead for double the mileage.

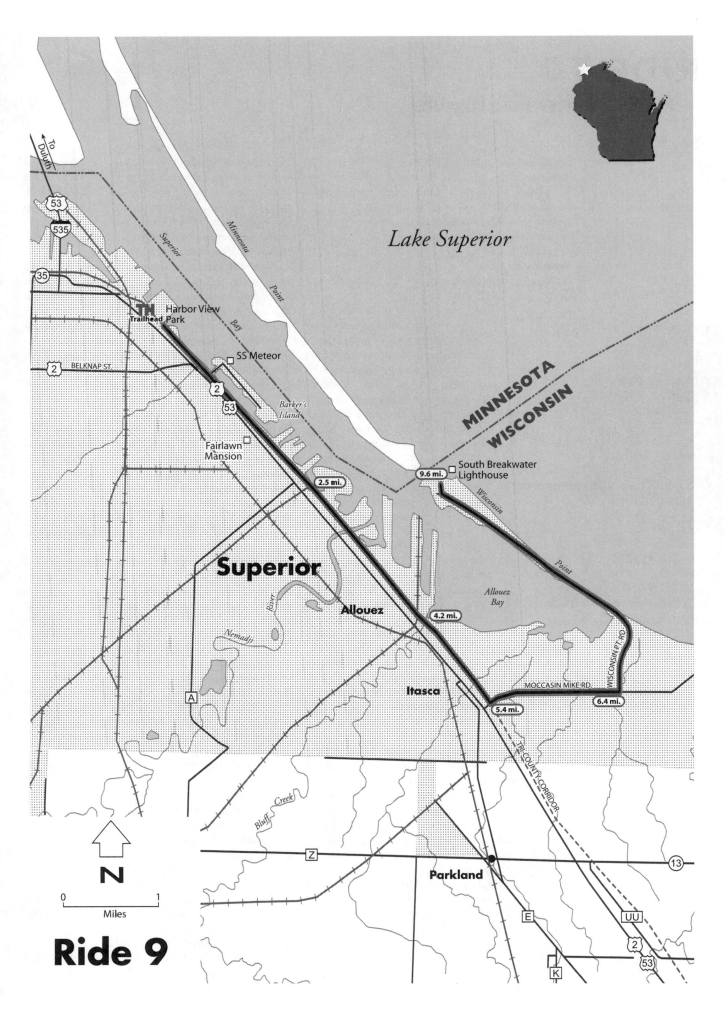

To Duluth

53

535

35

2 BELKNAP ST.

TH
Trailhead

Harbor View Park

SS Meteor

2
53

Fairlawn Mansion

Superior

River

Nemadji

Allouez

A

Itasca

2.5 mi.

4.2 mi.

5.4 mi.

Lake Superior

MINNESOTA

WISCONSIN

Barker's Island

Superior Bay

Minnesota Point

South Breakwater Lighthouse

9.6 mi.

Wisconsin

Allouez Bay

Point

6.4 mi.

MOCCASIN MIKE RD.

WISCONSIN P.T. RD.

TRI-COUNTY CORRIDOR

Bluff Creek

Z

Parkland

E

UU

13

2
53

K

N

0   1
Miles

Ride 9

RIDE 10
Fifty to the Firehouse

Location: County and back roads in the Chequamegon National Forest, including the towns of Grand View, Namekagon, Cable, and Drummond.
Distance: 49.8 miles.
Pedaling time: 4.25–5 hours.
Surface: Smooth, paved roads.
Terrain: Rolling.
Sweat factor: High.
Trailhead: The intersection of U.S. Highway 63 and County D in Grand View.

Four bikers on a road east of Cable.

For 24 years, the town of Grand View has hosted one of the most popular citizen bike races in the nation, the Firehouse 50. With touring rides, running races, and kids' events, this annual two-day affair attracts a loyal following that turns Grand View into a hotbed of cycling and related goings-on. The 50-mile race route follows dreamy county roads through stunning scenery thick with rugged forest and pristine lakes. Terrain is rolling throughout with some good hills between Cable and Drummond on scenic Lake Owen Drive.

Head south on County D from its junction with U.S. Highway 63. Almost immediately we pass the Great Divide ballpark and the official start line of the Firehouse 50. The route enters the Chequamegon National Forest at the 3-mile mark, then begins to test our legs with some consistent climbing, with a final mile-long grind up to the crest of the Great Divide.

On the descent down the other side, we pass the epic North Country Trail, a spectacular long-distance hiking trail stretching from North Dakota to New York State. Some of the path's most memorable miles pass right through the Chequamegon forest. Riding on, the road flattens, and we enjoy perfect road conditions all the way to a fine view of Trapper Lake at mile 8. From here the road begins a long stretch of fun twists and turns and is generally squiggly for the next 6 miles. Lake Namekagon appears at 9.6 miles with postcard-gorgeous views to the west. The road hugs the shoreline for another mile to a bridge crossing over a narrows area and a smaller bay to the east. Numerous cabins and resorts are tucked in the woods along this part of the lake.

We arrive at the junction of Garmisch Road, County M, and the Namekagon Town Hall at 14.6 miles. The official Firehouse 50 route follows County M, but we're going to stray from that a bit and hang a right on Garmisch Road, only a few bike lengths north of County M. Garmisch is a velvety-smooth ribbon of tarmac that is made to order for two-wheeled travel—it feels like your bike is floating. Thick woods crowd the sides of the road, with long branches embracing overhead.

The road rolls and curves up and over a few moderately steep hills to just over 15 miles, where we pass the entrance to Garmisch Resort, a unique lake retreat with hand-crafted old-world charm in its 1920s-vintage main lodge and guest homes. Breathtaking views of Lake Namekagon are standard features, and you can't beat relaxing on the deck to take it all in.

We arrive at the junction with County M at 17.3 miles, where we turn right and head west on a road with a nice shoulder and light traffic. The popular Lakewoods Resort is immediately on our right, and only a short distance farther along on the left is Rock Lake Road. At 23.5 miles, we pass the road to Telemark Resort, yet another spectacular North Woods hideaway and outdoor playground.

We roll into Cable at 25 miles, then take a right on Randysek Road, a left on Spruce Street, and another right on Kavanaugh Road. This will deliver us to a shade over 26 miles, where we turn right on Perry Lake Road. The route starts rolling and curving again at this point, and the fun continues for the next 16 miles. We reach the junction with Trail Inn Road, turn left, and ride just a mile farther to a right turn on McAully Road. This silky-smooth part of the ride is great fun but quickly ends in one short mile when we go left on South Lake Owen Drive at 29.4 miles. Watch for errant golf balls as you ride right between fairways of a golf course.

Then begins some of the most scenic riding in all of Wisconsin. No grand vistas, but this rolling terrain through the dense woods of the Chequamegon National Forest is equally distracting. Stands of pine, birch, poplar, and maple shade the road, parting now and again just enough to reveal the waters of Lake Owen. If there is a blemish on this otherwise delightful ride, it is a few sections of rough road on Lake Owen Drive. They are short-lived, however, and we sail on smooth seas past the Two Lakes campground road at mile 36, then coast down a long descent, roll over another bump or two, and speed by the entrance to the Drummond Ski Trail system. At the 42 mark, we arrive at the junction with Highway 63 and the town of Drummond. Food and drink are available at the convenience store across the road, and Drummond's main street is just a couple of blocks beyond.

We head northeast on Highway 63 for the home stretch of this great ride. There is a decent shoulder here, but passing traffic, albeit only sporadic, is still disturbing after so many miles of peace and quiet. The road rolls slightly for 4.5 miles, where we'll make an escape from the highway as we turn right onto Sweden Road. A quick, hard left takes us to Old Highway 63, a fantastic stretch of the road's original path. Here we are treated to some mild hills and gentle curves through quiet forest with only a rare appearance of a vehicle. The old highway rejoins Highway 63 at 49.5 miles at the west end of Grand View. A right turn and a dozen pedal strokes take us to the end of our version of the Firehouse 50.

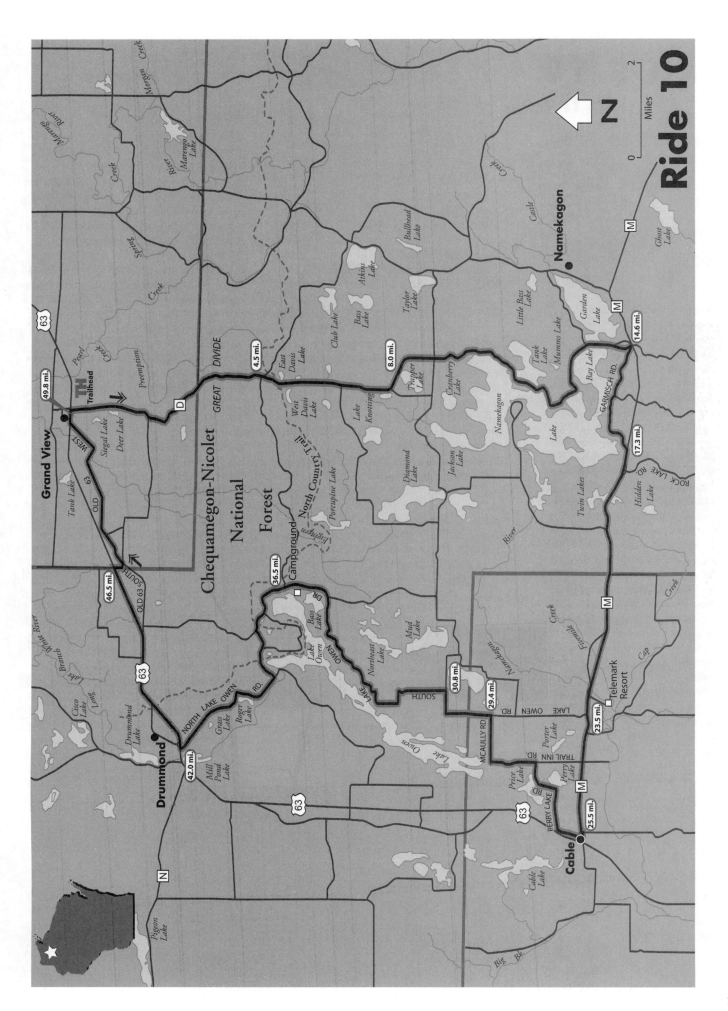

Ride 10

RIDE 11
Double D Tour

Location: County and back roads in the Chequamegon National Forest north and east of Drummond.
Distance: 40-mile loop.
Pedaling time: 3.5–4.25 hours.

Surface: Smooth, paved roads.
Terrain: Rolling.
Sweat factor: High.
Trailhead: Drummond Store on U.S. Highway 63 across from Lake Owen Drive.

Bibon Marsh

Situated in the basin of an extinct glacial lake, the 15-square-mile Bibon Marsh hosts a wide variety of plant and animal species. According to the Wisconsin Department of Natural Resources, portions of the area are forested with a wet conifer swamp of cedar, some of which are as old as 150 years. The ground layer consists of species like twinflower, bunchberry, bishop's-cap, and orchids. Bordering the cedar swamp is wet forest consisting largely of black ash, with alder and fern below. Look for Canada warblers, winter wrens, and red-eyed vireo. The scene changes dramatically north of the White River. Here is a large network of peat-land communities, including bogs, black spruce swamp, and tamarack. Palm warblers, yellow-bellied flycatchers, chickadees, and hawks call this part of the swamp home. Large portions of the wetland are covered by vast shrub swamps of willow, dogwood, and alder. The threatened wood turtle lives here, as do other rare animals like the great gray owl and the osprey.

Like Ride 10, this loop explores more of the striking beauty of the Chequamegon National Forest. Traveling north from Drummond, a town steeped in a long logging history, the route passes dozens of secluded lakes and the Rainbow Lake Wilderness Area. On the eastern portion of the ride, we will be close to the expansive Bibon Marsh. A stop in Grand View for ice cream and 10 more rolling miles rounds off a fantastic ride.

With 850,000 acres of rolling, glacial terrain and dense forest, the Chequamegon is a special place. Hundreds of clear lakes and streams are scattered throughout, and the forest is home to numerous unique attractions, both natural and manmade. The Smith Rapids covered bridge is a rare lattice, glue-laminate structure; the Mocquah Barrens Wildlife area is an expansive pine-barrens ecosystem; and the Penokee Range has rugged cliffs rising to 1,600 feet. Two wilderness areas, Porcupine Lake and Rainbow Lake, and two national scenic trails, the North Country and the Ice Age, make the Chequamegon even harder to resist.

Since this ride starts in Drummond, take some time to visit the historical museum in the library building. Interesting history and photos from the logging days of the mid-1800s are here. The relaxing town park sits on the shore of Drummond Lake and is a perfect place for some postride relaxation.

From the Drummond Store, we head west a short distance on U.S. Highway 63 to the first right turn on Delta-Drummond Road (FR 223). There is a trailhead a short way along for a group of trails in the CAMBA system. These trails are great fun; plan to come back for some off-road fun. We pass Star Lake Road at 4.5 miles and reach Perch Lake Campground at mile 5.5, an excellent place to set up for a bike-camp weekend. The 6,500-acre Rainbow Lakes Wilderness Area, one of two in the Chequamegon National Forest, is off to the west and needs to be on your list of places to visit. Rolling, glaciated terrain under a canopy of pine and mixed hardwoods make this one of the most scenic areas in the state. Dozens of lakes and ponds are hidden among oak, maple, fir, pine, birch, and aspen. Six miles of the North Country Trail pass through the wilderness.

We continue to curve and roll through this gorgeous glacial country to the little town of Delta at mile 10.3. We'll turn right here on County H, cruising past the Delta Town Hall. After rolling along for a few miles, the road makes a hard left and runs north for a mile, then turns back east to 15.9 miles and the junction with County E. We'll stay on our easterly course and begin a series of stair-step turns on County E to the south. After the last of four steps, the road straightens and delivers us to the small town of Mason at 24.2 miles. To the west is the Bibon Marsh, the largest wetland in Bayfield County. At Sutherland Road in Mason, we'll make a break for Highway 63 to the east, turning right on the highway at mile 25.2. This is a busier road, but there is a decent shoulder, and traffic is only moderate. We'll follow the highway on a long, sweeping bend to the town of Grand View at 32.2 miles. Now is a good time to stop for a break and something to eat at the corner store.

We then ride west out of Grand View a short distance to Old 63 Road and turn left. This is the same great road we enjoyed on the Firehouse 50 loop in Ride 10. Five miles of peaceful riding takes us back to Highway 63, where we will hang a left and finish this loop on rolling terrain. Back in Drummond at 40 miles.

If you're staying in Drummond, check out Bob's Bear Den, (715) 798-4406, or the Chequamegon House Bed & Breakfast, (715) 739-6665. Come for the annual Blueberry Festival in Iron River in July or the Bayfield Apple Festival in October.

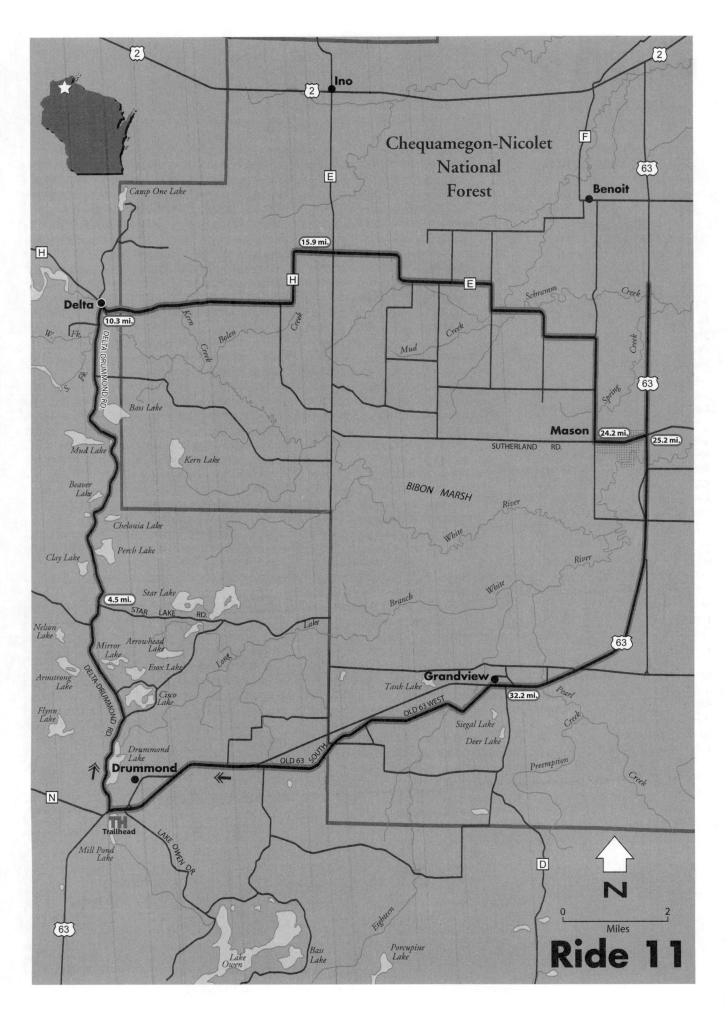

Ino

Chequamegon-Nicolet
National
Forest

F

2

63

Benoit

H

Delta

15.9 mi.

E

H

E

Schramm

Creek

10.3 mi.

DELTA-DRUMMOND RD.

W. Fk.

S. Fk.

Kern Creek

Bolen Creek

Creek

Mud

Creek

Spring

Creek

63

Bass Lake

Mud Lake

Kern Lake

Mason

24.2 mi.

25.2 mi.

SUTHERLAND RD.

Beaver Lake

BIBON MARSH

River

Chelonia Lake

White

Clay Lake

Perch Lake

River

White

4.5 mi.

Star Lake

STAR LAKE RD.

Branch

Lake

Nelson Lake

Mirror Lake

Arrowhead Lake

63

Armstrong Lake

Esox Lake

Long

Grandview

Tank Lake

32.2 mi.

Pearl

Creek

Flynn Lake

Cisco Lake

OLD 63 WEST

Siegal Lake

DELTA-DRUMMOND RD.

Drummond Lake

Deer Lake

Preemption

Drummond

OLD 63 SOUTH

Creek

N

TH
Trailhead

LAKE OWEN DR.

Mill Pond Lake

D

N

63

0   2
Miles

Lake Owen

Bass Lake

Porcupine Lake

Eighteen

Ride 11

RIDE 12
Ripe Mellen

Penokee

The Penokee Range, stretching for 80 miles from around Mellen into the Upper Peninsula, is billions of years old, with thousand-foot hills cloaked in dense forests of pine, maple, and hemlock. Narrow gorges and waterfalls only add to the natural beauty. Among the range's natural wonders is Copper Falls State Park, offering some of the most stunning scenery in Wisconsin. The Bad River winds north to Lake Superior, fed by dramatic Copper and Brownstone Falls; Devils Gate is an interesting jumble of prehistoric rock. Hundreds of species of birds and animals make their homes here as well.

Location: Along County GG between Clam Lake and Mellen.
Distance: 37 miles out and back.
Pedaling time: 3.25–3.75 hours.
Surface: Smooth, paved roads.
Terrain: Flat to rolling.
Sweat factor: High.
Trailhead: The junction of County M and County GG, two blocks west of the town of Clam Lake.

From the little town of Clam Lake and its surrounding lake country, this ride follows a quiet county highway north to the rugged hills of the Penokee Range and historic Mellen. The best thing about this ride is that it's just you and the bike and miles of uninterrupted road, presenting a long uphill grind on the way out and rewarding that effort with a nice coast down on the return trip. Several secluded campgrounds are on the way—for a potential extended cycling/camping trip—and the overlook just south of Mellen allows access to the magniWcent North Country Trail for unbeatable hiking. An optional short ride beyond Mellen leads to Copper Falls State Park, a Wne place to unwind from a long day in the saddle.

Our ride begins at the junction of County M and County GG, within sight of the tiny Clam Lake. We head north on GG on velvety-smooth tarmac, accompanied by dense pine and poplar stands of the Chequamegon National Forest. There is usually very little traffic on this entire route, but the road also lacks a shoulder; so take care not to drift off the edge and stay alert for occasional vehicles—their drivers won't expect to see a bike.

Just 1.9 miles up the road, we pass the quiet wetlands area of Day Lake to our port side. Keep an eye open for herons, ducks, turtles, and the like. At 4 miles is East Twin Lakes Campground, which offers gorgeous lake views from a rugged point above the water; it's an ideal place for a quiet rest stop. Back on the road, we are treated to a stretch of uninterrupted pedaling on curves, gentle hills, and straightaways. Although the terrain appears to be relatively flat, your legs will tell you otherwise, as the road climbs steadily and subtly all the way to Mellen. To make the going more difficult, the road deteriorates as it gets closer to Mellen. At about the 10-mile mark, more potholes and crumbling pavement, in addition to an overall unappealing look, lessen the ride's enjoyment.

The landscape also makes a transition as we travel north. The woods turn largely deciduous, and the terrain becomes hillier as we approach the Penokee Range. We stop at the scenic overlook at 15.9 miles to check out the sights. A toilet is available here, as well as interesting interpretive signs with information about the surrounding area. Gaze south and east at the 1.6-*billion*-year-old Penokee Range, once rising 4 miles above sea level. Also known as the Great Divide, this range diverts water north to Lake Superior and south to the Mississippi River. In addition, this overlook is close to the access point for the epic North Country Trail, which leads to two of Wisconsin's most scenic natural attractions, Morgan Falls and Saint Peter's Dome, approximately 10 miles to the northwest.

After a nice downhill and a cruise alongside a rail line, we arrive in Mellen at mile 18.5. A humble little town at first glance, Mellen is rich in history. Its city hall, a grand restored Victorian structure, is listed on the National Register of Historic Places. The town is also a hub for visiting a few nearby natural wonders. About 3 miles north of town via State Highway 169, Copper Falls State Park offers excellent camping, hiking, and scenic waterfalls. Three miles to the southeast is Mount Whittlesey, the second-highest point in the state; it's clearly visible from town. Mellen is also a "trail town" for the North Country Trail, which is just 2 miles west. It's a hiker-friendly place offering rest, supplies, good food, and more to long-distance hikers.

After a rest break and some rations, it's time to point our wheels back toward Clam Lake. The return will take advantage of the steady descent, and we arrive in Clam Lake at the completion of 37 miles.

Observing Copper Falls from a viewing platform.

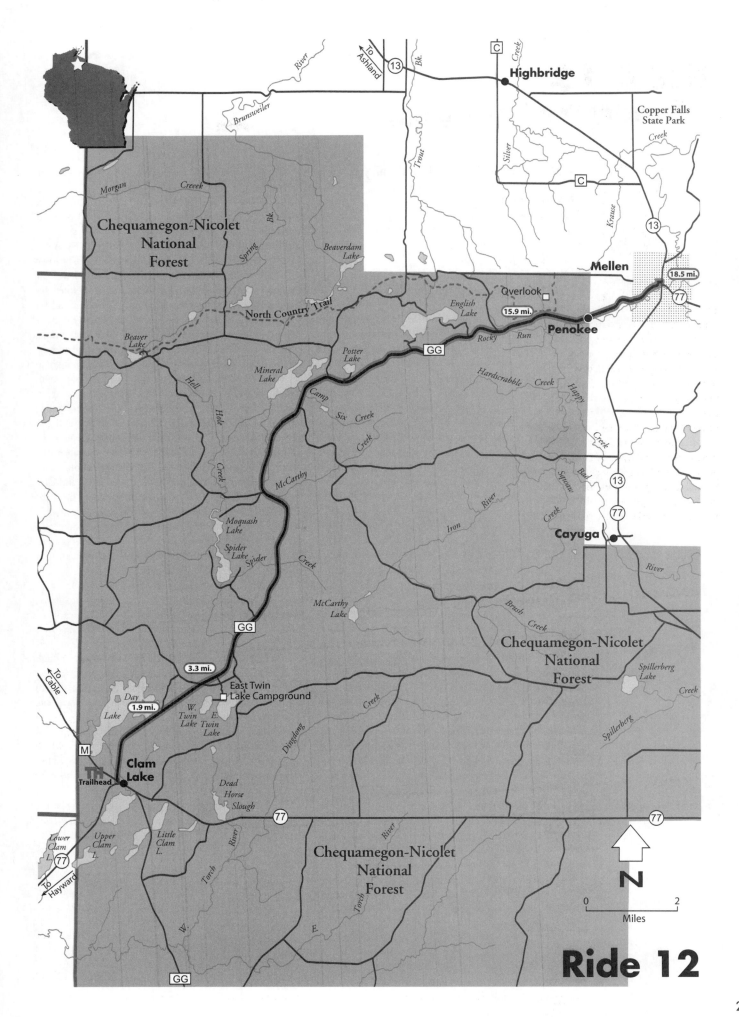

Copper Falls State Park

Highbridge

Chequamegon-Nicolet National Forest

North Country Trail

Mellen

Overlook

15.9 mi.

Penokee

18.5 mi.

GG

Cayuga

East Twin Lake Campground

3.3 mi.

1.9 mi.

Clam Lake

Chequamegon-Nicolet National Forest

Chequamegon-Nicolet National Forest

Trailhead

To Cable

To Hayward

N

0   2
Miles

Ride 12

RIDE 13
Frolic at the Flowage

Location: Secluded county highways south and east of Hayward near the Chippewa flowage.
Distance: 38-mile loop.
Pedaling time: 3.25–3.75 hours.
Surface: Paved roads.
Terrain: Flat to gently rolling.
Sweat factor: Moderate to high.
Trailhead: Herman's Landing Resort on Lake Chippewa, 5 miles south of County B on County CC.

Lake Chippewa is much more than just a lake. Call it a wilderness on water. With over 200 miles of undeveloped shoreline and 140 islands, the 15,000-acre Lake Chippewa Flowage is indeed the essence of the North Woods. Wisconsin's third-largest lake, the "Big Chip" came to be in 1924 when the Wisconsin/Minnesota Power and Light Company constructed a dam across the Chippewa River and the waters of many nearby natural lakes, rivers, streams, and ponds swelled to create this spectacular wilderness. Hidden bays, secluded coves, and hundreds of acres of woodland treat visitors to all sorts of adventure. Bald eagles, loons, beaver, otter, heron, deer, and bear all make regular appearances. Best of all, the flowage has been preserved and protected in much of its pristine state for generations.

Our ride in this special place starts at a marina on the road that splits Lake Chippewa right down the middle. An easy spin north from the lake delivers us to a wonderful loop on especially quiet back roads past many scenic streams and lakes.

We'll head off on our ride from Herman's Landing Resort, home of the world's record muskie, a 69-pound, 11-ounce monster landed back in 1949 by Louis Spray. Herman's is a hub of activity on the flowage, with a marina, guide services, boat rentals, and more. Our ride north on County CC is an easy cruise on flat terrain, with glimpses through the pines of Lake Chippewa's clear waters and several small islands far offshore. "Double C" makes a few bends, followed by a final straight stretch to the junction with County B at mile 5. If we turn left here and ride 4 miles west, we'll reach Grand Pines Resort and the original Famous Dave's Bar-B-Que restaurant. This is where the operation, which now totals well over 50 restaurants throughout the Midwest, all began, and the grub is as good as ever.

We'll save the feast for after the ride and turn right (east) on the wide, smooth shoulder of County B. About a half mile along, the road dips slightly and crosses the Chief River to mile 6 at the junction with County A. We'll turn north here and ride past the Chippewa Inn, a top-shelf steakhouse whose motto is "Where the Old World Meets the Northwoods" (www.haywardlakes.com /chippewa).

County A starts out blissfully smooth with a wide shoulder as it travels through an elegant stand of white pine. After about a mile or so, we lose the nice shoulder, but there is almost no traffic, and the riding is easy. A few small hills appear once in a while, and there are but two gentle curves on this otherwise straight initial stretch to the junction with Moose Lake Road at 9 miles. (Note: this road provides a bailout option if you're in the mood for fewer miles. It runs east for nearly 5 miles to where it meets County S, a road that we'll encounter later on the main route. This shorter loop then returns to County B and the trailhead.) Let's keep going on the longer route, though, to see what's in store. Cruising north on this arrow-straight section of County A, we'll pass several farmsteads and adjoining crop fields and pastures with small clusters of cows and horses lumbering hither and yon. The fields soon give way to woods with a mix of coniferous and deciduous trees, and at 11.8 miles we arrive at the junction with State Highway 77. We'll take a right here, riding a wide shoulder on good pavement past the little Spider Lake Motel and Café (www.haywardlakes.com/spiderlakecafe). After a mile, the road's wide shoulder gets narrow, but again we are riding with only sporadic vehicle traffic. A relaxed spin on generally flat ground takes us into the Chequamegon National Forest. Shortly thereafter, Forest Road 320 goes by, and our route crosses the Teal River at mile 16.2.

The best part of this loop starts at 17.8 miles, with a right turn onto County S. We roll south into dense woods straight away and lean into the first of nearly 10 miles of a road filled with curves and twists. Small hills hop up over low ridges and then drop past silent wetlands. The road doesn't ever straighten out long enough to see what's coming up. A lazy southwesterly course brings us close to the Teal River once again, and at 21.6 miles we cross the Teal just before its confluence with the west fork of the Chippewa River.

The east end of Moose Lake Road appears at 22.4 miles (if you chose the short-loop option, this is where you rejoin the main loop). From this point, County S follows a long S bend of the Chippewa River, then shoots to the west to the junction with County B at mile 27.7. Here we'll turn right back toward the flowage, passing scenic Drake, Hay, and Moss Creeks, all drifting into Lake Chippewa.

When mile 31.7 arrives, we'll be passing County A and the Chippewa Inn once again, and we reach our final turn onto County CC at 33 miles. From here it's a 5-mile repeat performance of our ride's prologue, and we're back at Herman's Landing and the end of a wonderful 38 miles.

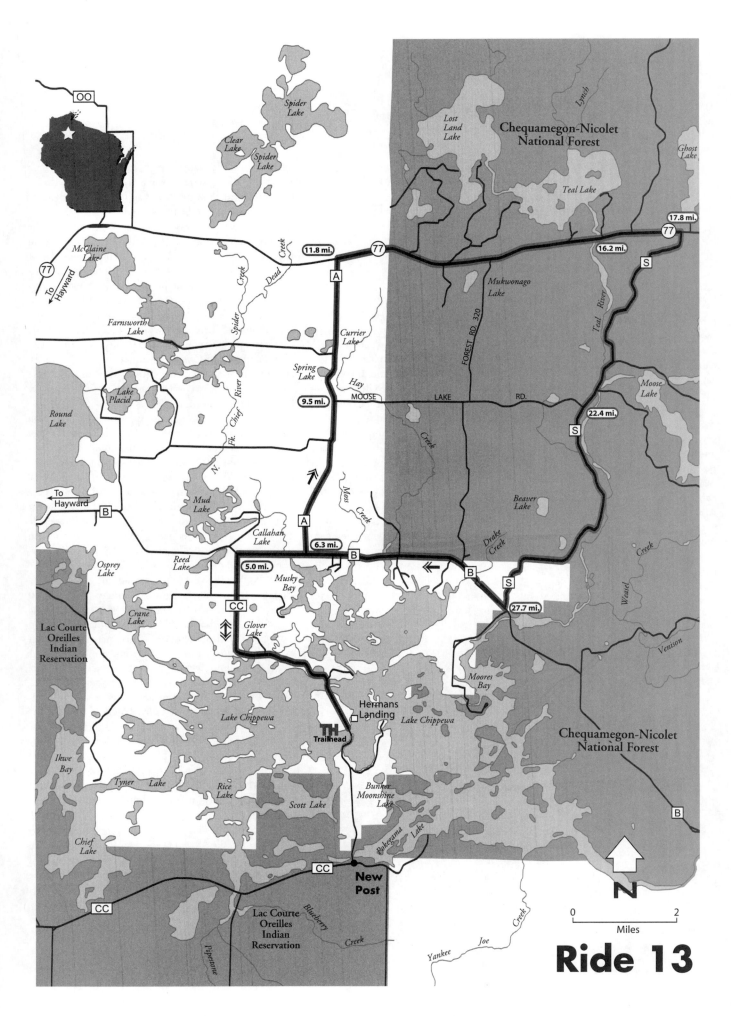

Ride 13

RIDE 14
Some Call Me Timm

Location: County roads near Timm's Hill, 4 miles east of Ogema and just south of State Highway 86.
Distance: 18.5-mile loop.
Pedaling time: 1.5–2 hours.
Surface: Paved roads.
Terrain: Flat and rolling.
Sweat factor: Moderate.
Trailhead: Timm's Hill County Park, a mile north of County RR.

Zany Art

"It's gotta be in ya to do it." So said Fred Smith, the creative lumberjack behind the uncommon outdoor art of the Wisconsin Concrete Park near Phillips, about 20 miles north of Ogema on State Highway 13. After his retirement, Fred worked between 1948 and 1964, building more than 250 sculptures made of concrete, glass, and other stuff. Fred probably was just goofing around at the outset, but now his work is internationally regarded as masterworks of American sculpture. Look for rock-solid images of Abe Lincoln, Ben Hur, Sacagawea, Paul Bunyan, various animals, and cowboys and Indians. Call (715) 339-4505 for more information.

Another fantastic ride on one of Wisconsin's Rustic Roads, this one takes you near Wisconsin's highest point, Timm's Hill, at 1,951.5 feet. Timm's Hill County Park is a beautiful place, and the observation tower at the top of the hill reveals impressive views of lakes and woods far in the distance. The trailhead is located in a former 187-acre logging camp that Price County purchased from Timothy Cahan, the park's namesake. A 300-yard trail leads to the top of Timm's Hill, with access to the tower from here. Quiet roads, a bed and breakfast, a small lake resort, and camping are all in the neighborhood. We'll ride on mostly flat terrain, with a few gentle rollers along the way.

How about a warm-up before the ride? A little stroll up to the top of Timm's Hill ought to do it. From the parking area at the county park at the north end of Bass Lake, follow the trail through maple, ash, and birch woods to the observation tower and climb the steps to the very top. Admire the great views and then trot back to the trailhead; you should be ready to go.

From the park, take the narrow exit road to the junction with County RR (Rustic Road 62). Follow it to the left, a sublime, forested road with slightly undulating terrain following the western shore of Pearson Lake. At 1.6 miles we come to the junction with State Highway 86. It's a left turn here. An occasional car might pass by, but for the most part this is a quiet road and there is a wide shoulder. There is a tree farm on our left as we ride west past forests of poplar, birch, maple, pine, and more. The junction with County C comes along at 3.7 miles, and we turn left here. Four miles to the west is the little town of Ogema, a former logging town settled by Swedish immigrants in the 1870s.

Riding south on County C, we pass Timm's Hill Bed and Breakfast, a century-old farmhouse with three distinct guest rooms and homemade food, (715) 767-5288, and abruptly ride into dense woods and more rolling land. The road is like velvet, and around each new curve is another postcard come to life. At 4.6 miles is the junction with the west end of County RR; we'll go right past and continue south. The one big climb in the ride arrives about a mile later, rising up past a large tree farm on the left. We stay on County C through a series of stair-step turns to the east and south, all the way to County YY (mile 9). There, take a left and head due east. This is a straight 2-mile stretch through younger forest. At 10 miles, we are joined by State Highway 102 from the south, and at 11 miles we'll turn hard left on northbound 102. This stretch follows flat ground to start and some mild hills farther on. A few farms, pasture, and cropland mix with the woods as we work our way north.

We come to the junction with Highway 86 at 14 miles. Follow this to the left back to County RR at 17 miles. A left here takes us back over our earlier path, past the county park's exit road. About a mile and a half down the road is High Point Village, a small lake resort with four free-standing chalets and a communal great room. Look to the right for fine views of Timm's Hill. We're back at the entrance to the park at mile 18.2. Head down the skinny, rolling road through woods so thick it seems as if the sun went down. Our ride ends at the parking area at 18.5 miles.

Rustic Road 62 near Timm's Hill.

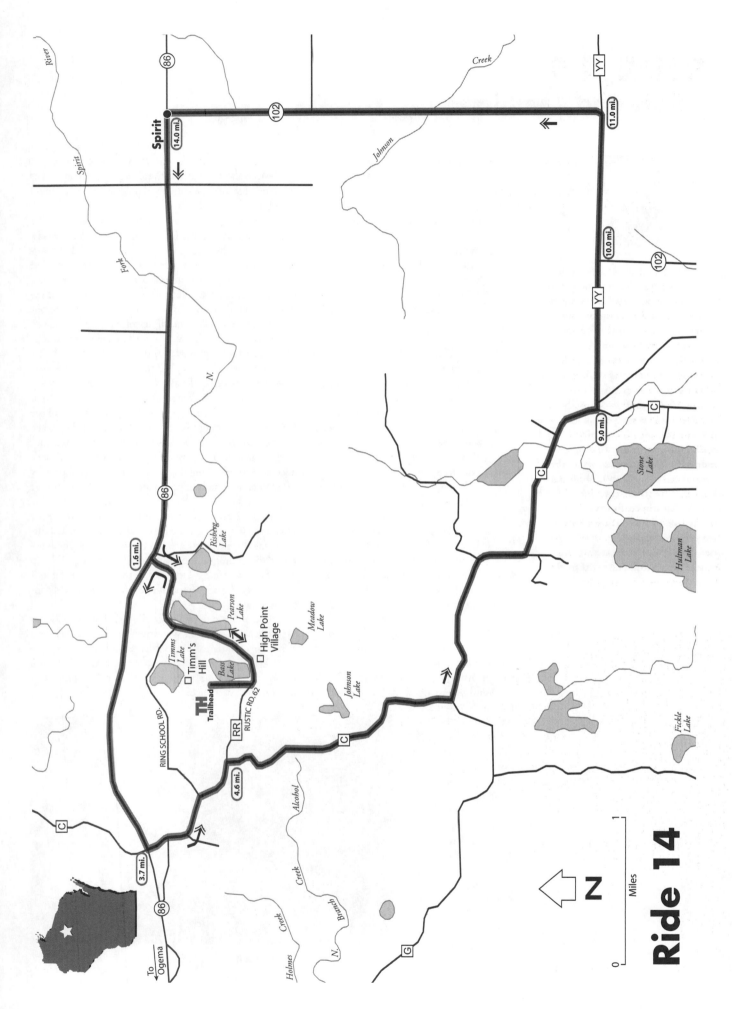

Ride 14

RIDE 15
Ruff and Tumble

Location: On County J, between Minocqua/Woodruff and Saint Germain.
Distance: 11.2 miles one way, or 22.4 miles round trip.
Pedaling time: 1–1.25 hours, one way.

Surface: Smooth, paved roads.
Terrain: Flat.
Sweat factor: Low.
Trailhead: At the junction of U.S. Highway 51 and County J in Woodruff. Ample parking is available in the lots west of the town shops.

Angel on Snowshoes

Dr. Kate Pelham was a dedicated physician who was famous throughout the Woodruff/Minocqua area for her determination to reach patients—no matter what the weather conditions were—and the distance she had to travel in the dead of winter when roads were clogged with snow. In the 1950s, the Angel on Snowshoes, as she was called, spearheaded a campaign to build a hospital in Woodruff and, along with local schoolchildren, made the dream come true. The kids set out to collect one million pennies to build the hospital, and the Million-Penny Parade caught the attention of the whole world. Donations poured in from all over, and soon Woodruff was home to a new hospital and a community that walked tall with pride.

This is the ideal North Woods cruising ride. County J meanders through especially scenic forestland and presents a nearly flat profile for its entire distance. Now, we cyclists really appreciate a nice piece of road, and the highway crews outdid themselves on this one. Your bike practically rides itself on flawless pavement, and the entire experience is a better one simply because of this splendid tarmac. Two campgrounds are located on the route, at Carrol Lake and Buffalo Lake, that provide rustic accommodations for bike-camp trips. Grab breakfast at a café in Minocqua or Woodruff, cruise the road to Saint Germain, and retrace your tracks back to town for ice cream!

The bustling Minocqua/Woodruff area has all sorts of shops loaded with tourist booty and lots of small-town cafés where you can fuel up before the ride. We'll leave all that behind, including the tourist traffic, on U.S. Highway 51. In Woodruff, we ditch the crowds and begin the ride on County J's wide and marked bike lane. Soon we enter the dense woods of the Northern Highland–American Legion State Forest, with over 220,000 acres of abundant lakes, streams, and wetlands. The forest was established in 1925 to protect the stream flow at the headwaters of the Wisconsin, Flambeau, and Manitowish Rivers. The forest is the largest state property in Wisconsin, and over two million visitors each year enjoy its scenery and recreation opportunities. There are more than 900 lakes, many miles of hiking trails, and a wide variety of wildlife. Be on the lookout for ruffed grouse, deer, beaver, fox,

and maybe even a black bear. A hundred or more bird species can also be seen and heard in the forest, as well as the venerable loon. Stately pines line the route, accented with birch and maple.

The road makes a couple of flimsy curves, and at 3.5 miles passes the Carrol Lake campground on the left. County J then bends slightly to the south on a lazy stair-step course to the second campground at Buffalo Lake (mile 7). These are two gorgeous sites to call home for a few nights while you take in some extra two-wheeled exploring around the area's more than 900 lakes. Numerous cabins and resorts line the shores of lakes such as Clear, Sweeney, Gilmore, Pickerel, as well as offer copious opportunities for water-related activities.

At 8.4 miles, we cross a short bridge over the narrows between Pickerel Lake and the Rainbow Flowage. The Rainbow is a swollen section of the Wisconsin River, which here is in the early stages of its long journey to the Mississippi. After completing mile 9, we see the landscape transformed from thick woods to more open space and wetland areas. Unfortunately, you could very well experience more traffic along this section of the road, especially on weekends. The lack of an adequate shoulder doesn't help matters either.

At 11.2 miles, we arrive at the junction with State Highway 70 on the south edge of Saint Germain. This little town's deceptive size offers much for North Woods activities, including skiing, snowmobiling, hiking, fishing, and of course, biking. Don't forget to sample some goodies at Cathy's Candy Shop, and the annual scarecrow contest is always a hoot.

End your ride here or do a U-turn and take County J back to Minocqua and Woodruff. I like that choice best. With the abundance of woodlands and lakes along the way, there's no doubt that you'll spy something that you missed the first time, making the 22.4-mile round trip a memorable experience.

County Road J east of Woodruff.

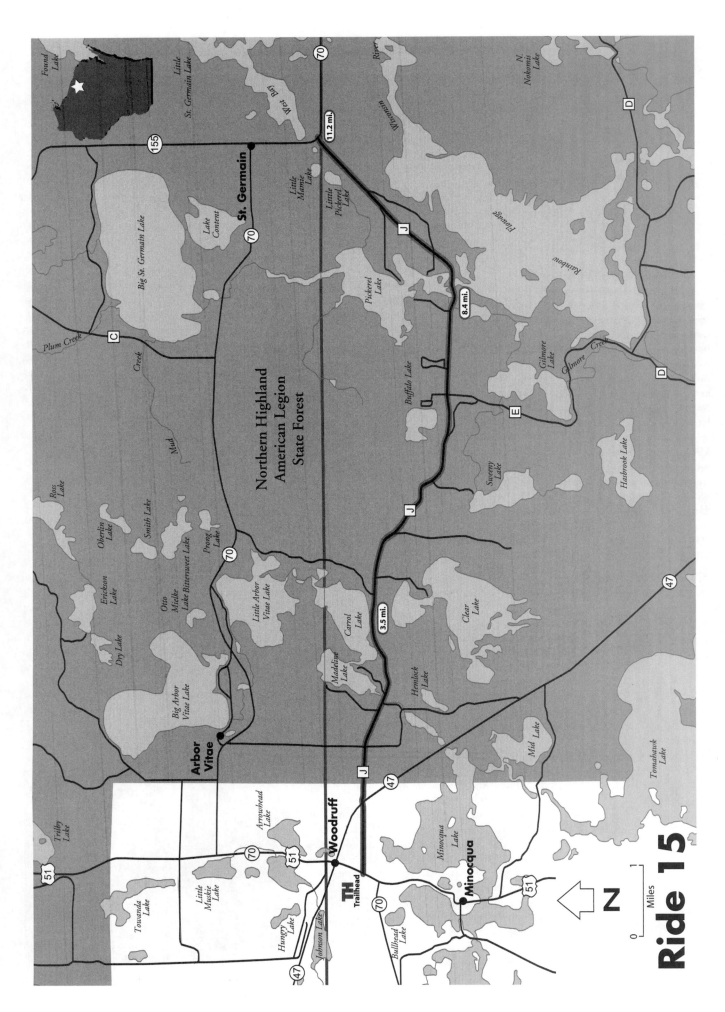

Ride 15

RIDE 16
Follow the North Star

Timber Dependent

The tracks of the Milwaukee Road made their way to Boulder Junction in 1903. Along with loggers came hunters and anglers, and both tourism and logging grew as the town was established. Coon's Resort and Camp McKinley were two of the first northern getaways in the area. But as the trees were systematically removed from the landscape, the railroad operation slowed and ceased altogether in 1932. Tourism in Boulder Junction also waned until Wisconsin began an aggressive reforestation effort in 1933 with the formation of the Civilian Conservation Corps. Their efforts returned the trees, and as the trees grew tall, they breathed new life into the town, bringing back visitors and new residents alike.

Location: County K between Boulder Junction and Star Lake, in Vilas County.
Distance: 26.4 miles, out and back.
Pedaling time: 2.25–2.75 hours.
Surface: Smooth, paved road; paved bike path.
Terrain: Flat to rolling, with a few medium-steep climbs.
Sweat factor: Moderate.
Trailhead: Parking area at the chamber of commerce building on County M at the south end of Boulder Junction.

On this pleasant out-and-back ride, we start with a nice warm-up on a scenic bike path lined with towering pines, then cruise through an enchanting woodland, and roll gently past pristine lakes on yet another Rustic Road. The setting is quiet, the road in perfect shape, and traffic extremely light—a perfect opportunity to experience the full North Woods mystique. The historic town of Sayner is just a few miles south of our main route, with numerous lodging and dining options and a museum housing the world's first snowmobile.

Before we begin, note that the location of the trailhead in Boulder Junction is ideal for getting to know more about this rugged area. The nearby chamber of commerce office is loaded with handy information for visitors, while next door, the Boulder Junction Historical Society and railroad depot museum offer numerous exhibits on the area's colorful past. The town was also voted one of the "Fifty Best Outdoor Sports Towns in America" by *Sports Afield* magazine. And how about being named "Friendliest Small Town in Wisconsin" by the readers of *Wisconsin Trails*? A combination of pristine natural lands, a variety of outdoor recreation, friendly residents, and great restaurants keep the accolades coming year after year. This is bona fide North Woods country.

But these diversions can wait. We'll head south on the paved bike path paralleling County M. This is a fun trail that sneaks through big pines on a twisty course and with a gradual descent all the way to County K. The trail can get busy on weekends, so use caution on some of the curves, and especially on the hill here, to avoid a collision with other riders. We arrive at County K at 1.5 miles. The bike path continues south; be sure to set aside another day to explore its entire length. The path ducks in and out of the woods, generally following County M, for nearly 12 miles to the Crystal Lake area. Watch for future expansion of the trail, too.

But today we'll turn left and ride east on County K, which is also Rustic Road 60. We're in for a treat on this quiet county road, which starts out straight and flat for 1.8 miles. At mile 3, the road curves into the deep woods of the Northern Highland–American Legion State Forest over casually rolling hills. For about the next 1.5 miles, the road passes between White Sand Lake to the left and, close by on the right, Lost Canoe Lake.

We roll on through this primeval scene over wrinkled terrain to the 8-mile mark, where we pass White Birch Lake and one of the many lake resorts on this ride. The road squeezes between an array of more lakes and at 11.3 miles passes Little Star Lake and climbs abruptly to Star Lake about 1 mile farther on. Look for the 1800s-era Hintz's North Star Lodge on your right, built by the Star Lake Lumber Company as a home and retreat for early railroad and company officials and guests. Two of the original buildings still stand on the property's 1,200 acres. Visit them at www.hintznorthstar.com

From here, it's less than a mile before we reach the town of Star Lake and the junction with County N. Star Lake was once a booming lumber town, giving way to the tourism industry after virtually all the trees in the area had been removed. All's quiet in Star Lake today, with just a general store, post office, and a couple of small restaurants along our ride route.

For an interesting side trip that will add about 12 (round-trip) miles to your ride, head south on County N to Sayner. Here you'll find ample evidence that the area has always been a hotbed of winter sports: the world's first snowmobile, invented by Carl Eliason, is on display at the Vilas County Historical Society. Also in Sayner is Eliason Hardware, now operated by Carl's grandson, which also boasts several early "motor toboggans." While you're in town, be sure to sample some scrumptious pizza at Vinchi's Hillside Inn.

Back in Star Lake, we'll cruise back along County K toward Boulder Junction. When County M again comes into view, we turn right on the bike path and take it back to the trailhead and the completion of 26.4 miles.

Rustic Road 60 on the way to Star Lake.

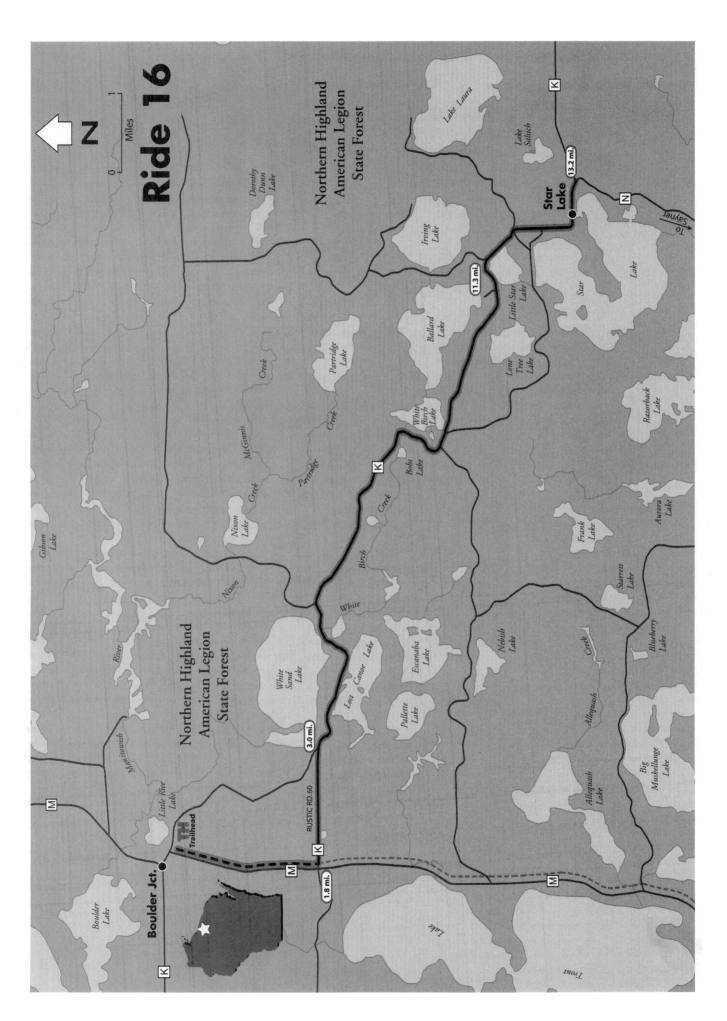

Ride 16

N

0   Miles   1

Boulder Jct.

M

K

Northern Highland American Legion State Forest

Boulder Lake

Manitowish River

Little Rice Lake

Gibson Lake

White Sand Lake

Nixon

Nixon Lake

McGinnis

Creek

Partridge

Creek

Creek

Partridge

Dorothy Dunn Lake

Partridge Lake

Northern Highland American Legion State Forest

Irving Lake

Ballard Lake

White Birch Lake

Bobs Lake

Birch

White

Creek

Lost Canoe Lake

Escanaba Lake

Pallette Lake

Nebish Lake

Frank Lake

Starrett Lake

Creek

Allequash

Blueberry Lake

Big Muskellunge Lake

Allequash Lake

Aurora Lake

Razorback Lake

Star Lake

Lone Tree Lake

Little Star Lake

Lake

Lake Salsich

Lake Laura

Star Lake

N

To Sayner

K

13.2 mi.

11.3 mi.

3.0 mi.

1.8 mi.

RUSTIC RD. 60

TH Trailhead

Trout   Lake

RIDE 18
Rural and Rustic

Chain O' Lakes

The glaciers of the last ice age left behind Waupaca's famous chain of 22 clear-water lakes. These spring-fed, interconnected lakes, named by the Menominee tribe for their exceptional clarity, have been a gathering place for generations. It is possible to take a canoe trip—via the Crystal, Wolf, and Fox Rivers and Lake Michigan—from here all the way to the Atlantic. But it's awfully tough to leave. With the serenity of the lakes and forests and the hometown values of nearby Waupaca, why not stay and play for a while? The Windmill Manor and the Lindsay House offer comfortable accommodations for some serious R and R. Or head for the action at Ding's Dock or the beaches at Hartman Creek State Park.

Location: Hartman Creek State Park area west of Waupaca.
Distance: 11-mile loop.
Pedaling time: 1–1.25 hours.
Surface: Paved roads.
Terrain: Flat, with one good hill.
Sweat factor: Low.
Trailhead: Hartman Creek State Park entrance, 1.5 miles south of State Highway 54.

Eleven miles might seem hardly worth it to some folks, but this loop through the scenic Chain O' Lakes area near Waupaca is worth every pedal stroke. If you want more miles, do the loop twice or move right on to Ride 19, which is in the same area. But be sure to add this one to your ride list. Nearly deserted roads wind through tall pines on the way to the Chain O' Lakes. Our route follows tight bends past the shores of several of the lakes en route to the tiny community of Rural, with an amazing collection of mid-1800s homes and the Crystal River Inn. The *two* Rustic Roads that we sample wander through quiet forests, and the beach at Hartman Creek State Park can't be beat for a postride cooldown. For more information on the Waupaca area, check out www.waupaca areachamber.com

This is another ride with so many attractions (it just wouldn't be right to call them distractions) at the trailhead that it's difficult to get started. Hartman Creek State Park is a 1,500-acre beauty containing three of Waupaca's Chain O' Lakes and a fascinating blend of northern and southern habitats. Pine and hardwood forests merge with southern oak and prairie meadows, and the result is a wonderful cast of wild critters and diverse plant life. Evidence of the park's glacial past is present in the kettles, ravines, and huge boulders in the area. In addition to four nearby spring-fed lakes, Hartman Lake is within the park itself and has a 300-foot beach, swimming areas, and picnic grounds.

We start our ride by heading east from the park on Rustic Road 23. First, we ride through an open meadow with woods on the fringe, then cross a one-lane bridge over Hartman Creek into thicker forest. There are excellent cross-country ski and hiking trails in these parts. And it must be said again: Wisconsin's Rustic

Road program is one of the best things that the state has done to further two-wheeled recreation. At 1.1 miles, we turn left on Whispering Pines Road, which affords us a quiet cruise northeastward through the small state park of the same name and past clusters of homes on Pope and Knight Lakes. There's a miniature golf course at 2.2 miles and another one-lane bridge.

Our road snakes right into the middle of this chain of lakes, and at 2.9 miles we arrive at County Q and the hub of lake-related activity. Ding's Dock is here for boat rentals and canoe trips on the Crystal River. The Wheelhouse Restaurant serves up great pizza, and you can top it off with goodies from Scoopers Ice Cream Parlour. To work off any excess calories we acquired at either place, we'll ride on County Q east to County QQ at 4.3 miles and turn right. Very soon, at State Highway 22, we head straight across, past the split with Smith Road, and ride south on Old State Highway 22.

Coasting into the little burg of Rural at 5.6 miles, we meet the junction with another segment of Rustic Road 23 (Rural Road). We follow that to the right, crossing the Crystal River and taking a step back in time. Here, there's an amazing collection of restored nineteenth-century homes and a huge barn that gives the whole area an extra down-home dimension. Also here is the enchanting Crystal River Inn, a bed and breakfast that ranks with the best.

Back in the present, Highway 22 appears again at 6.1 miles. We'll go straight across and follow R-23 for just half a mile to the split with Emmons Creek Road (Rustic Road 24). We take a left and soon encounter a rarity for this ride: a hill. Short but fairly steep, the hill climbs into a dense wood with big pines crowding in. A bridge crossing over Emmons Creek at mile 8 means we're getting close to West Road, where we'll turn right at 8.2 miles. The road runs through open land and makes a 90-degree turn to the east to meet back up with R-23 at 9.3 miles. A left here takes us back through the whispering pines to Hartman Creek State Park.

The Crystal River Inn near the town of Rural.

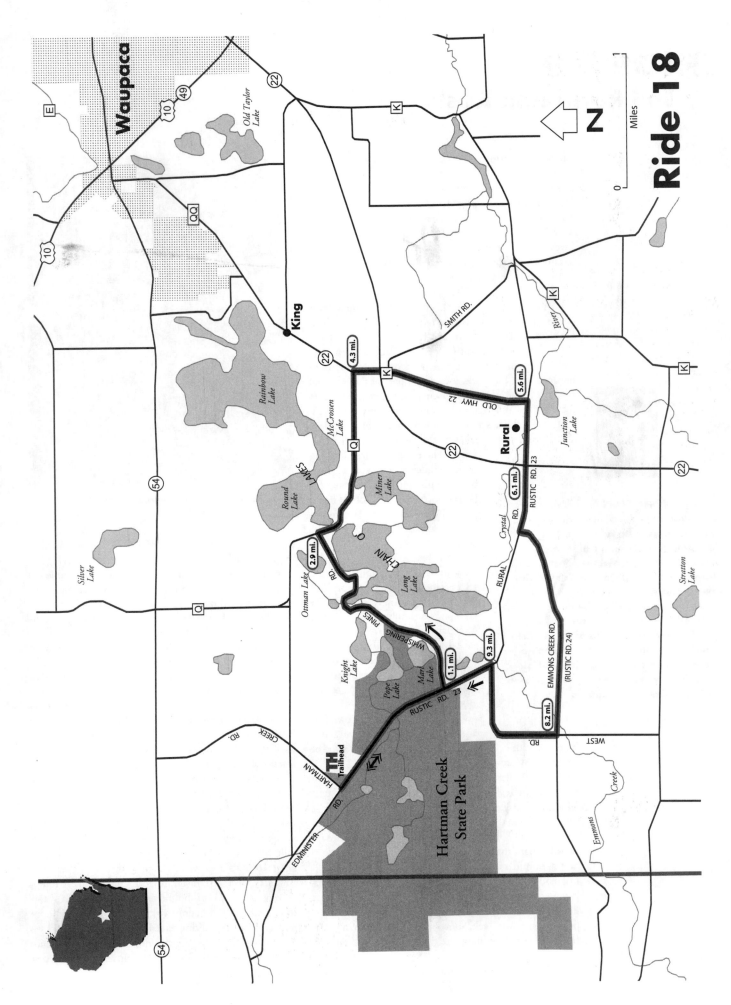

Ride 18

N

Miles

Waupaca

Old Taylor Lake

King

Rainbow Lake

McCrossen Lake

LAKES

Round Lake

Miner Lake

Silver Lake

Ottman Lake

CHAIN

Long Lake

Knight Lake

Pope Lake

Marl Lake

WHISPERING PINES

Hartman Creek State Park

TH Trailhead

HARTMAN CREEK RD.

EDMINSTER RD.

RUSTIC RD. 23

Smith Rd.

River

Rural

Old Hwy 22

Junction Lake

Crystal Rd.

Rustic Rd. 23

Rural Rd.

Emmons Creek Rd.
(Rustic Rd. 24)

West Rd.

Stratton Lake

Emmons Creek

4.3 mi.

5.6 mi.

6.1 mi.

2.9 mi.

1.1 mi.

9.3 mi.

8.2 mi.

RIDE 19
Still Rural and Rustic

Location: Hartman Creek State Park area west of Waupaca.
Distance: 11.2-mile loop.
Pedaling time: 1–1.25 hours.
Surface: Paved roads, with one short gravel section.
Terrain: Flat, with one good hill.
Sweat factor: Low.
Trailhead: Hartman Creek State Park entrance, 1.5 miles south of State Highway 54.

Along with Ride 18, this tour will give you a flavor of the wonderful variety of activities in Waupaca's Chain O' Lakes area, and a part of it travels over two different Rustic Roads. Hartman Creek State Park is the perfect place to begin and end a ride, with over 1,500 acres of outdoor fun. The park, located on part of the terminal moraine of the Wisconsin glacier, boasts seven clear lakes set aside for quiet recreation only—no motors allowed. Hartman Lake has a 300-foot sand beach, and the park also adjoins several lakes at the head of the Chain O' Lakes. There are 10 miles of hiking trails, 5 miles of unpaved, off-road biking trails, and 7 scenic miles for horses. It also boasts a robust heard of white-tailed deer. Year-round camping makes Hartman one of our favorites.

The first segment of the ride is the same as the beginning of Ride 18. From Hartman Creek State Park, we ride east on Rustic Road 23 (also known simply as Rural Road). After passing through open meadow, we cross a one-lane bridge into a more forested area. Take note of the trailheads here, and next time come back with your hiking boots (or skis in winter) and explore these quiet woods up close. Deer, fox, owl, lots of songbirds, and more are active here year round. In fact, the Waupaca area boasts one of the largest white-tailed deer herds in the state.

At 1.1 miles, we roll past Whispering Pines Road on the left, which takes a winding course northeastward past lakeside cabins and homes right to the buzz of activity at Ding's Dock in the heart of the Chain O' Lakes. The road also parallels Whispering Pines State Park, a small day-use-only park that was originally used for popular entertainment and relaxing in the 1940s. The 30-acre park originally opened as a privately owned public park; following the death of the landowner in 1975, the park was donated to the state, which now operates the land as a sibling to Hartman Creek. Some original stone steps and the faint remains of buildings are the only hints of the park's former appearance.

Our own route continues for about 2 miles to the

Rustic Road 23 near the town of Rural.

junction with Emmons Creek Road (Rustic Road 24) at mile 3. We take a right here and tackle a short, steep hill (the only real obstacle on the entire loop) and follow a gorgeous stretch west through fragrant woods, big pines, and over the bridge above Emmons Creek at 4.4 miles.

Just past the bridge is West Road, an intersection familiar from Ride 17. This time we head straight on R-24, riding for about a mile before entering the Emmons Creek Barrens. This is a state natural area consisting of oak savanna with scattered burr and white oaks. Look to the ground to see wild lupine, a favorite habitat of the endangered Karner blue butterfly. You would have a good chance to see the Karner if you were hiking on the Ice Age National Scenic Trail, which travels right through here on its way north. This is a perfect spot to pull over and just listen—and simply be glad you're here.

The road turns to gravel for the last mile of the Rustic Road, but the surface is typically hard-packed and very rideable. At 6.9 miles, we turn right (north) on Stratton Lake Road. (For an optional trip, we can instead head straight west on Fountain Lake Road, which leads to a 2-mile fun and curvy descent to County TT. That leads north to Badger Drive and a right turn; the road soon connects with Edminster Road.) On the main route, however, we stay northbound on Stratton Lake Road and soon roll to the junction with County D. Continuing north, we come to Edminster Road at mile 9.4, and we turn right here, following this quiet road through dense stands of pine back to the park entrance and trailhead at 11.2 miles.

Waupaca Fun

Waupaca is loaded with all kinds of fun things to do all the year through. If it's June, it's time to check out the annual Strawberry Fest, with a large art and craft fair, live entertainment, and strawberry shortcake! July means Hometown Day, Waupaca's July 4th celebration. A parade, barbecue lunch, concerts, and of course fireworks over Shadow Lake. The Fall-o-Rama in September is a family affair with food, entertainment, horse-drawn wagon rides, and pumpkin carving.

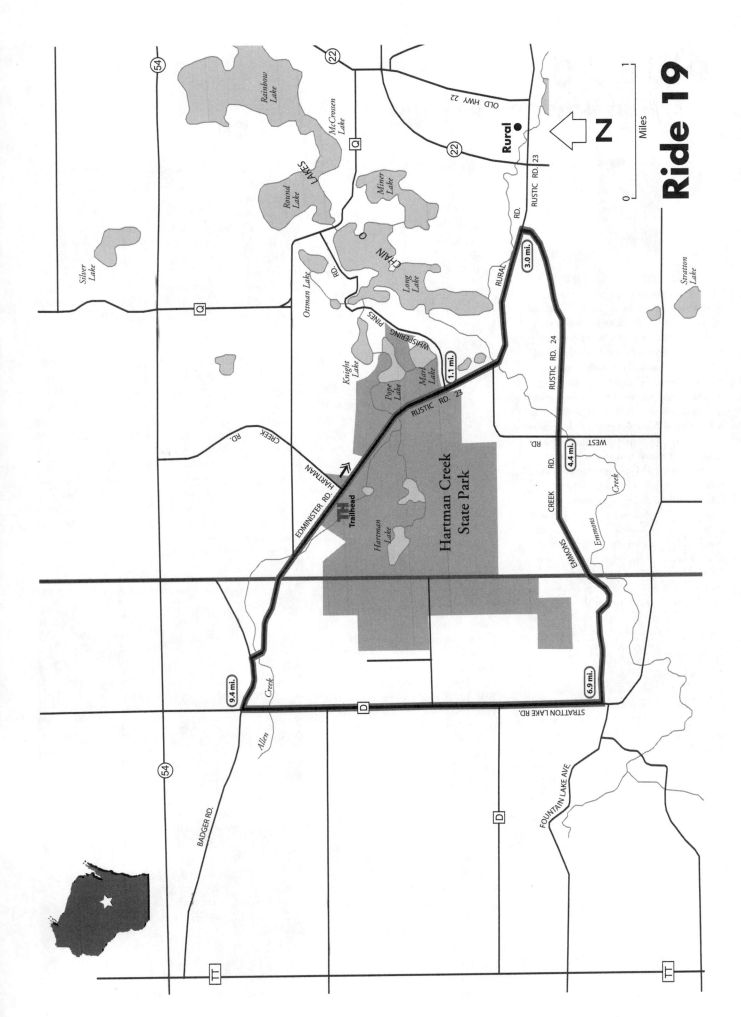

Ride 19

N

Miles

0 1

Rural

OLD HWY 22

22

22

RUSTIC RD. 23

RURAL RD.

3.0 mi.

1.1 mi.

RUSTIC RD. 23

RUSTIC RD. 24

4.4 mi.

WEST RD.

Stratton Lake

Emmons Creek

EMMONS CREEK RD.

6.9 mi.

STRATTON LAKE RD.

FOUNTAIN LAKE AVE.

D

D

Hartman Creek State Park

Hartman Lake

Marl Lake

Pope Lake

Knight Lake

WHISPERING PINES

CHAIN O LAKES

Long Lake

Miner Lake

Ottman Lake

RD.

Q

Q

54

Round Lake

Rainbow Lake

McCrossen Lake

Silver Lake

CREEK RD.

HARTMAN

EDMINSTER RD.

TH
Trailhead

9.4 mi.

Allen Creek

54

BADGER RD.

TT

TT

RIDE 20
Ellison Bay and Beyond

Location: Area north of Ellison Bay in Door County.
Distance: 14-mile loop.
Pedaling time: 1.25–1.5 hours.
Surface: Paved roads.
Terrain: Flat and rolling.
Sweat factor: Moderate.
Trailhead: Tourist Information Center in Ellison Bay on State Highway 42.

Death's Door

In the early days of shipping, with few navigational aids, hundreds of ships met their demise in the dangerous currents and shoals between the Door Peninsula and Washington Island in Wisconsin's early days. Death's Door, originally *Porte des Morts* in French, was the name given to this perilous strait, and that is one tale of how Door County got its name.

An Indian legend on the subject lends a bit more drama to it, and Wisconsin's 1851 Legislature noted this story in giving the county its name. The Cape Indians were the first to live in this area of the peninsula and were happily going about their daily lives when a large band of Potawatomi Indians forced them off their land. The Cape Indians retreated to Detroit Island, planning to retrieve their land by sending in sentries to light a signal fire to alert the rest when to attack. Alas, the spies were captured by the Potawatomi and tortured until they revealed the plan. The Potawatomi then lit the fire and waited. When the Cape Indians arrived they were ambushed and killed; the title "Death's Door" was associated with this fateful event ever since.

Door County, Wisconsin's much-celebrated—and increasingly populated—peninsula jutting out into Lake Michigan, is a marvelous place for two-wheeled jaunts. The Green Bay (north) side is edged with high, rugged cliffs and cozy bays, and Ellison Bay is one of the charming small communities tucked in along the coast. Founded in 1866, the village offers grand views of Green Bay and is home to many pottery shops and other artisans. This loop explores the peaceful roads along the bay and farther inland, clear over to the eastern coast of the peninsula at Gills Rock.

Heading out of Ellison Bay on State Highway 42, we turn left on Garret Bay Road, following the sign for Door Bluff Headlands County Park. This is a nice quiet road with woods of birch, maple, and pine and some seasonal lake homes on the left. Just a short way up the road is The Clearing, a small school of art, literature, and ecology situated in a pastoral woodland on the bluffs above Green Bay. At 2.2 miles, we pass Door Bluff Park Road and the entrance to the county park, which leads north to Deathdoor Bluff and some fun hiking trails running down to the water. There are no views from the road or the parking area, which keeps many auto tourists away and leaves the area blissfully uncrowded.

Garret Bay Road now continues east along the shore, providing opportunities for some fine viewing of Garret Bay on our left. We turn right on Garret Bay Hill Road and climb up a steep hill to a stop sign at Cottage and Blackberry Roads. We'll head left on Cottage Road at 3 miles, following the posted bike route sign. After an open meadow, we enjoy a long descent winding through more woods. At 4.2 miles, we roll into Gills Rock, a tiny community on the tip of Door County's peninsula, with a few shops situated on its main street and dozens of boats docked in a nearby marina. A long tradition of commercial fishing continues to be part of life here, and a mar-

itime museum displays memorabilia from the fishing industry and from many of the shipwrecks in the waters of Death's Door.

It's too early for a rest stop here, so we'll turn left on Highway 42, again following the bike-route sign. Down the road a bit is a sign for the ferry to Washington Island, the largest of Door County's islands and the oldest Icelandic community in the United States. For an enjoyable day-trip, take the short boat ride and enjoy the relatively uncrowded byways of the island. With the number of motorized vehicles limited by the ferry, this is a very bike-friendly place.

But for now, we'll press on and return to Highway 42, where we take a left and continue east on to Timberline Road at 4.9 miles. A right turn there brings us to a long, flat stretch past open fields and meadows. At the junction with County NP at 7.9 miles, we'll go left (east) at the sign for Newport State Park. A right at Newport Lane and another 0.5 mile deliver us right to the front door of the park. Stop by for spectacular views of Lake Michigan and Spider Island to the southeast.

After a short break, let's turn around and head back west on County NP, passing Timberline Road; after NP turns to the right, head north a short distance to the junction with Highway 42 at 11.9 miles. We're going to be adventurous here and take a left and ride the highway back to Ellison Bay at 14 miles.

Overlooking the harbor at Gills Rock.

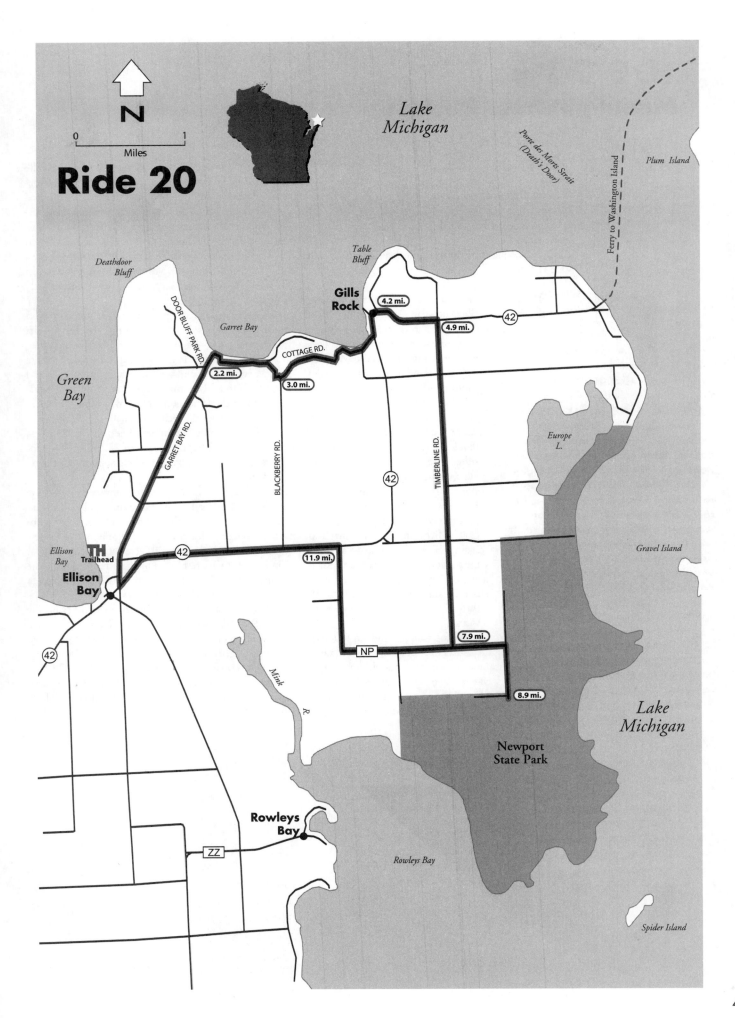

Ride 20

N

0   1
Miles

Lake Michigan

Porte des Morts Strait
(Death's Door)

Plum Island

Ferry to Washington Island

Table Bluff

Deathdoor Bluff

Garret Bay

Green Bay

Gills Rock

4.2 mi.

42

4.9 mi.

DOOR BLUFF PARK RD.

COTTAGE RD.

2.2 mi.

3.0 mi.

GARRET BAY RD.

BLACKBERRY RD.

42

TIMBERLINE RD.

Europe L.

Ellison Bay

TH Trailhead

Ellison Bay

42

11.9 mi.

Gravel Island

42

NP

7.9 mi.

Mink R.

8.9 mi.

Lake Michigan

Newport State Park

Rowleys Bay

ZZ

Rowleys Bay

Spider Island

RIDE 21
Moonlight over Michigan

Location: Eastern coast of Door County on County Q.
Distance: 15 miles one way.
Pedaling time: 1.25–1.5 hours.
Surface: Paved roads.
Terrain: Flat.
Sweat factor: Low.
Trailhead: Aqualand Camp Resort on County Q and State Highway 57.

What's in a Name?

One night in the fall of 1848, a cargo ship under the command of Captain Justin Bailey sailed into a furious Lake Michigan storm with high winds and heavy rain. Searching for a safe harbor along Door Peninsula, he found what he was looking for and was able to keep the ship safe and wait for calmer waters. The bay he used was named Baileys Harbor, as was the village that quickly grew up around it.

This is a lovely one-way ride on super-smooth roads along the shores of Lake Michigan. A side trip on a Rustic Road near Moonlight Bay allows access to the water and views of a lighthouse. At the end of the ride is Baileys Harbor, a bustling lake town filled with shops and eateries and loads of nautically themed activities.

We start this ride heading due east on straight, flat, and well-maintained County Q. The road has no shoulder, but there isn't much traffic either. The woods on both sides are filled with poplar, birch, and maple, along with a pine here and there. At 1.3 miles, the road angles to the right at North Bay Road. Brief glimpses of Lake Michigan appear now and again through the trees. We arrive at the junction with Cana Island Road at mile 6.1, where we take a left. This is a short side trip on Rustic Road 38 through a lush, green forest of spruce, cedar, and white pine.

We follow the sign for Cana Island Lighthouse, wandering along the shores of Moonlight Bay for views of the lighthouse and a chance to dangle our feet in Michigan's cold waters. The lighthouse was built in 1869 and is Door County's most recognizable light. It can be reached by walking across a causeway of smooth stones (or wading, if the water level is high). The keeper's house is open from mid-May through mid-October. The Moonlight Bay Bedrock Beach is a protected five-acre state natural area supporting rare plant and animal communities that depend on the significant influences of Lake Michigan. The dolomite bedrock beach hosts several plant species adapted to unstable shores. After the 5-mile round-trip to the lighthouse, we return to County Q and go left to continue on a southwesterly course.

The Ridges Sanctuary Wildlife Area appears on our left around mile 14.2, an outstanding area for wildlife viewing and home to many rare native plants. Established in 1937, this 1,200-acre natural area is the oldest private preserve in the state and is also a State Natural Area and National Natural Landmark. There are 5 miles of rustic trails and bridges and numerous environmental education events. Best of all, cyclists can help by taking part in the Ride for Nature, an annual bike tour on the area's scenic back roads, with distances of 25, 50, or 100 kilometers to choose from. Proceeds help support the Ridges and its programs.

After this it's an easy spin to Highway 57, where we turn left and cruise for one more mile to bustling and tourist-laden Baileys Harbor. The town has numerous options for lodging and dining. Among these are the New Yardley Inn, tucked among 10 acres of pines; the Inn at Windmill Farm, a restored Dutch farmhouse with the original windmill and barns; and the Blacksmith Inn, a romantic getaway right on the shore.

Before or after we settle in, there's another nearby Rustic Road that's worth exploring. Winding eastward from Baileys Harbor to the Old Lighthouse Point Natural Area via Ridges Road, R-39 is a 5-mile, round-trip jaunt offering lovely views of the cove known as Baileys Harbor and another section of the Ridges Sanctuary. Plan ahead and stay the night in this fun town or double back for a 30-mile trip.

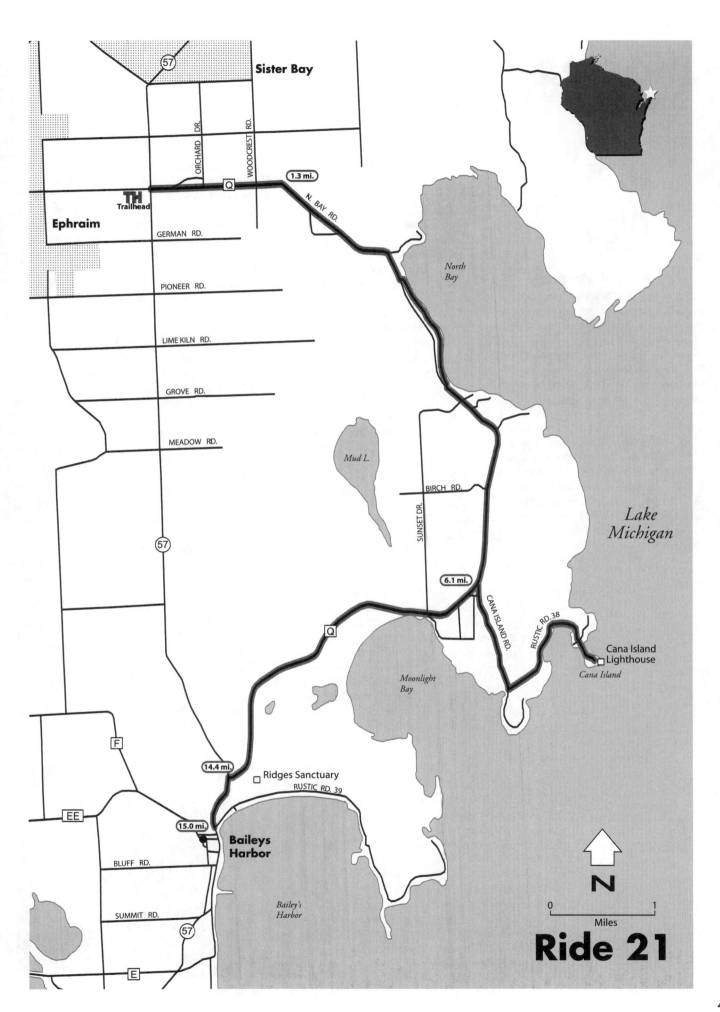

Sister Bay

57

ORCHARD DR.

WOODCREST RD.

Q 1.3 mi.

TH
Trailhead

Ephraim

GERMAN RD.

PIONEER RD.

LIME KILN RD.

GROVE RD.

MEADOW RD.

N. BAY RD.

North
Bay

Mud L.

57

BIRCH RD.

SUNSET DR.

6.1 mi.

CANA ISLAND RD.

RUSTIC RD. 38

Lake
Michigan

Cana Island
Lighthouse
Cana Island

Q

Moonlight
Bay

14.4 mi.

F

EE

Ridges Sanctuary

RUSTIC RD. 39

15.0 mi.

Baileys
Harbor

BLUFF RD.

SUMMIT RD.

57

Bailey's
Harbor

E

N

0   1
Miles

Ride 21

RIDE 22
Terrific T

A Proud History

The role that Sturgeon Bay has played in the history of Great Lakes shipping is proudly displayed at the Door County Maritime Museum, 120 North Madison Avenue, Sturgeon Bay. The town has been home to shipbuilding since the beginning of the twentieth century, producing trawlers, ore carriers, yachts, and naval vessels. Visit the Baumgartner Gallery to see scale models of boats and ships built in Sturgeon Bay, along with an exhibit on area lighthouses. The Founders Gallery provides a chronological history of shipbuilding, starting in 1800 with Indian dugout and birch-bark canoes and continuing to present-day shipbuilding operations.

Location: Shores of Lake Michigan on County T in Door County.
Distance: 13.2 miles one way.
Pedaling time: 1–1.25 hours.
Surface: Paved roads.
Terrain: Flat.
Sweat factor: Low.
Trailhead: The junction of State Highway 57 and County T in Valmy.

Just the mere fact that this ride travels on two different Rustic Roads earns it the distinction of being my favorite ride in Door County and one of the best in the state. Plus, the scenery is outstanding, the road is surreal, and there are numerous access points to Lake Michigan along the way. The ride concludes at a Coast Guard lighthouse and a ship canal that connects Green Bay with Lake Michigan. In terms of size, the lake takes the number-two spot behind Lake Superior, but it stands alone as the only one of the Great Lakes to lie wholly within the United States. The southern section of its 1,600 miles of shoreline contains large metropolitan areas like Chicago and Milwaukee, while its northern section is less populated and its pristine beauty better preserved. Lake Michigan's cold, deep waters are host to various fish and plant populations, and its massive drainage basin spills into Illinois, Indiana, Michigan, and Wisconsin.

From the small town of Valmy at the junction of State Highway 57 and County T, head east on County T, which is also called Whitefish Bay Road, straight toward Lake Michigan. At mile 2, just before reaching the lake, we come to a T intersection. If you wish, you can head left and take a 2-mile jaunt to Whitefish Dunes State Park, with its huge white sand dunes and rugged shoreline. The ever-present wind is the main sculptor of the big piles of sand along this part of the lake. Established in 1967, this 865-acre park was set aside to protect the fragile shoreline environment. The shore extends about 3 miles and is lined with rocky bluffs as well. A boardwalk allows access to interior wetlands, and several trails wander through the adjacent forest. There are also eight Native American villages in the park that are listed on the National Register of Historic Places.

Back at the T intersection, we turn right on County T, which is also Rustic Road 9. We immediately enter dense forest on a straight, flat road to start, then the fun begins with one curve after another, passing some extraordinary real estate mixed in among lightly rolling hills. We'll start to see short dirt roads, more like driveways, splitting off the main road toward the water. These are public access points and are labeled with small white signs with names like Bittersweet Lane and Evergreen Lane. Check one of these out for views or a swim.

At 6.7 miles, we cross scenic Shivering Sands Creek and continue on R-9 to the 8-mile mark, where we turn right, then left on North Lake Michigan Drive, which marks the end of R-9. Continuing south on North Lake Michigan Drive, we are joined by County TT and the start of Rustic Road 77, the second half of our rustic doubleheader. This road hugs the shoreline for its entire length, but with a buffer of private property between the road and the water, nice views can be had only from the access roads. Nonetheless, this continues to be one of the premier rides in Wisconsin.

The trip comes to an end at 13.2 miles at the U.S. Coast Guard Station and the North Pierhead Lighthouse. A right turn here and three-quarters of a mile away is a parking area for the Sturgeon Bay Ship Canal. This is a good place for a trailhead if you decide to do the ride in reverse, and it's an excellent spot to watch big old ships mosey on through on their way to and from Lake Michigan. The short portage between the big lake and Green Bay attracted at least nine different Indian tribes to settle or visit here, and the first European settlers also chose this area as a place to live and conduct trading activities.

Sturgeon Bay is right down the road from the end of this ride and offers a boatload of things to do and places to stay. Try the Creative Soul Café for coffee and delectable soups and sandwiches, Perry's Cherry Diner for 1950s-style fun and handmade malts, or Sonny's Pizzeria for the best pizza in Door County. Stay for a while at the romantic Barbican B&B in the historic district or maybe the White Pines Victorian Lodge, the oldest house in the historic district with 132 years of Victorian charm.

Rustic Road 9 near Sturgeon Bay.

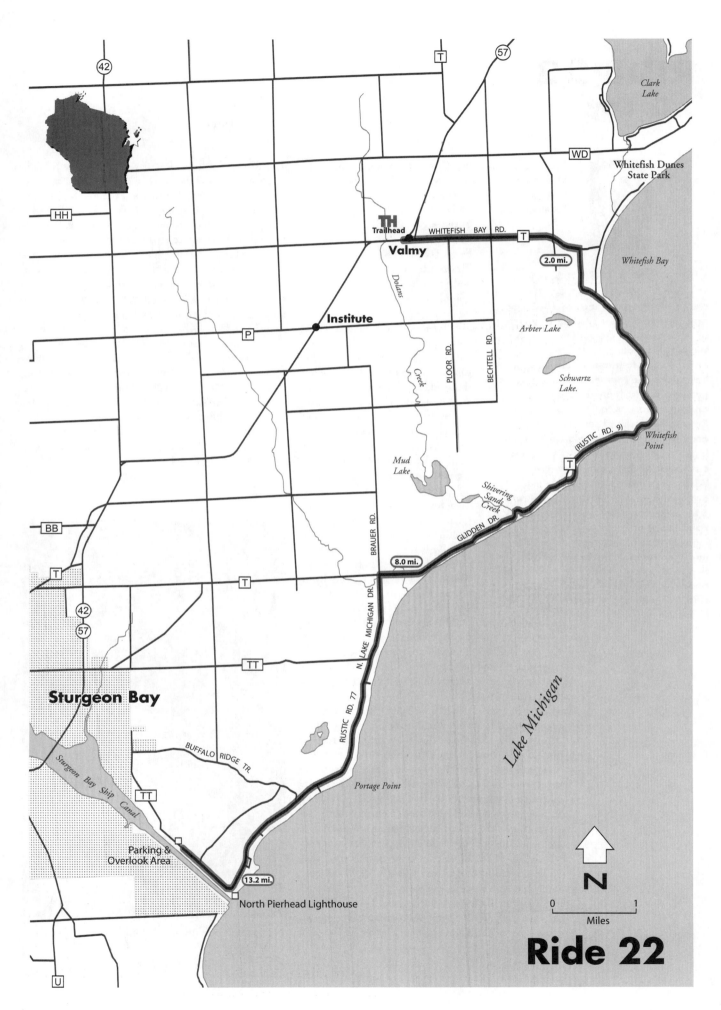

42

Clark
Lake

T

57

WD

Whitefish Dunes
State Park

HH

TH
Trailhead
WHITEFISH BAY RD.
T

Valmy

2.0 mi.

Whitefish Bay

Dolans

P

Institute

Arbter Lake

PLOOR RD.

BECHTELL RD.

Schwartz
Lake.

Creek

(RUSTIC RD. 9)

Whitefish
Point

T

Mud
Lake

Shivering
Sands
Creek

BB

GLIDDEN DR.

T

BRAUER RD.

8.0 mi.

T

42

57

N. LAKE MICHIGAN DR.

Lake Michigan

TT

RUSTIC RD. 77

Sturgeon Bay

Sturgeon Bay Ship Canal

BUFFALO RIDGE TR.

TT

Portage Point

Parking &
Overlook Area

13.2 mi.

North Pierhead Lighthouse

N

0   1
Miles

Ride 22

U

RIDE 23
O, Boy

Two Rivers

Two Rivers is where the first ice cream sundae was made in 1881. Today, the event is honored by a replica of Ed Berner's Ice Cream Parlor in the Washington House, which sports an antique soda fountain where you can belly up to the counter and order a genuine, old-fashioned sundae. There are other reasons to linger a bit in Two Rivers. The docks of several marinas are summer homes for pleasure boats big and small and are hosts to numerous charter-fishing outfitters. Two of Wisconsin's most scenic bicycle trails are right here. The Mariner's Trail runs 5 miles to Manitowoc, and the Rawley Point Trail heads north from town using a portion of this very route. Lake Michigan remains the center of attention, with many sections of white sand beach for volleyball, picnics, sun worship, swimming, and general summer laziness.

Location: Rustic Road 16 (Sandy Bay Road) along Lake Michigan north of Two Rivers.
Distance: 12.6 miles out and back.
Pedaling time: 1–1.25 hours.

Surface: Paved roads.
Terrain: Flat.
Sweat factor: Low.
Trailhead: Junction of County V and Sandy Bay Road at north end of Point Beach State Forest.

Here's a short spin on a Rustic Road through Point Beach State Forest along the shores of Lake Michigan. Six miles of sandy beach border the road, in addition to the 2,900 acres of woods. The lake, of course, is a big attraction in these parts, and such close access on this ride calls for an extended rest stop to hunt for driftwood or simply bury your feet in the sand and watch the waves drift in. At the halfway point is the city of Two Rivers, home of the first ice cream sundae, a fine place for a midride rest stop.

We'll start this short ride by heading south on Sandy Bay Road (Rustic Road 16, also County Road O), just inland from Lake Michigan. The road is in great shape, and traffic is nearly nonexistent as we roll through the fabulous woods of the Point Beach State Forest, which is very similar to the lands up north in the Hayward area—towering red and white pine, blue spruce, and occasional clusters of aspen.

At 1.8 miles on the left, we pass the entrance to the campground area of Point Beach State Forest. Also down this road is the U.S. Coast Guard lighthouse at Rawley Point. Situated on a tower 113 feet above the lake, this is the biggest and brightest light on the Great Lakes, sending a two-million-candlepower twinkle across the water. Past the campground, it's an easy, enjoyable cruise on a pancake-flat road past dense woods on our right and stubby shoreline foliage on our left. Lake Michigan shows itself in fleeting glimpses, then disappears again behind the trees. Sandy Bay Road follows this routine all the way to mile 4.3 and Molash Creek. This is a pretty cool spot to stop and soak in some nice views of this small stream on its last winding turns to the big lake.

After crossing the creek, we begin to see scattered homes of a residential area at 5.8 miles as we get closer to Two Rivers. Getting a clear view of the lake is still difficult here because of the woods and private residences. We roll into the heart of Two Rivers at 6.3 miles, named for the south-flowing East and West Twin Rivers. There is a bike path along the road here and in town is an A&W—how can you beat an ice-cold root beer after a ride?

Two Rivers has a few other great places to check out. Down the street is a store called Unique Flying Objects, filled with all kinds of cool things that allegedly fly. Visit the Red Forest Bed & Breakfast for a cozy night in an early 1900s antique-adorned home, www.redforestbb.com Just a few blocks past the end of County O is the Historic Rogers Street Fishing Village, (920) 793-5905, the site of an early French Canadian and Indian fishing community. A museum includes fishing and boating antiques, and there is also an old fishing tug and lighthouse. Check out the *Buddy O,* a 1936 wooden tug, and the shipwrecks exhibit.

After more exploring in Two Rivers, we'll turn around and head back the same way we came, arriving back at the trailhead at 12.6 miles.

The lighthouse at Rawley Point.

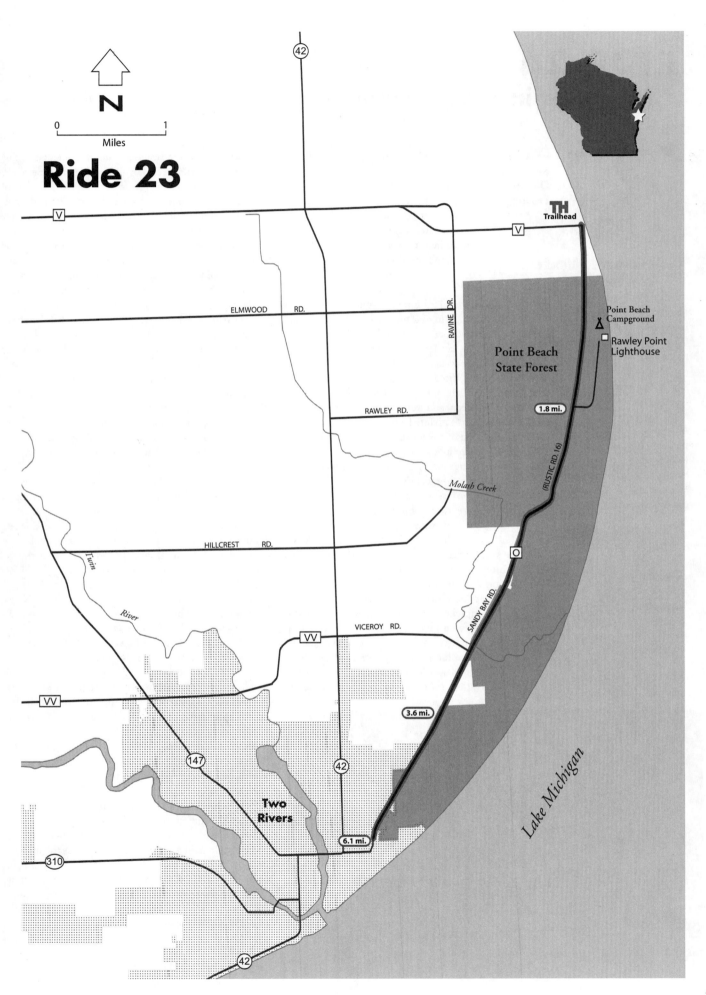

Ride 23

N

0   1
Miles

42

V

V

TH
Trailhead

ELMWOOD RD.

RAVINE DR.

RAWLEY RD.

Point Beach
State Forest

Point Beach
Campground

Rawley Point
Lighthouse

1.8 mi.

(RUSTIC RD. 16)

Molash Creek

HILLCREST RD.

Twin

River

O

SANDY BAY RD.

VICEROY RD.

VV

3.6 mi.

VV

147

42

Two
Rivers

6.1 mi.

Lake Michigan

310

42

RIDE 24
Meander in the Moraine

Historic Wade House

In 1851, in the tiny town of Greenbush halfway between Sheboygan and Fond du Lac, the Wade House opened as a convenient rest stop and inn for travelers on the Plank Road. Today the site is home to an impressive collection of restored buildings, including the Wisconsin Carriage Museum, one of the nation's largest collections of restored horse-drawn carriages. The site is open May to October, and demonstrations of old-time chores are given regularly.

Location: South of Greenbush on county roads in the Kettle Moraine State Forest.
Distance: 14.9-mile loop.
Pedaling time: 1.25–1.5 hours.
Surface: Paved roads.
Terrain: Rolling, with one tough climb.
Sweat factor: Moderate +.
Trailhead: Parking area for Parnell Tower on County U, south of State Highway 67.

The Kettle Moraine State Forest is tough to beat for straight-up cycling fun. The roads are smooth as silk and roll past the kettles, eskers, and moraines left in the wake of the glacier that covered most of Wisconsin thousands of years ago. The northern unit of the forest is rugged, lush green, and wet with streams and swamps, all remnants from the enormous glacier that blanketed the state 20,000 years ago. Two lobes of the glacier banged into each other on a northeast-to-southwest bearing. The debris from their collision, billions of tons of rocks, gravel, and sand, were left behind when the ice finally melted away.

In 1937, the Wisconsin Legislature noted the special character of this place and established the state forest, preserving a fabulous outdoor resource for recreation and education. In addition, part of the Ice Age National Scenic Trail's extensive path travels through this area. A comprehensive visitor center for the trail is located in Dundee on Highway 67, a few miles southwest of the area covered in the ride. The center includes information on the forest, interpretive displays, an ice age film, and naturalist programs.

An observation tower at the trailhead serves up panoramic views of the forest and rolling countryside. The counterclockwise direction of this loop means one tough climb followed by a long, fast descent. At the north end of the loop is the Old Wade House Historic Site and a collection of wonderfully restored buildings from the 1800s.

Like Ride 14, the trailhead begins at an observation tower. The 60-foot Parnell Tower is set in the midst of the state forest and presents views far and wide of the surrounding landscape. And it's another chance to warm up for the ride by climbing a substantial set of stairs. (If you're really in great shape, do the stairs *after* the ride.)

Leaving the Parnell Tower area, we turn left onto County U and ride east 0.3 mile to County A, where we turn left, following the sign for the Kettle Moraine Scenic Drive. There is no shoulder, but the road surface is good and traffic is nowhere to be found. County U turns to the right at 0.8 mile, but we keep going straight on County A. We head up a small hill, then cruise down a nice descent into more open farm country to mile 2.2 and State Highway 67. A right here and a quick left gets us back on County A heading north through more farm country (the heavily forested area is just to the west and we'll be there soon). County Z goes by at 4.1 miles, followed by a nice long descent to 5.9 miles and the junction with Plank Road. We'll lean left, staying on County A.

On the left at 6.3 miles, we arrive at the Old Wade House Historic Site in Greenbush (see the sidebar), a stately stagecoach inn from days past. Turn left at the entrance to the site, then take a right on County T, still following signs for Kettle Moraine Scenic Drive. At 7.1 miles, we'll leave County T and take a left on Kettle Moraine Drive. This is where the real fun starts, on velvety pavement rolling through dense stands of pine.

A pretty good little hill takes us past the Greenbush Group Camp, and then we're in for a tough grind way up to 8.7 and the Greenbush Picnic Area. Catch your breath and lean over your bars for a long and fast downhill, flying past the Greenbush Kettle before the road finally levels out around 9.8 miles. If you've been looking around, you'll have noticed the impressive glacial features left over from 20,000 years ago. Some of the resulting kames rise more than 350 feet. Eskers and kettles are plentiful here as well, and it's awe inspiring to ride past remnants of this ancient scene.

We curve to the right at Summit Road, staying on our southbound course. The forest on the left gives way to farmland, and we reach the junction with Highway 67 at 10.5 miles and a right turn. We stay on the highway only to 10.9, where we follow Forest Drive to the right, on the way to the Kettle Moraine Correctional Institute. We'll turn left at 11.9 on County U and take this to yet another junction with Highway 67, at 12.3 miles. We'll cross the highway and follow County U east and south to a final curve up a long, gradual climb to Parnell Tower at 14.9 miles.

The Old Wade House in Greenbush.

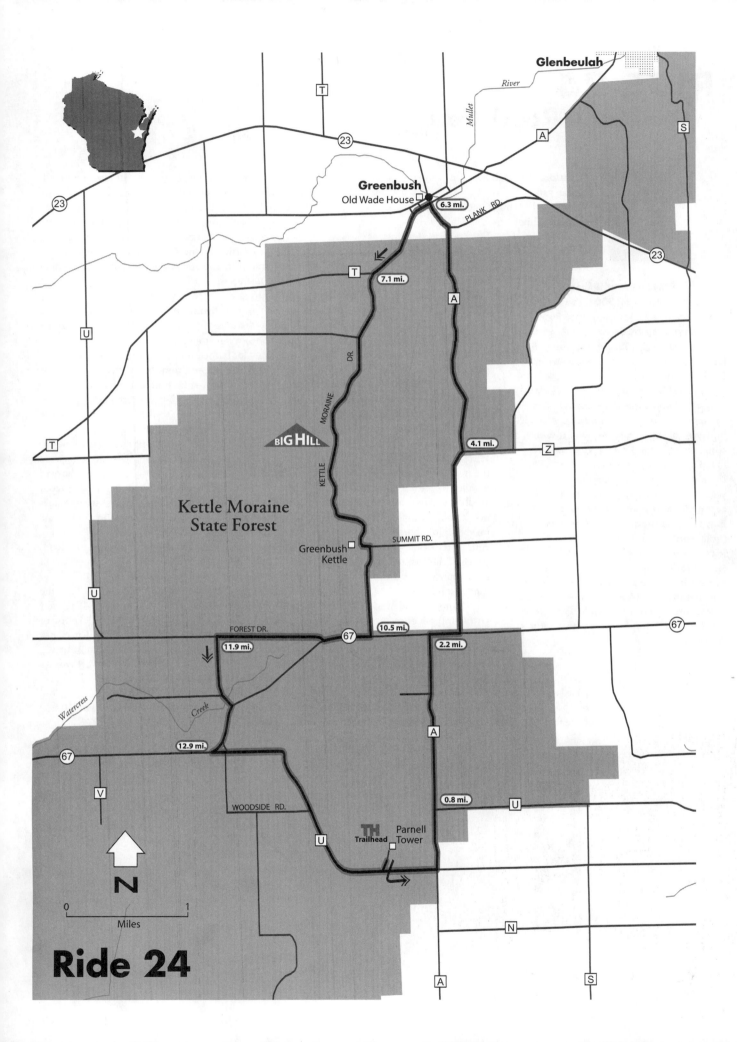

Glenbeulah

Mullet *River*

(23)

T

Greenbush
Old Wade House

6.3 mi.

PLANK RD.

A

23

S

T

7.1 mi.

U

A

MORAINE DR.

BIG HILL

KETTLE

4.1 mi.

Z

**Kettle Moraine
State Forest**

Greenbush
Kettle

SUMMIT RD.

U

FOREST DR.

67

10.5 mi.

67

11.9 mi.

2.2 mi.

Watercress *Creek*

67

12.9 mi.

A

V

0.8 mi.

U

WOODSIDE RD.

U

TH
Trailhead

Parnell
Tower

N

0   1
Miles

N

A

S

Ride 24

RIDE 25
Old Plank Road Trail

Location: Paved bike path between Greenbush and Sheboygan.
Distance: 17.5 miles one way.
Pedaling time: 1.5–1.75 hours.

Surface: Paved path.
Terrain: Mostly flat, with a few small hills.
Sweat factor: Low.
Trailhead: Old Wade House Historic Site in Greenbush.

Plank Road

In the late mid-1800s, the dirt road between Sheboygan and Fond du Lac was a busy trade route but was often impassable. To remedy the problem, wooden planks were laid from Sheboygan to Greenbush to allow more reliable passage for horses and wagons. Even after the improvement, the journey was still arduous. An oasis halfway along this route was a welcome sight indeed for travelers, thanks to Sylvanus Wade, who built a stately inn at tiny Greenbush. Wade was sure his establishment would become the mainstay of a thriving city, but alas, the wooden road was eventually replaced by more modern surfaces, and the heyday of the Wade House faded along with it. But the name Plank Road survives to this day, and the historic Wade House continues to welcome guests to experience what life was like in mid-nineteenth-century Wisconsin.

This is the only ride in the book where we a use a paved bike path for the entire trip. This isn't a converted rail bed, so we generally follow the natural terrain, and there are a few ups and downs that add a little fun to the trail, which shadows State Highway 23 the entire way. Historical sites are at both ends of the trail, and Lake Michigan is only 4 miles past the eastern trailhead. We'll be sharing the trail with runners, walkers, roller bladers, and maybe even a horse or two, so use your best trail manners. Rest benches, shelters, toilets, water, and emergency phones are all along the trail, just in case.

From the Old Wade House in Greenbush, we begin the ride by following County A south a short distance to Plank Road. There, we turn left and go straight to the Old Plank Road Trail, and we jump on the paved path and start heading east, with Highway 23 at our left. Only a mile into the ride, the trail follows Julie Lane for a very short while, then it's back to business. For the most part, we're riding in an open meadow-type landscape, with some woods off to the south. At 2.3 miles, we cross County S, and at 3.3 we roll by Pioneer Road, then County C. At 4.2 miles, a spur trail splits off to the south, leading to one of Plymouth's city parks. From here the trail curves north underneath Highway 23, crosses Highway 67, and then returns back to the south side of Highway 23, where we stay to the end.

At around mile 16.2, a spur trail goes south along County Y into Kohler, a name you might have seen on plumbing fixtures. Way back in 1873, John Kohler bought Sheboygan Iron and Steel and began producing implements for farmers and other heavy-duty items. Ten years later, Kohler slapped some baked enamel on a horse trough—and presto!—a bathtub appeared. The Kohler plumbing reign began. The homestretch of the ride takes us underneath Interstate 43 to the parking area on Erie Avenue on the far west side of Sheboygan.

Sheboygan and the surrounding area offer ample opportunities for postride relaxation. The city offers the Kohler Arts Center, as well as the nearby Sheboygan County Museum; and the Lakefront Promenade has a paved trail along Lake Michigan. Also close to the lake is Kohler–Andrae State Park, with rolling sand dunes, pine forest, wildlife aplenty, and loads of recreational activities. This park, which celebrated its 75th anniversary in 2003, is an important natural preserve along this portion of heavily developed Lake Michigan shoreline.

Sheboygan also offers fun diversions like the Bratwurst Day festival. If you're hungry, try Blackwolf Run in Kohler, in the log clubhouse at the golf course of the same name, or Cuccina, with old-world Italian charm and great food. Numerous inns and B&Bs are scattered around Sheboygan for a memorable weekend. Favorites are English Manor, a 1908 Tudor-style home that oozes elegance; the Brownstone Inn, a luxurious 1907 inn; and the Lakeview Mansion B&B, a 1912 shanty with 10,000 square feet of opulence.

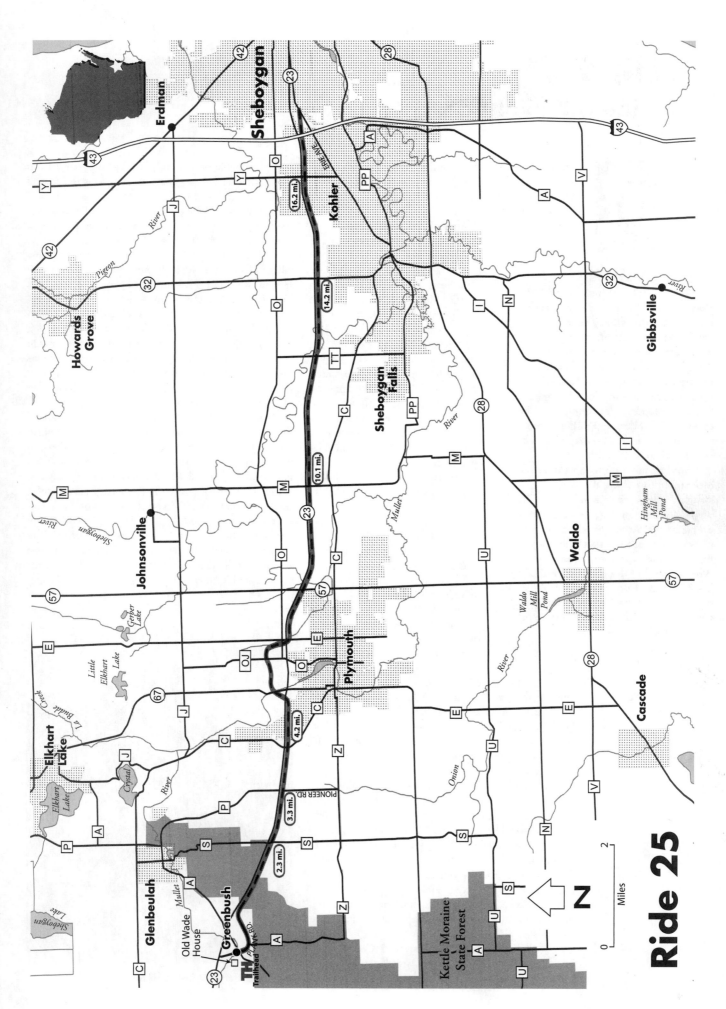

Ride 25

Sheboygan

Erdman

Kohler

Howards
Grove

Johnsonville

Sheboygan
Falls

Gibbsville

Waldo

Elkhart
Lake

Plymouth

Glenbeulah

Greenbush

Cascade

Old Wade
House

Kettle Moraine
State Forest

Trailhead

TH

16.2 mi.

14.2 mi.

10.1 mi.

4.2 mi.

3.3 mi.

2.3 mi.

PIONEER RD.

ERIE AVE.

N

Miles

0   2

RIDE 26
Divine Intervention

Holy Hill

There is a lot of history behind Holy Hill's Gothic-style spires rising above the surrounding countryside southeast of Hartford. In the mid-nineteenth century, after learning of Marquette's and Joliet's expeditions through Wisconsin in the late 1600s, a young Frenchman named François Soubris noted that Marquette had located and climbed a high hill in the area, erected a cross there, and dedicated it as holy ground.

Soubris set out for this hill to seek atonement but along the way was stricken with paralysis in his legs. He pressed on, struggling to the summit on his knees. After spending the night praying, he rose the next morning to find he could again walk normally. Word spread of the miracle, and people flocked to Holy Hill to seek their own cures. Today there is lodging set aside for pilgrims who come here to visit the shrine.

Location: County roads south of Pike Lake State Park and State Highway 60 in Washington County.
Distance: 25-mile loop.
Pedaling time: 2–2.5 hours.
Surface: Paved roads.
Terrain: Hilly, with several long and difficult climbs.
Sweat factor: High.
Trailhead: Pike Lake State Park on Kettle Moraine Drive and State Highway 60 east of Hartford.

After plodding up some of these hills, you might be hoping for a little help from above. The centerpiece of this ride is the impressive Holy Hill monastery, and the roads on this ride are also nothing less than divine. We'll climb some long, tough hills and go down some bigger ones. (If you're feeling particularly energetic, reverse the loop for a considerably greater challenge.) At the south end of the loop, we'll be on Rustic Road 33. There, Emerald Road is a slice of heaven all on its own. This is a challenging and scenic route you're sure to enjoy.

This ride has a lot of hills. One of them comes up soon after leaving Pike Lake State Park on Kettle Moraine Drive. It's a long, steep and wooded affair tough enough to get your attention, and the views from the top are beautiful. A fun descent follows on the heels of the first climb, then we hit another one that goes past Pike Lake at 0.9 mile. We hit the junction with County E at 1.7 miles and ride right across, still heading south. We cruise on a couple of flat sections here to 2.7 miles, where we'll go right on Waterford Road. It's a little more open here, with some agricultural land mixed with the trees.

We tackle another big hill and some downhills, too, on the way to the junction with County K at 3.8 miles. We go left here and might see a few more cars, but there is a good shoulder on this up-and-down stretch. At 5.9 miles, we meet Highway 167 (Holy Hill Road) and turn left on an excellent road running through dense woods. It's difficult to leave this fine road, but we'll do just that at 6.5 miles, the entrance to Holy Hill. Rounding a bend to the left is an open view of the towering spires of this magnificent church. It sits high atop a glacial kame, Scottish for *steep hill*.

We'll drop down the steep exit road (Carmel Road) into thick woods to the junction with Donegal Road at 7.6 miles. (Be sure to look behind you on the way down for an incredible view of Holy Hill.) Let's go left here on a short, flat section past some wetland areas to Emerald Road (Rustic Road 33) at 8.5 and take a right. This is a marvelous cruise through a heavily wooded area on absolutely perfect pavement. The road drops down on a winding descent back to County K at 11.4 miles.

After a left on County K, we pass through the tiny village of Monches to 12.9 miles and another left on Hartley Road. At 13.3 miles, we ride straight across County Q to Monches Road, which is also a continuation of Rustic Road 33. Some more climbing takes us up to Saint Augustine Road at 15.6 miles. We will go left here and enjoy another great view of the church spires in the distance before a long, steep descent leads back into the open flats and farmland. Continuing on Saint Augustine, we'll make a couple of turns and hit the bottom of a long climb, the toughest one so far.

Finally, at 19.2 miles, we cross Highway 167, and the road we're on becomes County CC. We'll ride north on a long straightaway to 22.3 miles and the junction with County E. We turn left here, ride up a sizeable hill past Powder Hill Road, and take a right at Kettle Moraine Drive (23.3 miles). Powder Hill is a large glacial kame, the second-highest point in southeast Wisconsin. A half-mile hiking trail leads to the top, and a 60-foot observation tower affords gorgeous views. Kettle Moraine Drive takes us back to the park entrance at 25 miles, ending one of the most difficult rides in this book—and one of the most enjoyable, too.

A view of Holy Hill from a distance.

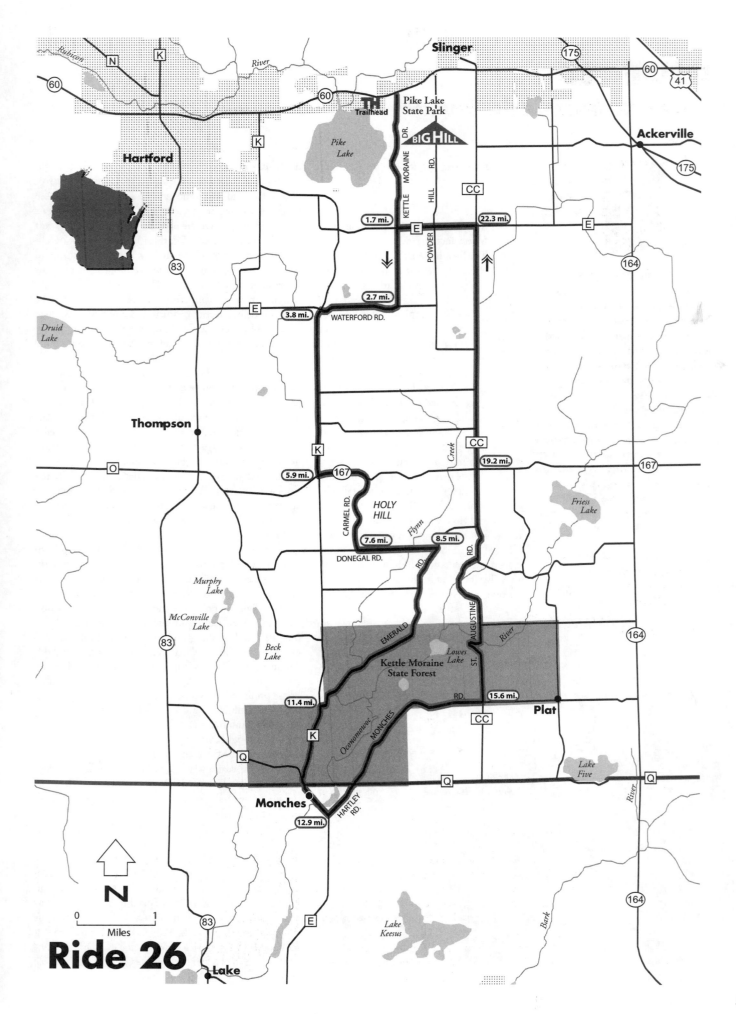

Ride 26

RIDE 27
See You in Cedarburg

Location: Quiet country roads northwest of Cedarburg.
Distance: 22.3-mile loop.
Pedaling time: 2–2.25 hours.
Surface: Paved roads.

Terrain: Flat, with a few small hills.
Sweat factor: Low.
Trailhead: Cedar Creek Settlement shops at Washington Avenue and Bridge Road in Cedarburg.

After completing this ride, you may want to go back home to pack your bags and move to Cedarburg, especially if you're a fan of main streets designated as a National Historic District. Thanks to the efforts of concerned residents, many of the treasured buildings from the town's early beginnings have been saved, and Cedarburg's residents remain committed to preservation.

There are over one hundred buildings considered historically significant. The 1864 woolen mill that serves as our trailhead is now home to small shops and a winery. The five-story Cedarburg Mill on Cedar Creek dates to 1855. The Stagecoach Inn is a grand stone building that offered rest and good grub to folks traveling the long road from Milwaukee to Green Bay. Of course, the highlight of the ride is the last remaining covered bridge in Wisconsin.

Our trip begins by heading west out of town on Bridge Road. We'll ride through dwindling residential areas to mile 1.8 and turn right on Horns Corners Road. As we pass through open farmland, look for the century-old farmhouses and barns. The junction with State Highway 60 is at 3.3 miles, and we'll ride straight across to a mile of flat road past some newer residential areas. At 4.3 miles, we turn right on Cedar Creek Road and ride east past Washington Avenue at mile 4.7 (a right here leads back into downtown Cedarburg), continuing straight ahead. At 5.4 miles we reach Covered Bridge Road and turn left. A wooded park is situated in the lowland across the road along Cedar Creek. The last covered bridge remaining in Wisconsin, erected in 1876, sits just off the road. In the nineteenth century, by some estimates, there were 300 bridges like this in the state. Although the actual number is probably closer to 50, the end result is the same: today we are left with only one.

We continue our ride heading north to Kaehlers Mill Road at 6.1 miles and turn left. This is a smooth road wandering past pasture and quiet fields, with no traffic in sight. After winding around some turns, we arrive back at Horns Corners Road and roll south to Cedar Creek Road once again. This time, we'll take a right and head west, passing a beautiful stone-foundation farmhouse on a relaxing cruise on a flat and curvy stretch along Cedar Creek. We pass Grandville Road (County Y) at 8.5 miles, and now we begin to roll up and down some moderate hills, all the while passing one amazing old farmstead after another.

We reach the junction with County M (North Country Aire Drive) at 10.2 miles, where we turn right, crossing Cedar Creek and stair-stepping north on a couple of tight turns. At Pleasant Valley Road and 11 miles, we keep right on going for another mile to the junction with County NN and continue straight ahead. Finally, at mile 12.7 and Washington Drive, we will turn and head east (look for the big electric substation for a landmark). An uneventful 2 miles brings us to County Y, where we take a right turn and head south, past a vintage stone house protected by an equally antiquated split-rail fence. At Cedar Sauk Road and 15.6 miles, we turn left.

After another short, flat, woodsy stretch to mile 16.4, take a right turn on Horns Corners Road (but a different segment of it than the one we were on earlier). A few more turns and some downhill runs bring us back to Pleasant Valley Road at 17.7 miles. Here we turn left. A unique octagon-shaped house and adjoining farm buildings sit to the left as we ride on to the junction with Covered Bridge Road at mile 18.5. Turn right.

Take another look at the covered bridge we saw earlier as we sail past on the way back to town. The junction with Highway 60 arrives at 20.6 miles. Here we'll go on straight across (look for traffic) and continue south on Highway 181 to its split with Washington Avenue. Continue southeast on the Washington side, which brings us back to the trailhead at 22.3 miles. If you've got a craving for goodies, maybe a trip to Mary Jane's Cedarburg Confectionery is in order or perhaps the Chocolate Factory ice cream shop.

The covered bridge north of Cedarburg.

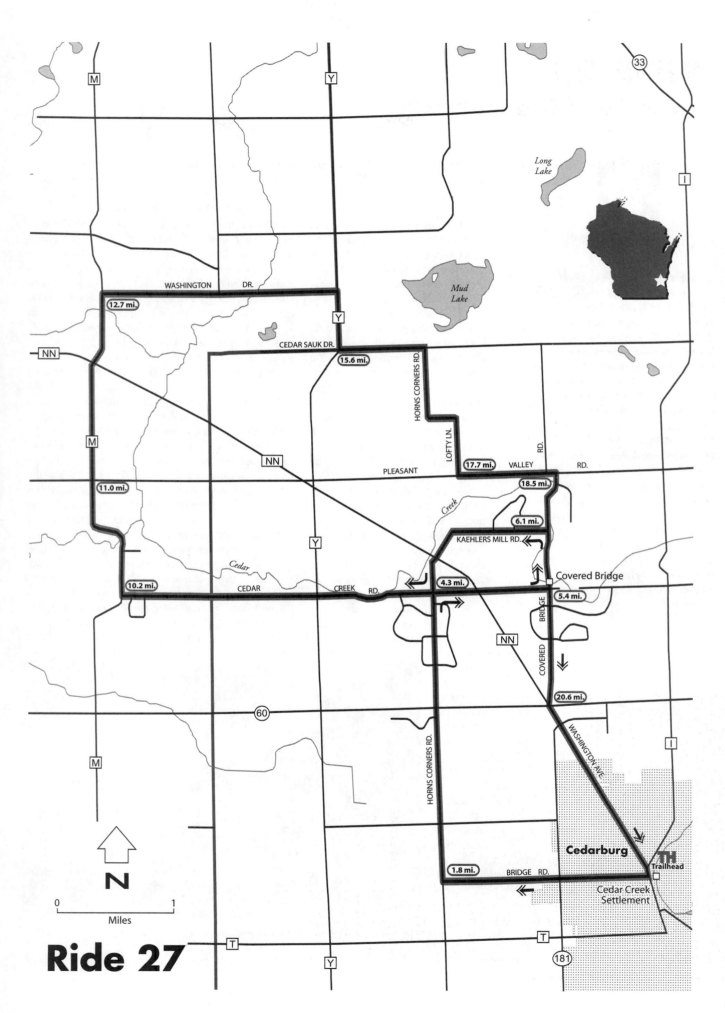

WASHINGTON DR.

12.7 mi.

NN

M

11.0 mi.

CEDAR SAUK DR.

15.6 mi.

Y

Long Lake

Mud Lake

HORNS CORNERS RD.

LOFTY LN.

PLEASANT

17.7 mi.

VALLEY RD.

RD.

18.5 mi.

NN

6.1 mi.

Creek

KAEHLERS MILL RD.

10.2 mi.

Cedar

CEDAR

CREEK

RD.

4.3 mi.

Covered Bridge

5.4 mi.

COVERED

BRIDGE

NN

20.6 mi.

60

M

Y

HORNS CORNERS RD.

WASHINGTON AVE.

I

Cedarburg

TH
Trailhead

N

0   1
Miles

1.8 mi.

BRIDGE   RD.

Cedar Creek
Settlement

Ride 27

T

Y

T

181

I

33

RIDE 28
Oak Leaf Tour

Ethnic Milwaukee

Few cities in the United States can boast of a richer ethnic heritage than Milwaukee. Starting with an influx of Germans in the mid-nineteenth century, a group most closely associated with the city, Milwaukee has prospered through the hard work of other ethnic groups that have settled here: Poles, Irish, Italians, and African-Americans to name a few. Recently the city's ranks of Mexican-Americans have swelled considerably. To honor the various groups, the city sponsors several large festivals every year. Usually held on the lakefront, the celebrations include Irish Fest, German Fest, Polish Fest, Indian Summer Fest, and African World Fest. There are so many, in fact, that Milwaukee has earned the nickname City of Festivals.

Location: Shore of Lake Michigan along Lincoln Memorial Drive in Milwaukee.
Distance: 5.8 miles out and back.
Pedaling time: 30–40 minutes.
Surface: Paved roads and bike path.
Terrain: Flat, with one gradual climb.
Sweat factor: Low.
Trailhead: Veterans Park on Milwaukee's lakefront. Start at the marina at the end of the entrance road.

The Oak Leaf Trail is a fantastic long-distance bike path meandering all the way around Milwaukee County, including segments through scenic river corridors and along parkways lined with historic mansions. Stretching inland from the sandy beaches of Lake Michigan, the trail was designed in 1939 with 64 miles. Continued expansion has made the trail what you see today: approximately one hundred miles in length, with 42 miles of off-road paths, 31 miles of parkway drives, and 26 miles on connecting streets. This particular ride follows the Lake Loop segment along Lake Michigan. Check www.countyparks.com for additional information.

From the marina parking lot in Veterans Park, we can spin around on the paths near the shore and close to McKinley Marina, watching rookie sailboat skippers practice on an inner bay and maybe a big freighter steaming offshore. During the summer, dozens of masts of sailboats, yachts, and other skiffs docked nearby clatter in the wind like giant wind chimes. A short distance to the south is the Milwaukee Art Museum and the War Memorial, two attractions housed in one building that are well worth a visit. The art museum has been described as "Jetsonesque" and features many fine-art exhibits. Built in 1957, the War Memorial honors Milwaukee's war vet-

erans. Its express mission is "To Honor the Dead by Serving the Living" through a diverse program of arts and cultural activities.

To begin our ride, we follow the bike path along Lagoon Drive, the park entrance road, to Lincoln Memorial Drive and hop on the Oak Leaf Trail heading north. Look for the handy brown signs emblazoned with the oak-leaf emblem to lead the way. This is a popular recreation area and is loaded with trail users and beachgoers. Watch for other cyclists, walkers, runners, even kids on tricycles. We roll past McKinley Beach and Marina, with its huge sand beach speckled in the summer with people lounging beneath the sun, bobbing in the water, or playing on a cool play-gym in the shape of a ship.

Bradford Beach is only a little farther along, and shortly past this point the trail curves inland and climbs a long, gradual hill, revealing stunning views of Lake Michigan as we climb. A stately mansion is perched at the top, and we'll cross Lincoln Memorial Drive here to the Oak Leaf Trail sign and then ride south along Lake Drive. We can ogle the palatial homes along this street until we arrive at the entrance to Lake Park. Here we'll follow the squiggly line on the road sign to our left and head down Ravine Road's steep hill through a short section of dense woods back onto Lincoln Memorial Drive. This is a good hill to tackle the opposite way for some climbing practice.

Back on the main drag, we're simply going to follow the path on the west (uncrowded) side of the road back to Veterans Park and our starting point for a short 5.8-mile ride. There are any number of jumping-off points on this trail from almost anywhere in the city, and your ride can be a little one like this or can take the entire day and be topped off with a cool dip in the big lake.

The marina in Veterans Park, Milwaukee.

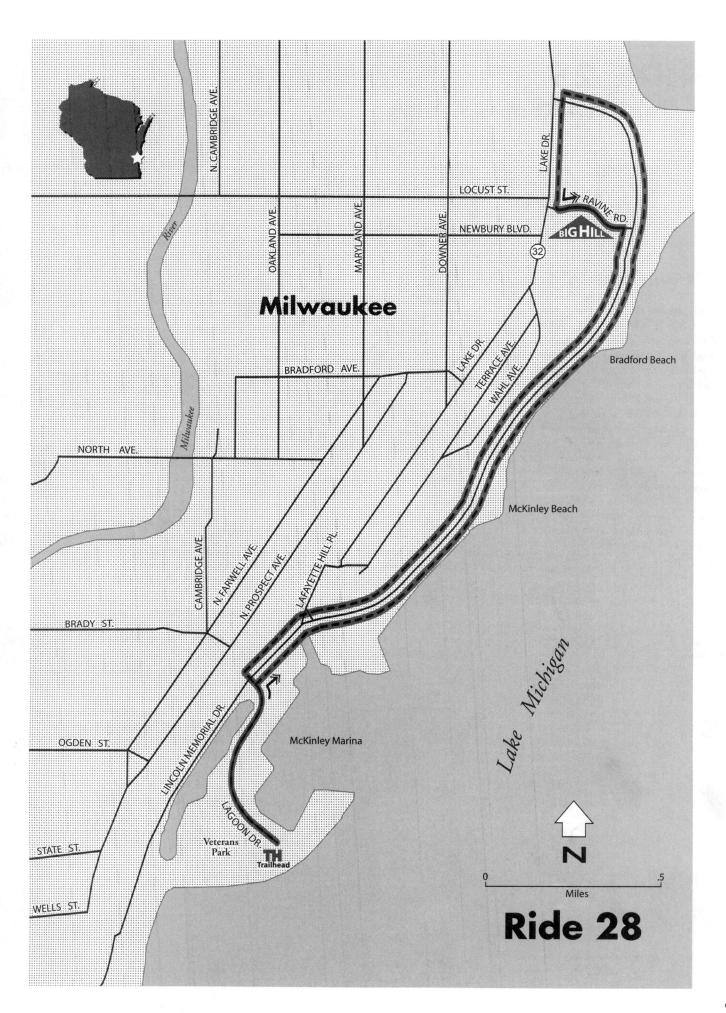

Milwaukee

N. CAMBRIDGE AVE.

LOCUST ST.

RAVINE RD.

NEWBURY BLVD.

BIG HILL

32

OAKLAND AVE.

MARYLAND AVE.

DOWNER AVE.

LAKE DR.

Bradford Beach

BRADFORD AVE.

LAKE DR.

TERRACE AVE.

WAHL AVE.

River

Milwaukee

NORTH AVE.

McKinley Beach

CAMBRIDGE AVE.

N. FARWELL AVE.

N. PROSPECT AVE.

LAFAYETTE HILL PL.

BRADY ST.

Lake Michigan

OGDEN ST.

LINCOLN MEMORIAL DR.

McKinley Marina

STATE ST.

LAGOON DR.

Veterans
Park

TH
Trailhead

WELLS ST.

N

0   .5
Miles

Ride 28

RIDE 29
Southern Kettles Cruise

A Step Back in Time

The starting point for this tour, Old World Wisconsin, re-creates Wisconsin rural life in the nineteenth century. There are more than fifty historic buildings that have been moved piece-by-piece from their original locations throughout the state and reassembled here. There are farmsteads with furnished houses representing various ethnic groups that migrated to the state, rustic outbuildings, and crossroads villages, among other structures. Plan on spending at least four hours to tour the whole site.

Location: County roads between Palmyra and Eagle, through the Kettle Moraine State Forest–Southern Unit, southwest of Milwaukee.
Distance: 18-mile loop.
Pedaling time: 1.5–2 hours.
Surface: Paved roads.
Terrain: Flat to rolling, with only a couple of short, steep hills.
Sweat factor: Moderate.
Trailhead: Old World Wisconsin historical village on State Highway 67, southwest of Eagle.

This ride roams through a small part of the 30-mile-long, 20,000-acre Kettle Moraine State Forest–Southern Unit, so expect to see pine and hardwood forest, glacial hills and kettles, and restored prairies. A 31-mile stretch of the Ice Age National Scenic Trail meanders through the forest, in addition to over 160 miles of other recreational trails. Three historic cabin sites are available for tours. Forest headquarters, located on State Highway 59 between Eagle and Palmyra, has a museum and an auditorium, where visitors can listen to a narrated slide presentation about the area. The terrain for our ride is mostly rolling, with only moderate climbs to contend with.

We leave from Old World Wisconsin, riding west on State Highway 67. Traffic can be heavy, but the shoulder is pretty accommodating; nevertheless, stay alert. Dense woods are mixed with open patches of meadow on this first stretch. We pass County S at 1.5 miles, and at 1.7 miles the junction with County NN appears. We leave Highway 67 and turn right on NN, following the signs for Palmyra. This is a smooth road on gently rolling terrain all the way to County Z at 3.4 miles. We head straight across to Little Prairie Road, passing a sprawling horse-stable complex at 5.2 miles. From here we'll encounter some hills of the more rolling variety until things flatten out on the way into Palmyra at 6.5 miles.

In Palmyra, turn right on Main Street (which is also State Highway 59 and County H) and coast through this historic town. Follow the Kettle Moraine Scenic Drive if in doubt. Just out of town, Lower Spring Lake sits off to our right, and just past the lake we take a left turn on County H at mile 8. Now we're riding through a more open area of mature oak trees mixed in with other hardwoods and pines. Excellent road again, and traffic is light.

The junction with County Z arrives at 9.8 miles, and we ride across it to County ZZ on the other side, continuing in a northeasterly bearing. This is smooth stretch of road, sporting well-maintained pavement as it curves beneath canopy oaks draping their branches overhead. At the junction with County N at 11.2 miles, we'll turn right and enjoy a long, straight, and flat stretch of lustrous road through wide-open fields and wetland areas. Farther along, we cross Scuppernong Creek and reenter thicker woods.

At 13.6 miles, we meet Paradise Springs Nature Area, a DNR-managed fishing and biking area. A short trail leads to the springs, which yield 5,000 gallons of water per minute. A springhouse from the 1930s still stands here, built by the land's original owner. About another half mile brings us back to Highway 59 at 14.1 miles. After a right turn here, we coast on a nice wide shoulder to County S at 15 miles. After a left turn there, we're back in the woods again and continue on to the junction with Highway 67 at mile 16.5. A left here and 1.5 miles later, we're back at our trailhead at Old World Wisconsin. Total mileage is 18.

Enjoying the sights at Old World Wisconsin.

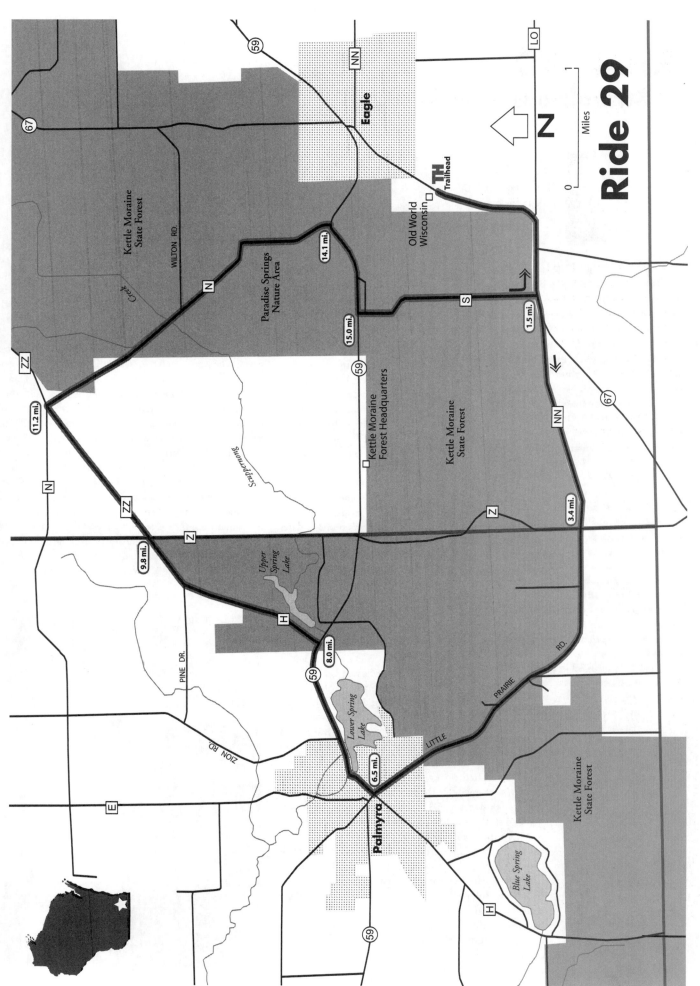

Ride 29

N

Miles

RIDE 30
Schoolhouse Rock

Location: Bike trail and rural roads south of Fort Atkinson.
Distance: 11.6-mile loop.
Pedaling time: 1–1.25 hours.

Surface: Paved and gravel trail and paved roads.
Terrain: Flat and rolling.
Sweat factor: Low.
Trailhead: Parking lot at Farmco Lane and Janesville Avenue in Fort Atkinson.

America's Dairyland

When people hear the name Wisconsin, they often think cheese and milk (well, maybe snow, cold, and the Packers, too). Wisconsin is indeed America's Dairyland, a title known worldwide thanks in large part to William Hoard. A native New Yorker, Hoard learned the best ways to make cheese and butter from his grandfather in the early 1800s. He came to Wisconsin in 1857 in search of work and became a farmer. He was soon encouraging area farmers to raise dairy cattle and try new farming methods, and in the process he formed several dairy associations. One byproduct of this work is *Hoard's Dairyman* magazine, and it is still published today. Hoard was elected governor of Wisconsin in 1888, all the while supporting the dairy industry and promoting effective farming practices. Known as the Father of Modern Dairying, William Hoard is honored in the Hoard Historical Museum and National Dairy Shrine in Fort Atkinson. The facility is housed in Hoard's Gothic Revival mansion, which contains exhibits, artifacts, clothing, and presentations on the area's rich history.

This is a quick ride on the short Glacial River Trail and quiet back roads near Fort Atkinson, a classic small town in the fertile farm country of south-central Wisconsin. Only 4 miles long, the Glacial River Trail travels south to Koshkonong Lake Road near the lake of the same name. From there the route runs on scenic paved roads past dairy farms and cornfields back to town. Expect some easy riding, most of it on flat roads.

Fort Atkinson's heritage dates back to the early 1800s and the war between the Sauk and Fox Indians, led by Chief Black Hawk, and the federal government. In 1832, General Henry Atkinson's troops defeated Black Hawk's forces in a decisive battle near the Mississippi River. The town, by the way, was named in the general's honor and is the site of a replicated U.S. fort.

Fort Atkinson is also at the center of a large group of Native American effigy mounds; some estimates put the original number at more than 500. One of the most significant groups is the Jefferson County Indian Mounds, located on Lake Koshkonong about 6 miles southwest of town. Of the estimated 72 mounds created about 1,500 years ago, 11 survive, including four in the shape of turtles and two in the shape of birds.

Our ride leaves the parking lot at Farmco Lane and heads south on the Glacial River Trail, which parallels Janesville Avenue, crossing Allen Creek and cruising along to Groeler Road at mile 1. After turning right onto Groeler, we follow the road as it works its way around the State Highway 26 interchange. Our route passes very close to the Rock River here, which flows clear down to Illinois and ultimately into the Mississippi. On the west side of the highway, we access Schwemmer Lane to rejoin the trail, which turns to smooth, crushed gravel at this point. We then follow it southwest along Highway 26 to mile 4 at Koshkonong Lake Road, which leads west a short distance to, not surprisingly, Lake Koshkonong.

This is the end of the bike trail, so we'll turn left and make a careful crossing of Highway 26 to go east on Pond Road (Rustic Road 87). By the way, 10,000-acre Lake Koshkonong was created by the construction of the Indianford Dam on the Rock River in the 1800s. The maximum depth of this sprawling lake is only seven feet, and it holds good populations of walleye, channel catfish, and white bass. Pond Road provides an enjoyable spin through a mix of quiet woodland, wetland, and farmland, with a good chance to see critters like deer, wild turkey, hawks, and herons.

We climb the only real hill on the loop shortly after passing the woods, and then reach the junction with Poeppel Road at 5.7 miles, where we take a hard left. There's another steady hill here as we ride north for 1 mile, then turn east onto Star School Road. This area is a mix of rolling farmland, some of it wide open, some wooded. The large population of cows in those fields reminds us that we are deep in dairy-farm country, near the town where the state's dairy industry was born (see sidebar).

At 7.2 miles is the junction with McIntyre Road. We'll continue straight ahead on Star School Road, cruise on a short, flat stretch, then enjoy an exhilarating downhill run to County K at 8.4 miles. It's a left turn on County K, heading north again on rolling terrain past several farmsteads to Hackbarth Road at mile 10. A left here takes us back to Janesville Avenue and the trailhead at 11.6 miles.

Wide-open road near Fort Atkinson.

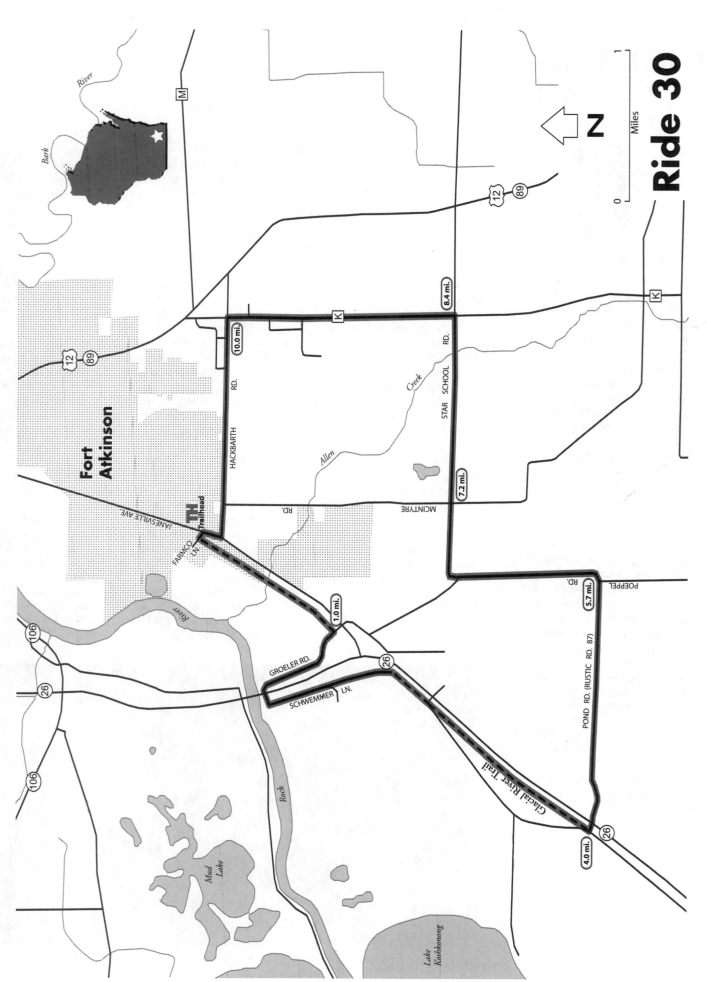

Ride 30

N

Miles

0   1

RIDE 31
Swiss Miss

Switzerland in Wisconsin

Arriving in New Glarus for the first time is akin to rolling right into Switzerland. This is one of the most picturesque towns in Wisconsin, loaded with authentic Swiss buildings. Swiss settlers moved into this area in the early 1800s, and it looks like they brought along one of their old-world towns. The Swiss Historical Village offers a wonderful view of pioneer life, with 14 separate buildings representing everyday life in the nineteenth century, including a log church and cabin, blacksmith shop, and general store. Naturally, there's some good ethnic food in this town, too. For the real deal, be sure to check out the New Glarus Hotel restaurant for dishes prepared by a Swiss-trained chef; the Glarner Stube, which serves up some great old-world dishes; and Deininger's, with a superb continental cuisine. The Chalet Landhaus Inn and Puempel's Tavern (occupying one of the oldest buildings in town) are other spots worth checking out. For lodging, the New Glarus Hotel and Chalet Landhaus Inn offer charming accommodations. Check www.swisstown.com for more information on America's Little Switzerland.

Location: Sugar River State Trail and county roads south of New Glarus.
Distance: 16.5-mile loop.
Pedaling time: 1.5–1.75 hours.
Surface: Crushed gravel trail and paved roads.
Terrain: Flat on the trail, rolling on roads.
Sweat factor: Moderate.
Trailhead: Sugar River State Trail access in New Glarus.

The Sugar River State Trail follows an old Milwaukee Road rail bed 23 miles between New Glarus and Brodhead, traveling over the Sugar River and numerous trestle bridges and through rolling hills, meadows, and wildlife areas. This ride starts at the northern end of the trail and combines on-road riding for a 16-mile loop. One of the highlights of the trip is New Glarus's charming Swiss ambience, with virtually the whole town sporting Swiss-style architecture.

From the century-old railroad depot that houses the trail headquarters, we ride south on the paved bike path toward the south end of town. (Bike rentals are available at the depot in season.) At the sign and the split for New Glarus Woods State Park, we curve to the left and cross State Highway 39 carefully to the Sugar River State Trail. As we cruise along this wooded path, we cross no fewer than six trestle bridges along the way. The trees give way to open farmland at around mile 3, and views of high rolling hills can be seen to the west. This trail is a busy wildlife corridor, and riders are likely to see deer, fox, rabbits, squirrels, chipmunks, and numerous bird species. Less visible are coyote, bobcat, beaver, and otter. Diverse terrain exists along the trail, including remnants of former prairies; wetland areas are scattered among stands of oak, walnut, hickory, and chokecherry.

At mile 5.8, we reach County C. Here we exit the trail with a right turn and climb a short hill into Monticello. Following County C through town, we arrive at the junction with Highway 39 at 7.2 miles. Cross this road—carefully again—and continue westbound on County C. Moderate-sized hills are more in evidence along here, with gradual climbs and a series of short rollers. In a little farming community at 10.2 miles, we'll go right on County N, coasting downhill to start, then grinding up a mile-long, steady climb. At the top are splendid views of the rolling farmland, followed by one more stretch of up-and-down travel before reaching the junction with County NN at 13.7 miles.

We turn right here and follow curvy NN east toward New Glarus Woods State Park. The road nearly disappears into a dark wood and descends a fun hill to the park's ranger station at mile 14.7. The 411-acre park has hiking trails, camping, and picnic grounds. Three areas of the park are undergoing a process of burning, mowing, and seeding to restore them to their original prairie condition.

Here we'll make a hard left and jump onto the paved bike path leading north past several campsites on a long downhill run back into New Glarus. We return to the trailhead depot at 16.5 miles.

Rolling on the Sugar River State Trail.

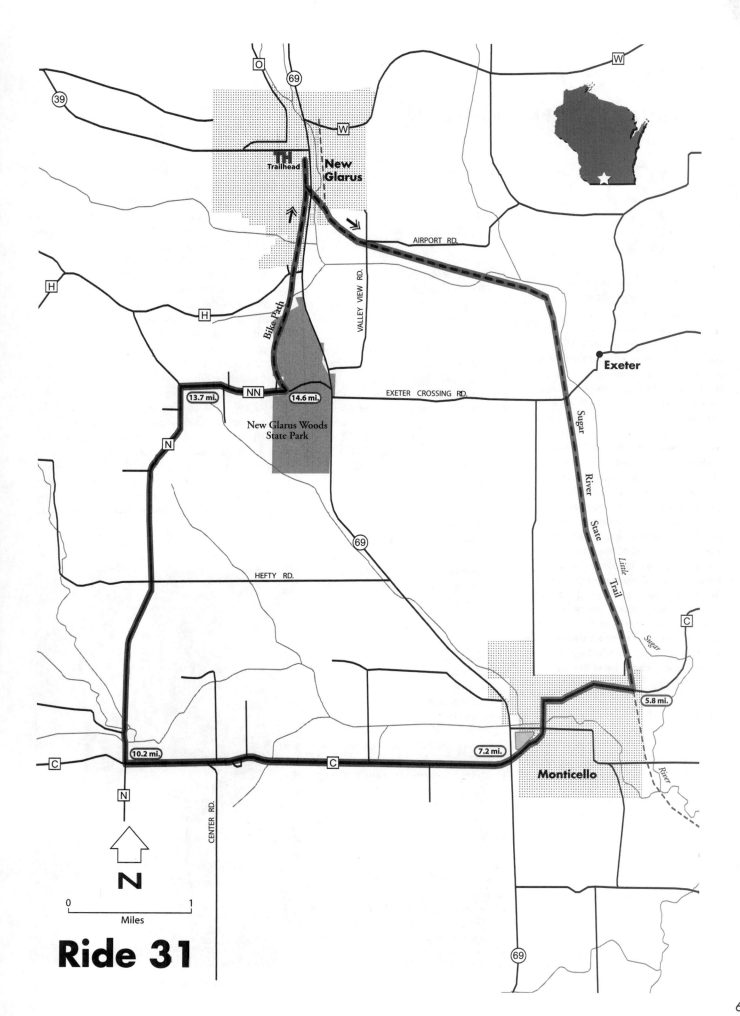

Ride 31

RIDE 32
Mount Horeb Homage

Fun Times in Mount Horeb

Mount Horeb is a town with a well-deserved reputation for the off-beat. Immediate evidence of this comes in the form of the large wooden troll carvings perched around town. This being a Norwegian community, the presence of these imps shouldn't come as a surprise to visitors. Then there's the Mustard Museum, with over 2,000 varieties to choose from (many of them for sale), along with free samples. More than a store or museum, the building is a testament to one man's quest to make mustard the world's premier condiment. The town also boasts of a couple of antiques malls and an interesting folk museum. For good, cheap eats, try the recently reopened Schubert's on Main Street. Several quaint cottages and bed-and-breakfast inns offer room and board for extended stays. Try the Arbor Rose B&B for historic Victorian charm close to town or the Othala Valley Inn tucked in a secluded valley.

Location: County roads near U.S. Highway 18/151, south and west of Mount Horeb.
Distance: 21.1-mile loop.
Pedaling time: 1.75–2.25 hours.
Surface: Paved roads.
Terrain: Rolling, with two long climbs.
Sweat factor: High.
Trailhead: Parking lot at Blue Mounds fort historical marker at the junction of County Roads F and ID.

This ride not only follows silky-smooth roads through scenic forest and bluffs—there are numerous bonus attractions to divert your attention as well. The ride itself is rolling throughout, with one tough switchback climb near Mount Horeb and another biggie at the end of the loop. Deep, wooded valleys and stunning panoramic views are all part of this fun tour.

Even before we begin, this spectacular ride tempts us with a number of alternate routes and attractions, but we'll wait to divulge those until the end of the ride. Let's start by going east on County ID for 1.3 miles to County JG, where we'll turn left at the sign for Little Norway. A long descent drops us to 2.2 miles and the entrance to Little Norway, a pioneer homestead of Norse architecture and antiques, nestled in a small, densely wooded valley. Stop in, now or later, for an unforgettable experience. Farther along, the road is impeccable. It's so smooth it doesn't even seem real, and it twists and winds through beautiful wooded hills and sloped farmland, following close to Moen Creek on the right.

After JG curves east, then south, we enter Stewart Park and pass a small dam on the left at 6.9 miles. Then begins a long, steep climb up through the park into Mount Horeb. We follow County JG through town to Highway 78 at 8.2 miles and turn right. The town is full of surprises, so you may want to wait until the end of the ride to take it all in.

We then follow 78 west out of town to County E at 9.8 miles (be careful—when 78 turns left, continue straight for a short distance to E). Turn left, crossing the Military Ridge State Trail, then very carefully crossing the four lanes of busy Highway 18/151. The Military Ridge trail is a wonderful 40-mile path connecting Dodgeville with Madison. It travels past Governor Dodge and Blue Mound State Parks through farmland, woods, wetlands, and small towns. It's just another of the wonderful side trips available on this trip.

County E continues south and drops into a scenic valley, curving past farms and thick forest. We reach County Z at mile 16 and turn right, following Blue Mounds Creek. After going 2 miles north, we begin a climb and keep going up all the way to 19.6 miles and the junction with County F. Continuing north on County F brings us back to the junction with Highway 18/151. Cautiously cross the busy highway to County ID and take a left back to the trailhead at 21.1 miles.

For those who want to see more of the marvelous local terrain, whether by bike or motorized conveyance, start by checking out Blue Mound State Park, only 2 miles west of the trailhead, with a huge climb leading to the entrance. The park is a popular family destination and offers a variety of hiking trails, biking, camping, and the like. Cave of the Mounds, a giant limestone cavern, is 1 mile north on County F. This is a fascinating National Natural Landmark that has attracted millions of visitors since opening in 1940. The cave was accidentally discovered when quarry workers set off a dynamite blast that tore the face off the quarry and revealed a giant underground tunnel, a large cavern, and many other hidden rooms and alleyways.

Crossing a bridge at Blue Mound State Park.

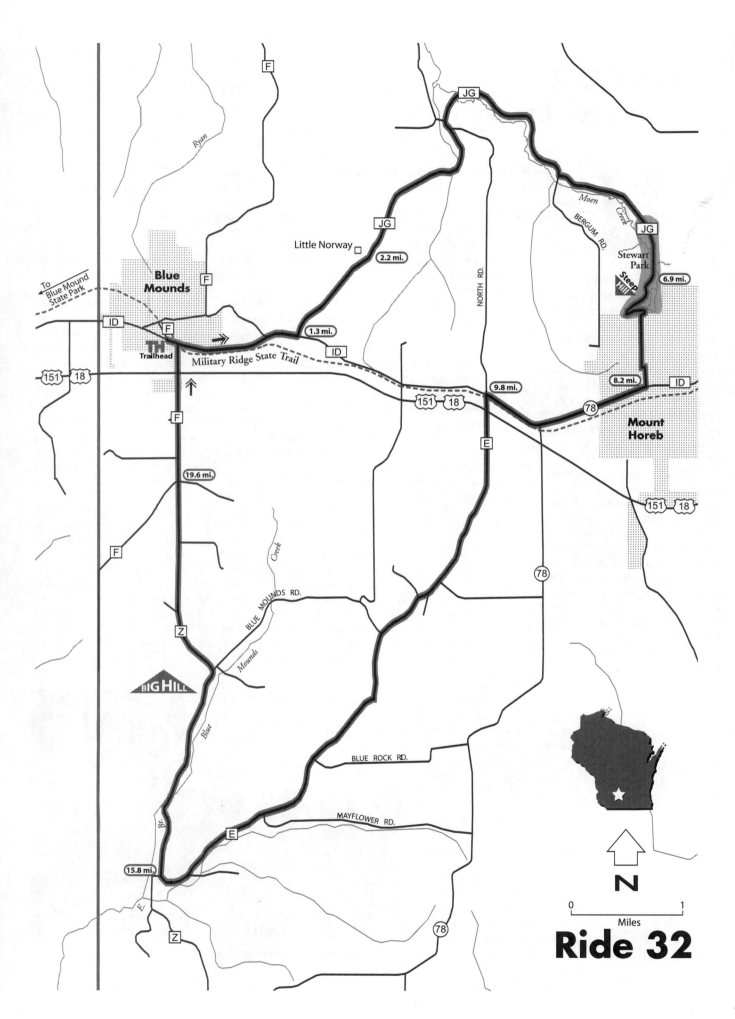

Ride 32

RIDE 33
Tower Hill Loop

Taliesin

One of the twentieth century's greatest architects, Frank Lloyd Wright, was so enamored of the rolling hills near Spring Green that he chose them as the site of his residence and studio workshop. Begun in 1911, Taliesin ("shining brow" in Welsh) has developed over the years into a 600-acre complex that includes a host of Wright-designed structures. It was here that aspiring architects flocked from all over the world to train under the master's critical eye. As part of their apprenticeship, they lived and performed daily chores on the grounds. They also took part in numerous educational and cultural events sponsored by Wright and his wife.

Several different tours of the complex, which is no longer in use, are available; call (608) 588-7900, or check www.taliesinpreservation.org

Location: In and around Tower Hill State Park, south of Spring Green.
Distance: 20.6-mile loop.
Pedaling time: 1.75–2 hours.
Surface: Paved roads.
Terrain: Mix of rolling hills, flat valley roads, and two significant climbs.
Sweat factor: Moderate +.
Trailhead: Tower Hill State Park, 2 miles east of State Highway 23 on County C.

This ride should rank as one of your favorites in the book. Starting out with a long, tough climb, the loop drops back into a valley, climbs up again, and then delivers us into a wooded hollow of extraordinary beauty. With the second half of the loop featuring flat valley roads, easy, rolling hills, and even more ravishing natural wonders, this ride is a special one. To top things off, the trip ends at the Frank Lloyd Wright Visitor Center and the historic shot tower in Tower Hill State Park; both are worth a visit.

From the entrance to Tower Hill State Park, we turn right on County C and then make a quick left onto Golf Course Road. In addition to the Springs golf course and the House on the Rock Resort on the right, we pass the American Players Theater on the left, which stages performances of classic plays in an outdoor amphitheater. Then comes a long, steady climb on a rough road in the midst of pine and hardwood forest all the way up to High Point Road at 1.7 miles. The trees give way to fields, and here we go right, rolling past croplands and pastures. Then we get to glide down a mile-long descent to Coon Rock Road at 3.4 miles, where we turn right. The first stretch of this road is gravel, but never fear; the bumpy, dusty surface quickly gives way to pavement, and then the road offers another steady climb to 4.3 miles, where we turn left onto Amacher Hollow Road. Follow the short rise and let fly on a long and steep descent into the hollow.

The exquisite beauty of the area is in full evidence here. In a corridor of high, thickly wooded bluffs, a stream wanders through soft fields bordered by hedgerows of large trees. Pastoral farmsteads that appear to be painted on the landscape are partially hidden in folds in the bluff. The road curves ever so slightly in just the right places on a gradual downhill path to the junction with County H at 7.2 miles. These last 3 miles are ones that you won't soon forget.

A right turn on County H takes us on a nice cruise on a flat valley road to 10.3 miles and County T, where we go right again. Rolling hills curve through dense forest along the bottom edges of bluffs to 13.3 miles, where we turn hard left, then right again down a long, curvy descent. This part of the ride might be even more gorgeous than the last, with bucolic farms watched over by high hills as the road lazily drapes over lightly rolling terrain.

At 17 miles we are joined by County Z from the left, and shortly afterwards a curve to the west goes past a unique and historic private cemetery. At 18.6 miles, just before we reach Highway 23, we dart off the road onto a paved bike path. Across Highway 23 is Frank Lloyd Wright's Taliesin (see sidebar).

The bike path runs parallel to the highway through a cornfield to the Frank Lloyd Wright Visitor Center and County C. Turn right on C and complete the homestretch back to the entrance to Tower Hill State Park at 20.6 miles. Before moving on, you should take a look at the park's nineteenth-century lead-shot manufacturing structures. A short hiking trail leads to a bluff top where a 120-foot-deep shaft connects to a 90-foot tunnel leading to the banks of the Wisconsin River. Inside the tower building, you can view a brief video presentation on the process.

Amacher Hollow Road southeast of Spring Green.

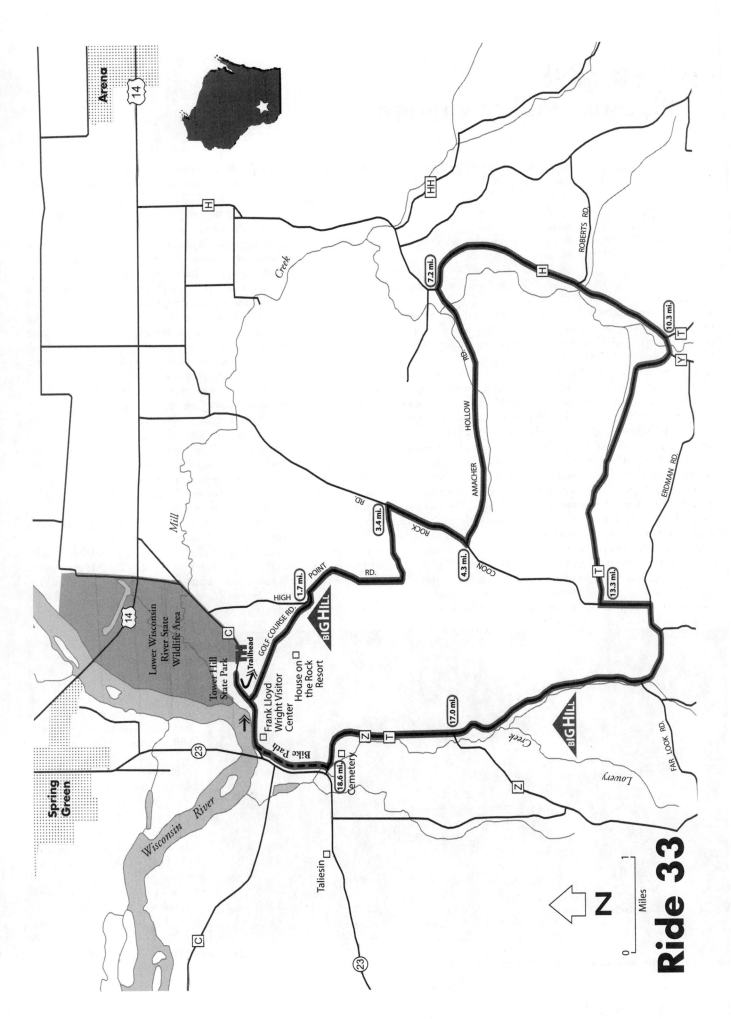

Ride 33

RIDE 34
Pleasant Valley Voyage

Location: Military Ridge State Trail and county roads east of Dodgeville.
Distance: 17-mile loop.
Pedaling time: 1.5–1.75 hours.
Surface: Paved roads.
Terrain: Flat to rolling, with two long, tough climbs.
Sweat factor: High.
Trailhead: Wisconsin DNR office and trail access on County YZ, a half mile east of State Highway 23.

Ho boy, this short ride sure packs a punch. It starts innocently enough, cruising along the flat Military Ridge State Trail and dropping way down into a valley. But after leaving the trail, two climbs of a mile or more each turn the route into a challenge. The valley scenery is unforgettable, and the woods along the arrow-straight section of the trail harbor wildlife of many types that often step out to greet the passersby. Nearby Dodgeville has a number of lodging and eating establishments, and the main entrance to sprawling Governor Dodge State Park is a couple of miles north on Highway 23. The park boasts over 5,000 scenic acres of steep hills, valleys, and forested ridges, 450 million-year-old sandstone bluffs, and a couple of lakes. The park is named after General Henry Dodge, one of the area's original white settlers and Wisconsin's first territorial governor.

Buy a trail pass or self-register at the kiosk next to the Military Ridge State Trail and head east on its flat, smooth, crushed limestone surface. This 40-mile path connects Dodgeville and Madison, skirting the southern boundaries of Governor Dodge and Blue Mound State Parks. The diverse scenery along the way includes farms, woods, wetlands, prairies, and small towns. Most of the trail follows the old Chicago & North Western railroad corridor, with easy two percent to five percent grades. The section we're riding on runs along the top of Military Ridge, a geographic divide between north-flowing tributaries of the Wisconsin and south-flowing tributaries of the Mississippi and Rock River watersheds.

A row of trees lines both sides of this early stretch of the trail, and rabbits, deer, wild turkey, grouse, fox, and many songbirds are all common visitors here. Several viewing platforms along the trail offer a chance to see some of these wild critters or to just sit a bit and admire the views. We stay the course to the junction with County Z, then keep on riding to the next junction at County Y and the 3-mile mark. There, we leave the bike trail and turn left. County Y wastes no time in serving up some fun: a long, fast downhill takes us into a stunning valley below, with round, densely wooded bluffs garnishing a slender stream. At 5.9 miles, we lean left at the junction with Ridgevue Road and follow a series of bends that reveal another breathtaking scene with each turn.

The junction with County ZZ comes up at 7 miles; we turn left here, following a nicely maintained road through a narrower valley. Look for an aging farm and outbuildings at 7.5 miles, and at 8.3 the road points upward and begins a climb of more than a mile, with grades in the six percent to nine percent range. At the top, the hill eases into a gradual incline past a farm to the junction with County Z and the Pleasant Ridge Store at 10.6 miles. This signals a left turn onto County Z, which forms the eastern border of Governor Dodge State Park. This section is pleasant enough to start, with an easy coast to a flat area near the bottom of the next bluff. But you know what that means—the road takes us into the woods and goes up again, steeper than the last one with no respite for another mile.

On level ground again, the road coasts back to the Military Ridge State Trail crossing at 15 miles. Just before reaching the trail, we pass a paved path running north and west. This is an access to the state park, leading riders to the Cox Hollow Lake beach area about a mile away—not a bad way to spend a little extra time before completing this loop.

But let's jump back on the Military Ridge trail and enjoy an easy cruise back to the trailhead to close out this 17-mile ride.

Bikers viewing the local cows along the Military Ridge State Trail.

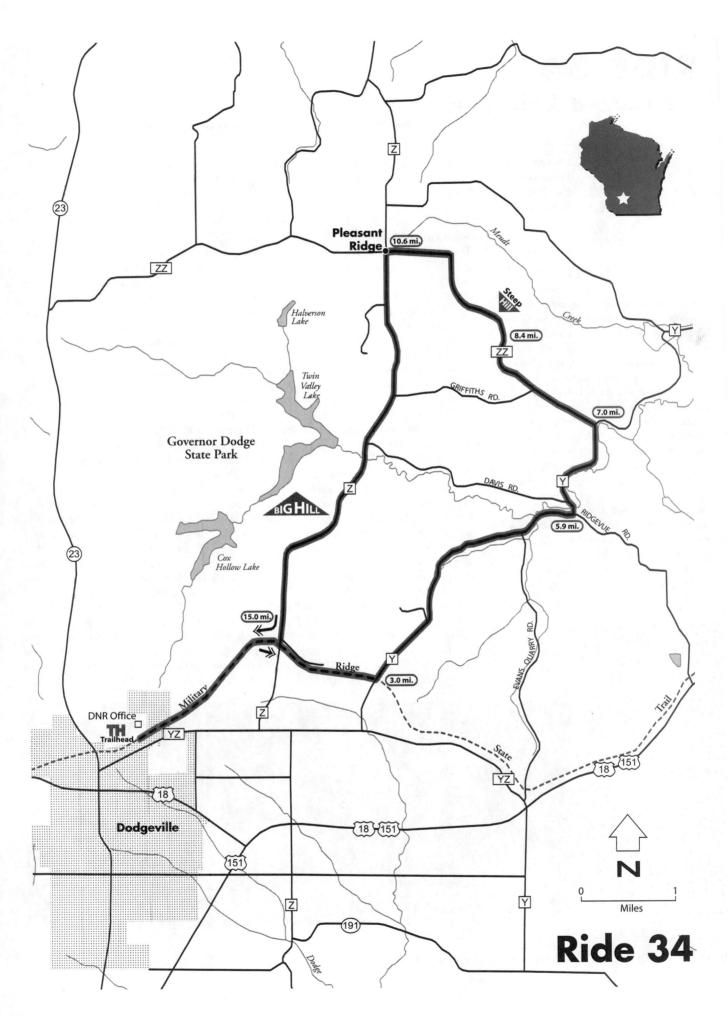

Pleasant Ridge

10.6 mi.

Steep Hill

8.4 mi.

Meudt Creek

Z

ZZ

Halverson Lake

Twin Valley Lake

Governor Dodge State Park

BiG HiLL

Z

Cox Hollow Lake

GRIFFITHS RD.

7.0 mi.

DAVIS RD.

Y

RIDGEVUE RD.

5.9 mi.

Y

15.0 mi.

EVANS QUARRY RD.

Ridge

Y

3.0 mi.

Military

DNR Office

TH Trailhead

YZ

Z

State

YZ

Trail

18 151

18

Dodgeville

18 151

151

Z

Y

191

Dodge

N

0   1

Miles

Ride 34

73

RIDE 35
Shake-a-Rag Ride

Location: County roads east of Mineral Point.
Distance: 18.5-mile loop.
Pedaling time: 1.5–2 hours.
Surface: Paved roads.

Terrain: Rolling.
Sweat factor: Moderate.
Trailhead: Pendarvis state historic site on Shake Rag Street in Mineral Point.

Pendarvis

In the 1830s, skilled miners from the Cornwall region of England learned of the lead rush here and ventured to Mineral Point to work the area's mines. They brought their considerable masonry skills and built the attractive homes seen today at the Pendarvis state historic site (www.wisconsinhistory.org/pendarvis). Rock walls, gardens, and lush foliage surround these treasures from the past, and a museum shop offers a selection of Cornish foods and wares. Merry Christmas Mine is directly across the street and has a footpath leading through a restored prairie. The site features exhibits of mining machinery and equipment used in the area, as well as one intact shaft of the original mine. It's open from May through the end of October (www.mineralpoint.com).

Mineral Point has so many historic sites that it was the first city in Wisconsin to be listed on the National Registry of Historic Places. In the early 1800s, lead was discovered in this area, and the sudden influx of people hoping to strike it rich, including a large group of Cornish miners, established mining camps that eventually became the village of Mineral Point.

This ride takes us over terrain that displays all the ups and downs of your favorite roller coaster, except here the only thing propelling us up the hills are our own pedal strokes. A departure from the wooded lands of previous rides, this loop rolls through open farm country. There are enough hills to make this a taxing ride, but the swimming pool at Soldiers Memorial Park near the trailhead offers a cool end to the trip, and a visit to the Pendarvis state historic site across the street rounds out a perfect day.

We begin this rolling ride innocently enough, by riding south on Shake Rag Street to State Highway 23/39 and going left. A short climb up from town brings us to where Highways 23 and 39 split at 1.2 miles; we will turn left onto Highway 39 and head east. This is an easy, smooth road that we follow for 1 mile to the junction with County DD. A right turn here takes us down a fun hill and back up a decent climb on the other side, all the while continuing east past quiet pastures and cropland. The historic Pleasant View Community Church sits atop a hill at 3.4 miles, and beyond that we climb up Proctor Hill. Riding up over a rise we see what is to come—a long stretch of sizeable roller-coaster hills.

The junction with County D goes by at 5.8 miles, and as we roll up a small hill between two scenic farmsteads we reach the junction with County W at 7.8 miles. Follow W to the left, where you may be treated to the fresh smells of crops and manure in the air. We're still riding up and down hills of various sizes and do so all the way to Highway 39 at 9.1 miles. Here we'll take a left at Bethel Church, an 1880 house of worship. With its flat terrain, this part of Highway 39 provides a breather from the steep hills that we've seen for much of the ride.

We come to the junction with County D on the left (southbound) at 11.1 and keep on truckin' west. We next come to where County D turns right (northbound) at 13.2. Here we'll take the turn and head north on County D, back on hilly terrain. When Antoine Road (which is also County S) appears, we'll take a left there and begin to head back to Mineral Point. Things are pretty quiet and laid back out this way. A herd of cattle crossing the road might be the only traffic you encounter, and the road should be in excellent condition, making for an ideal stretch of bucolic serenity. A couple of additional steeper climbs pop up before we reach the final downhill stretch leading back to Shake Rag Street at 18.3 miles. A left here takes us right back to the trailhead for a total of 18.5 miles.

The Pendarvis state historic site in Mineral Point.

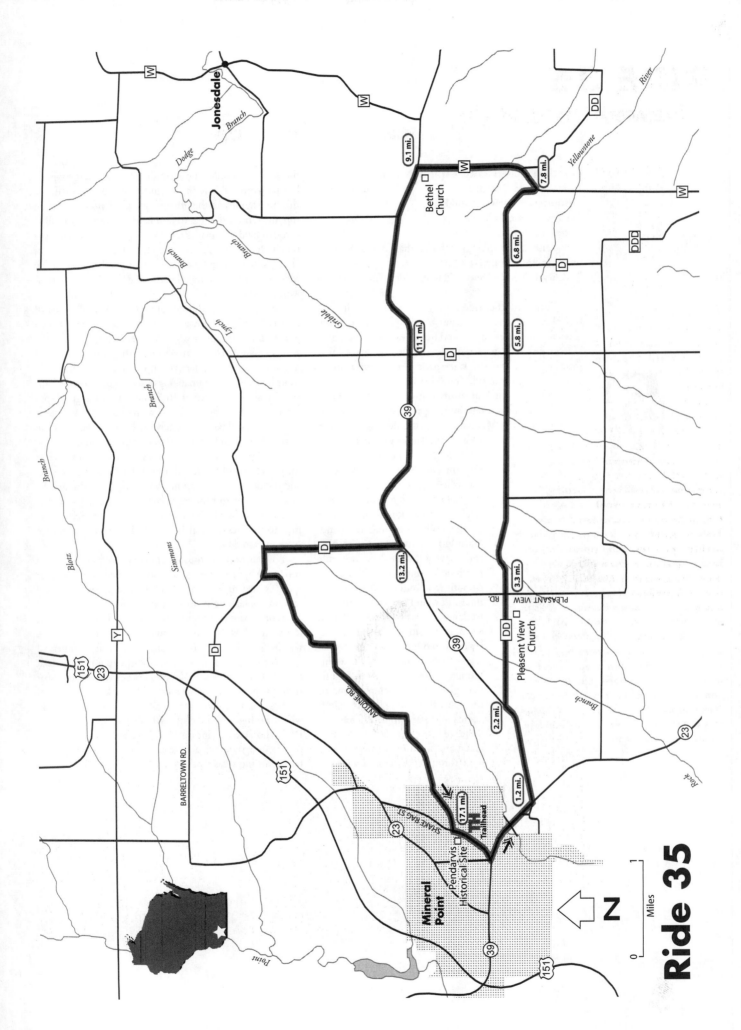

Ride 35

Jonesdale

Bethel Church

Pleasent View Church

Pendarvis Historical Site

Mineral Point

9.1 mi.
7.8 mi.
6.8 mi.
5.8 mi.
11.1 mi.
13.2 mi.
3.3 mi.
2.2 mi.
1.2 mi.
17.1 mi.

TH Trailhead

ANTOINE RD.
SHAKE RAG ST.
PLEASANT VIEW RD.
BARRELTOWN RD.

Point
Dodge Branch
Branch
Lynch Branch
Gribble Branch
Simmons Branch
Blotz Branch
Branch
Yellowstone River
Rock
Branch

N
Miles
0   1

RIDE 36
Dewey Does It

Location: County roads north of Nelson Dewey State Park, north of Cassville.
Distance: 21 miles out and back.
Pedaling time: 2–2.25 hours.
Surface: Paved roads.
Terrain: Flat and rolling, with one challenging climb.
Sweat factor: Moderate +.
Trailhead: Nelson Dewey State Park on County VV.

This is another ride through an area rich with historical significance. A true Mississippi River town, Cassville, just south of the trailhead, was settled in 1827. Wisconsin's first governor, Nelson Dewey, was a longtime resident, and the state park bearing his name is where we begin the ride. The area is also one of the nation's finest viewing sites for bald eagles, and many of them spend the winters hunting for fish in the nearby open areas of the Mississippi River. Bald Eagle Days in December, January, and February offer the best times to view these magnificent birds. Check www.cassville.org for more details.

This ride starts out in relatively sedate fashion, then serves up a big climb to rolling farmland. Starting from the entrance to Nelson Dewey State Park, we ride north on County VV, rolling along smooth road and easy flats for 2.5 miles. Lowland crop fields and the wetlands of the Muddy Creek drainage are situated along the valley floor to our left, with gently rising terrain beyond. To the right, though, are the steep wooded bluffs that give such dramatic flavor to this area. But a long, steady climb begins and presents a different experience altogether. A relentless grade and a couple of switchbacks wind through the trees, taking us all the way to 4.5 miles. This 2-mile hill is an energy sapper, but remember this is an out-and-back ride, so we'll ride this monster going the other way—a *downhill* jaunt. On top, the terrain changes to farmland, and we begin riding through fields of corn as far as the eye can see. There isn't much chance to fully recover after that first monstrous climb, as the terrain here is consistently rolling, with a few hills presenting enough length and height to keep us working hard.

A few country homes are gathered in the area of Badger Road as County VV takes a hard left and then points north again, with farm fields dominating the scenery. We reach the junction with County V at 7.5 miles. Turn left here, then ride up more hills, some small, some bigger, before a final long descent into the tiny community of Glen Haven at 10.5 miles. This is a good spot for a rest before the trip back, with excellent river views and plenty of small-town charm. Check out Parson's Inn Retreat (a bed and breakfast) for a quiet escape.

For the return trip, we follow the same route, so let's turn around and follow County V back up the long hill and continue east to County VV. A right on the two Vs takes us back across the roller-coaster hills, past the miniature neighborhood, and at about the 16-mile mark we return to the crest of that big old hill we came up earlier. Now for some fun.

The elevation drops in a hurry as we round the first turn, and by the time the second switchback arrives, our speed is nearing 40 mph. After exercising caution going around the last, tight turn, we drop into a tuck-and-take flight on the long, straight home stretch. This is more like it—sailing downhill for two miles, coasting almost all the way back to the start at the park entrance at 21 miles.

A perfect end to the ride is to spend a few hours at Stonefield (see sidebar), Nelson Dewey's vast estate across from the park bearing his name. The park offers some of the best secluded campsites in all of Wisconsin, several of which are high on the bluffs overlooking the Mississippi River and across it into Iowa. There are also 20 acres of prairie designated as a state natural area, scenic hiking trails, birding areas, and Indian burial mounds.

Stonefield Village

Nelson Dewey ventured west from Connecticut to Wisconsin and made a fortune in land and lead-mining investments and became the state's first governor. He built a vast estate called Stonefield near the Mississippi River. Today, Stonefield Village is a sprawling complex of buildings designated as a state historic site. In addition to Dewey's mansion, visitors can see the original stone stable where he boarded his horses. A museum shop is located in the 1870 stone barn, and visitors can explore a re-created 1900 village. Much information and excellent histories are online at www.stonefield.wisconsinhistory.com

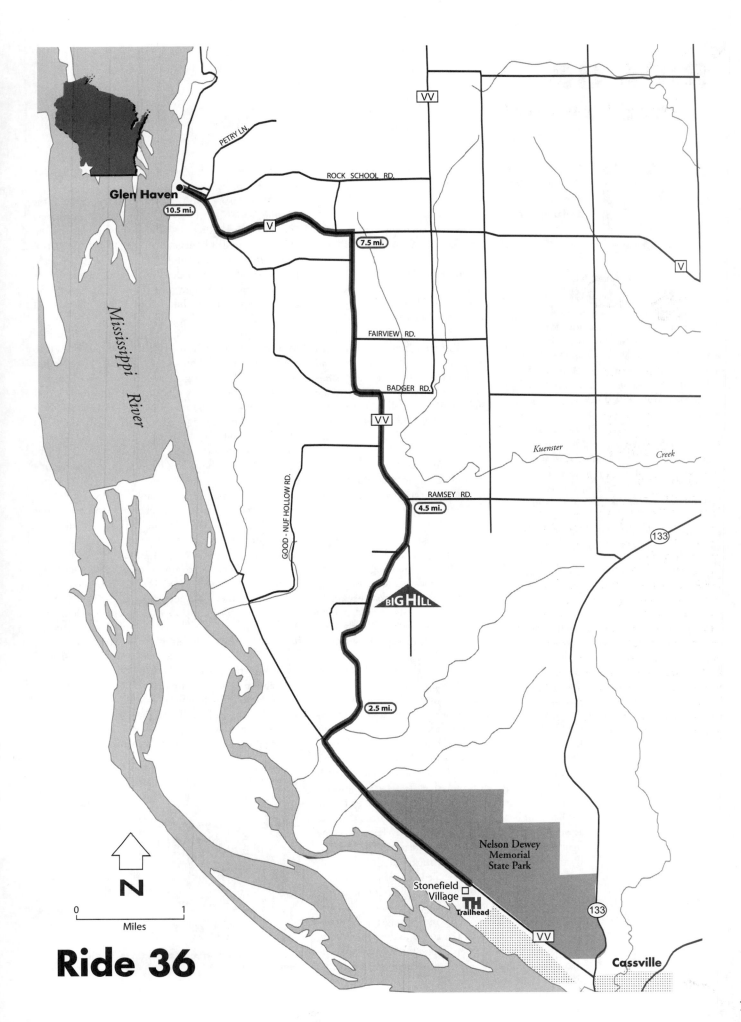

Glen Haven

10.5 mi.

PETRY LN.

ROCK SCHOOL RD.

V

7.5 mi.

FAIRVIEW RD.

BADGER RD.

VV

Mississippi River

GOOD - NUF HOLLOW RD.

Kuenster *Creek*

RAMSEY RD.

4.5 mi.

BiGHiLL

2.5 mi.

VV

VV

V

133

Nelson Dewey
Memorial
State Park

Stonefield
Village

TH
Trailhead

133

VV

Cassville

N

0   1
Miles

Ride 36

RIDE 37
Road to Riches

Location: Hills, ridges, and coulees east of State Highway 56 and Richland Center.
Distance: 23.2-mile loop.
Pedaling time: 2–2.5 hours.

Surface: Paved roads.
Terrain: Rolling, with several huge, tough climbs.
Sweat factor: High.
Trailhead: The historic Richland County Building on County N in Richland Center.

Two Local Rocky Sights

Richland Center has a couple of notable geological curiosities close by. Pier Park is the site of a natural rock bridge that rises 60 feet over the Pine River, which gradually cut through the original rock over a period of millions of years; a half-mile walk to the top provides superb views of the Pine River Valley. The park is located less than 8 miles north of Richland Center. Eagle Cave, about 12 miles southwest of town, is a 2,400-foot-long onyx cave with amazing rock formations, including those in the shape of toadstools, a shark's head and jaws, and an eagle (the cave's namesake). The cave is also known for its diamond stalactites and 2,000-year-old stone carvings.

Richland Center is in an area called the Ocooch Mountains, and while you might question the *mountains* part of that name, there are hills here that will test even the strongest legs. The region is largely made up of sloped woodland, with the rest of the terrain suited for agriculture. For cyclists, it's simply out-of-this-world gorgeous. Roads wind up folds in steep, wooded bluffs and wander through valley farmland with little vehicle traffic.

It's difficult to simply ride right through Richland Center, with its many historic buildings and cozy neighborhoods, without stopping to enjoy its charm. Before beginning this ride, it may be a good time to explore the sights of this town of 5,000 by simply spinning along the town's quiet residential streets, warming up for the big ride ahead.

Warmed up or not, we begin the ride by rolling east through a friendly neighborhood on Haseltine Street, named for Ira Haseltine, the young man who purchased and named the land that would become Richland Center. On the east side of town, we take a half turn to the left at the County N sign and head toward the bluffs farther east. In short order we climb above the streets and homes, and all around are breathtaking views of high, wooded hills. A glance up ahead reveals what's in store for us: a long, steady, steep climb. Bushy tops of trees mottle the flanks of deep coulees dropping away from the road as we climb higher and higher. A big gravel pit sits on the right side of the road about three-quarters of the way up. Listen and watch for hulking trucks entering the road, and be sure to steer clear of spilled gravel in the path.

After a mile of laboring uphill, we're finally at the top, and our reward is sweeping views of rolling countryside as we cruise along on a winding ridgetop. We continue to follow County N as it curves to the right. A long, meandering descent delivers us past the Sunset Apple Orchard and through farmland tucked between the bluffs.

This 1.5-mile stretch of welcome downhill cruising has some sharp turns, so watch your speed.

After crossing Little Willow Creek, we arrive at the junction with County NN at 5.1 miles. We go left here and head north along this valley road, bending around the high, rounded bluffs and passing picturesque farmsteads set into the folds of the hills. At mile 10, we begin to climb gradually through a heavily wooded mix of pine and hardwood forest crowding the road. This isn't quite as steep as our first big hill, but it's still another mile of uphill pedaling.

At the top, the trees once again give way to fields of corn and beans, and the road roller-coasters all the way to the junction with County D at 11.7 miles. There, we turn left (follow the NN sign) and ride west. We continue straight on County D as County NN turns north. After a couple of stair-step turns, we reach 13.3 miles, where County DD turns to the right. Turn left here and begin to head downhill. After only a half mile, just as DD starts a steep descent to the right, a road splits off to the left. There isn't a sign, but this is Pleasant Ridge Road, a title most fitting for this scenic stretch of the ride, as it provides great views of the area's many rounded bluffs.

The road is smooth and uncrowded with traffic as it curves through bluff-top farmland. At about 16 miles, the road begins to descend back into the woods, then pops back into farm fields. We pass a beautiful log home at Cooper Hill Road and continue to follow Pleasant Ridge to the left. At 19 miles, we pass Morris Valley Road to the right. Down there is a gorgeous, slender valley, which affords the opportunity to experience an exhilarating downhill coast, followed by a torturous uphill struggle on its nearly 2 miles of 10 percent to 18 percent grades.

At 24.2 miles, we pass the Sunset Apple Orchard again and arrive at County N. We take a right turn, head west, and soon reunite with that monster hill we rode up earlier. Hold on tight and be careful. Speeds can easily reach 50 mph on this hill, and there is a hard right turn close to the bottom. Before we know it, we are back at the starting point after more than 23 exciting miles.

A long and winding road on the way to Richland Center.

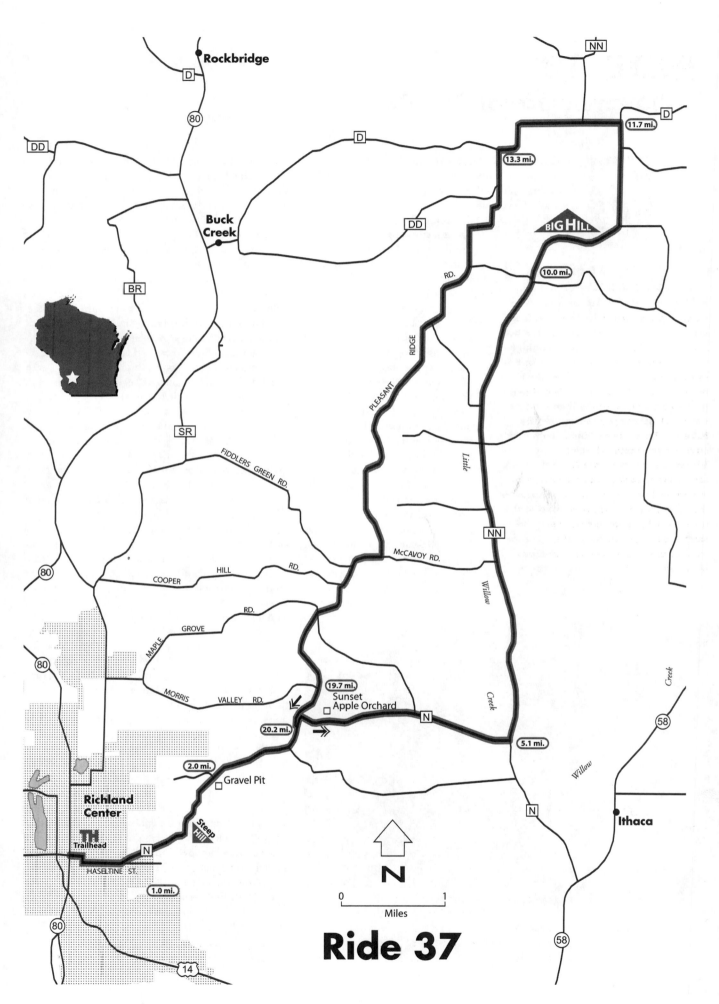

Rockbridge

D

80

DD

Buck
Creek

BR

D

13.3 mi.

D

11.7 mi.

DD

BIG HILL

10.0 mi.

PLEASANT RIDGE RD.

Little

SR

FIDDLERS GREEN RD.

Willow

NN

McCAVOY RD.

COOPER HILL RD.

80

RD.

MAPLE GROVE

Creek

80

MORRIS VALLEY RD.

19.7 mi.

Sunset
Apple Orchard

N

Creek

20.2 mi.

N

5.1 mi.

2.0 mi.

Gravel Pit

Richland
Center

58

TH
Trailhead

Steep
Hill

N

N

Ithaca

HASELTINE ST.

1.0 mi.

N

80

Miles
0   1

14

58

Ride 37

RIDE 38
Clown Prince of Baraboo

Location: Scenic county roads southeast of Baraboo.
Distance: 15.3-mile loop.
Pedaling time: 1.25–1.5 hours.
Surface: Paved roads.
Terrain: Hilly.
Sweat factor: High.
Trailhead: Old Schoolhouse Restaurant at County DL and Bluff Road.

Devils Lake

The Baraboo Hills offer numerous hidden glens and quiet rural roads to explore. One can't-miss trip idea is to use Devils Lake State Park as your hub and wander the area's many squiggly roads. Located a few miles west of this ride's trailhead, Devils Lake is one of the most scenic areas in the state, with towering 500-foot bluffs lining a mile-long gorge that holds spring-fed Devils Lake. The bluffs are popular with rock climbers from all over the Midwest. The 2.5-mile entrance road to the park is sublime, passing through dense forest with views of a huge lowland to the south. Circling the south end of the lake, a colossal climb presents quite a challenge to get to the high side of the gorge, and another thrilling descent leads into Baraboo and its circus-oriented attractions.

As this ride shows, the Baraboo Hills are full of unforgettable scenery and plenty of challenges for the cyclist. Over a *billion* years old, these steep, wooded bluffs rise 200, 300, even 500 feet and are an impressive sight from miles away. Nearby Devils Lake State Park is one of the most visited parks in the state system (see the sidebar for more information). To the north, Baraboo offers a wagonload of attractions for everybody. This is the hometown of the Ringling brothers, who created the most famous circus show in the world. Visit the Circus World Museum for a trip through generations of fun and to see live shows. Additional area information is available at www.baraboo.com

We start this ride from the Old Schoolhouse Restaurant (more on that later) and head eastbound on County DL. Although the road is in great shape, there is no shoulder, and there are more cars than we would like, so ride smart. Almost right off the bat, we get an up-close look at one of Baraboo's hills. After a gradual downhill to warm up a little, we begin to climb and do so for a little over a half mile. Cresting the top, we are treated to stupendous views of bluffs; we then sail all the way down to where we join State Highway 78 at 1.8 miles. We continue straight east on 78, which is a higher-trafficked road, for a little more than a mile.

Durwards Glen Road comes up at the 3-mile mark, and we turn left on this smooth bit of road as it winds upward into the hills. We pass McLeisch Road at mile 3.8 and continue riding along the lower flanks of steep, wooded bluffs. At 4.7 miles, we begin to climb in earnest on a steep grade, but then it levels a bit and becomes merely a steady, relentless ascent. At the top, the road levels somewhat and we cruise through cornfields; then it climbs one more small ridge before a big drop on the other side. The surface isn't the best here, so you'll have to dial back your speed a touch. After riding clear of the woods, we get a first-rate view of another bluff to the right. We finally get to coast downhill, arriving at County W (7.1 miles) where we turn left.

This road is without a shoulder, as well, so ride single file and stay alert. Now heading west, we are met with a long, steady climb straight away, passing the old Tucker Cemetery before cresting yet another rise and dropping down again. We follow County W to the left at 7.8 miles, riding on a gradual descent with fine views of farmland with high hills in the background.

We reach Bluff Road at 10.2 miles and turn left, heading back south. The pavement is in good shape, just in time for the next huge hill, which climbs steeply all the way to 10.9 before offering any relief. Once on top, there is an easy cruise on a flat section to enjoy, and we pass through woods and meadows to a fork in the road at 13.1 miles. We lean right here and begin a most spirited descent; foliage formerly in focus is now just a green, 45 mph blur. After about a mile and a half of hurtling downhill, we finally level out at about 14.5 miles. Speeds exceeding 50 mph are easily attainable on this homestretch—hold on tight! After passing Devils Head Resort (offering downhill and cross-country skiing in the winter, golf in the summer) on the left, we arrive back—exhilarated—at County DL. We also have a chance to revisit the Old Schoolhouse Restaurant. No ordinary eatery, it's a unique combination of historic schoolhouse, jailhouse, church, and caboose, all pieced together to make one fun place to eat. In good weather, sit on the outdoor porch, take in the view of this lovely area, and enjoy memories of one great ride.

Enjoying the view atop a bluff at Devils Lake.

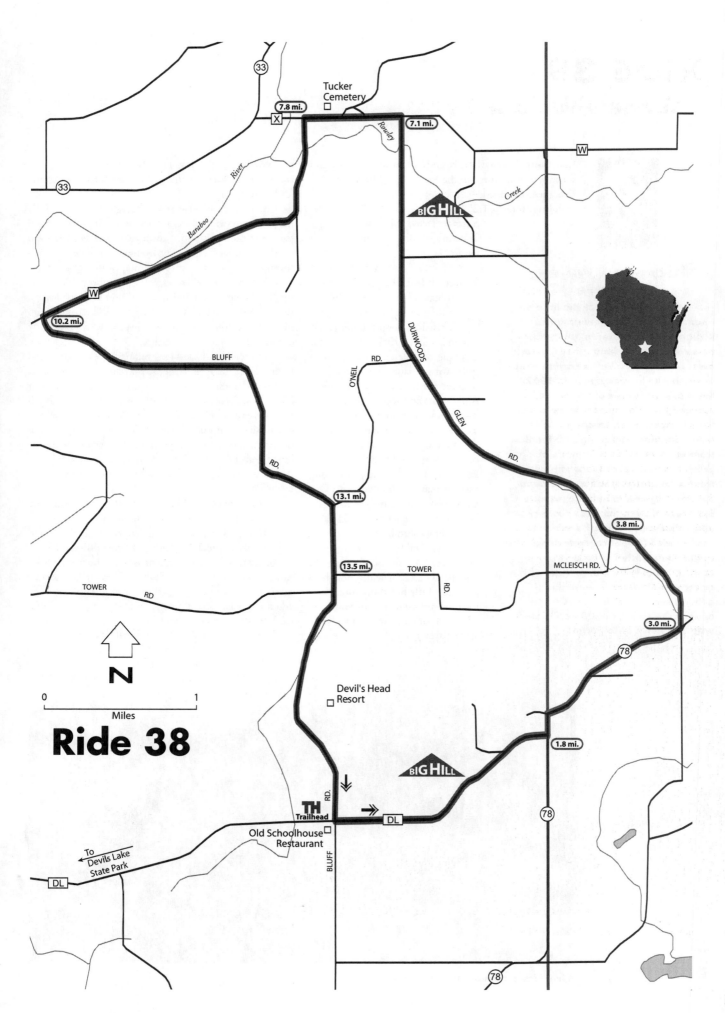

Ride 38

N

0   1

Miles

RIDE 39
Tunnelville Tour

Kickapoo Valley Reserve

A few miles north of the little town of La Farge is the wonderful Kickapoo Valley Reserve, an 8,600-acre complex of rolling woods, meadows, and streams. But the area's tranquility belies its rocky past. In 1962, the U.S. Army Corps of Engineers planned to build an earthen dam on the Kickapoo River, creating a lake 12 miles long and displacing 140 families from the valley. After 13 years of protests and legal challenges by environmental groups and local residents, the corps agreed to halt the project. But it was only in the last couple of years that the land has been reclaimed. A 110-foot concrete tower, originally intended to be part of the dam, is the only visible remnant of the government's plan. A two-million-dollar visitor center is scheduled to open in the spring of 2004 on Highway 131 north of La Farge.

Location: Wooded bluffs and ridges adjacent to and southwest of La Farge in the Kickapoo Valley.
Distance: 12-mile loop.
Pedaling time: 1–1.25 hours.

Surface: Paved roads.
Terrain: Rolling, with one big climb.
Sweat factor: Moderate.
Trailhead: In La Farge, at the junction of State Highways 131 and 82.

This short loop follows gentle terrain along the Kickapoo River for a couple of miles, then adds some spice with a jaunt on one of the steepest Rustic Roads in the state. Amid quiet and scenic environs, we delve into a narrow fold in a bluff, pass picturesque farmland, and coast down a long valley road. At the end of it all is the laid-back town of La Farge, ideal for some unwinding time or maybe a ride north to Ontario to connect with Ride 38.

We make tracks out of La Farge by heading south on State Highway 131. There will be a moderate number of vehicles on this first stretch, but the shoulder is wide enough to provide a little breathing room, and the road surface is in excellent shape. The road parallels the winding Kickapoo River just off to the right, a pretty waterway flowing down from near Tomah all the way to its confluence with the Wisconsin River in Crawford County.

At mile 2, we make a quick right turn onto Tunnelville Road, which is also Rustic Road 55, and we soon pass over the Kickapoo. Rustic Road indeed! We head northwest on old, cracking pavement that fades away altogether and turns to gravel, but mercifully only for a short stretch. We roll through lowland forest over a few small hills, with a wetland area and short scrub willow on the left and steep bluffs on the right. Solid pavement returns after 1 mile as we pass a large farm where big, burly oxen lumber about their pasture.

The road heads up a long hill past an old abandoned farm into dense, scenic woods. The climb gets steeper as it goes and doesn't let up until 4.4 miles. We can recover a little as we coast to the junction with County SS at 4.8 miles. We turn right here and begin a section of ups and downs that continue to test our legs. Stunning views of tidy farmland and woods packed into deep creases in the bluffs grab our attention. Chances are good along this stretch for spying a hawk or eagle overhead; keep an eye to the sky.

At 6.9 miles, we reach State Highway 82, where we turn right. This is a busier stretch of road than what we just left, with only a small shoulder, so ride single file and stay alert for traffic. Despite the vehicular distractions, we can enjoy this nice long descent after all the work we did earlier, coasting all the way into La Farge at the 12-mile mark. In terms of distance, this is a short trip (although you might have a hard time convincing your legs of that fact), but the scenery is beautiful and the land surrounding La Farge is loaded with additional ride routes.

A long descent amidst the hills near La Farge.

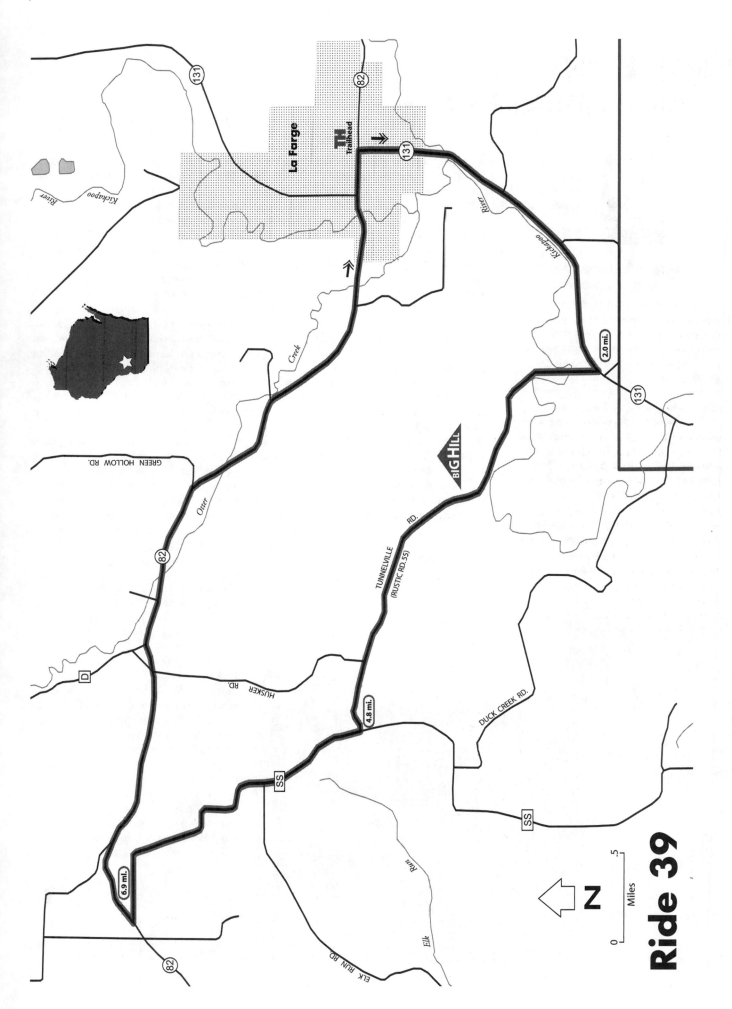

Ride 39

RIDE 40
Hollow Valley Hideaway

Location: Bluff roads west of State Highway 131 between Rockton and Ontario in the Kickapoo Valley.
Distance: 19.2 miles out and back.
Pedaling time: 1.75–2 hours.

Surface: Paved roads.
Terrain: Rolling.
Sweat factor: Moderate.
Trailhead: Town of Rockton at the junction of State Highway 131 and Dutch Hollow Road.

The Skinny on the Kickapoo

On its way south to the Wisconsin River, the Kickapoo River is so full of twists and turns and curves that the folks around here call it "the crookedest river in the world." The word *Kickapoo* means "he who moves about" in Algonquian. And Ontario bills itself as the Canoe Capital of the Kickapoo, with three major outfitters providing canoes, kayaks, and other gear for a memorable float on the squiggly river. The town is also known as the Gateway to Wildcat Mountain State Park, an especially scenic park on a high bluff to the east. The bluff is part of the Ocooch Mountains—hills, really, which are distinguished by sandstone slopes and limestone tops and which frame the river valley below.

Like Ride 38, this is a short trip that is long on fun, and we get to enjoy another Rustic Road. Part of the pleasure comes from a jaunt up a long valley road and a cruise through quiet farmland on an open ridge top. There are plenty of scenic views, including Wildcat Mountain State Park to the east. The park and surrounding area are made up of miles of unbroken forested hill and dale with rocky bluffs. This is an ideal habitat for mountain lions, and there are hundreds of reports, some even reliable, of sightings in these hills. The elusive mountain lion used to roam freely throughout Wisconsin but today is rarely, if ever, seen. "Officially," the last of the big cats was seen here over a century ago. Consider yourself very lucky if you spot one, in Wisconsin or any other state.

Our turnaround point in Ontario offers a variety of midride recreational opportunities, including canoeing, visiting an open-air museum, or sightseeing historic round barns. Check out www.visitvernoncounty.com for plenty of information and contacts.

On the northern fringe of tiny Rockton, we head west on Dutch Hollow Road, also known as Rustic Road 56. We immediately start a long, tough climb that challenges riders at the same time that it distracts them with lovely views of the rolling countryside. Finally we sail down a curvy stretch on the other side, passing Indian Creek Road at 2.1 miles, then steadily working our way back up the ridge. If we're lucky, we should be able to spot hawks and eagles soaring overhead, with some of them floating only a few dozen feet off the ground in search of prey.

There are all kinds of inviting roads splitting from our main route that look like great fun, too—Fish Valley, Wolf Valley, Twenty-Four Valley, all draped in pine, birch, oak, maple, and poplar. For now, though, we'll continue on Dutch Hollow Road for a short distance, then ride in a northwesterly direction on the same road, although it's now Sand Hill Road. We roll up and down some smaller hills to 4.8 miles, then begin to descend. Our Rustic Road turns off at 5.1 onto Lower Ridge Road, but it's gravel and we're having fun on our main route. So we keep heading downhill on what is now Hoff Valley Road, a long, curving descent through thick woods, all the way to State Highway 33 at 8.1 miles. A right turn here leads into Ontario at 9.6 miles.

At the halfway point of this up-and-back trip, let's take a break at the town that calls itself the Canoe Capital of the Kickapoo, then turn around and return to Rockton via the same route. This time, of course, we do things in reverse. Starting the climb back up Hoff Valley Road, we can get energized by thinking of the flyer waiting at Dutch Hollow Road and a speedy entry back into Rockton. Total mileage for the round trip is 19.2. (Another option is to head southbound from Ontario on Highway 131 all the way back to Rockton.)

Rustic Road 56 near Ontario.

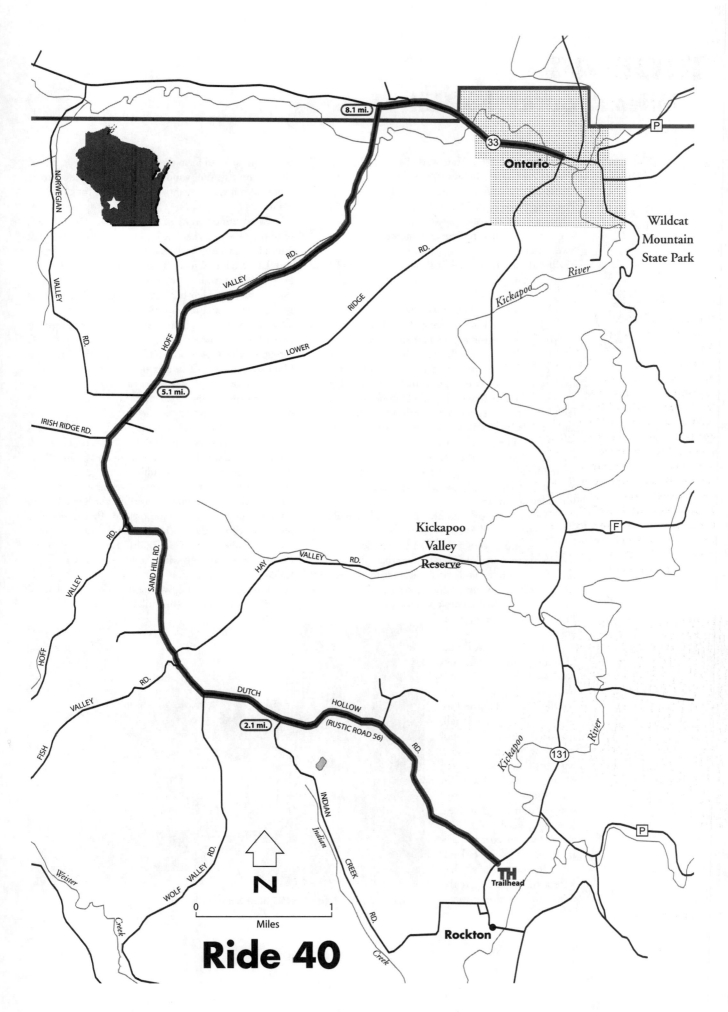

NORWEGIAN

VALLEY

RD.

8.1 mi.

33

Ontario

Wildcat
Mountain
State Park

P

VALLEY

RD.

RIDGE

RD.

HOFF

LOWER

5.1 mi.

IRISH RIDGE RD.

Kickapoo

River

Kickapoo
Valley
Reserve

F

RD.

SAND HILL RD.

VALLEY

RD.

HAY

VALLEY

RD.

HOFF

VALLEY

RD.

DUTCH

2.1 mi.

HOLLOW

(RUSTIC ROAD 56)

RD.

Kickapoo

River

131

FISH

INDIAN

Indian

CREEK

RD.

P

Weister

WOLF VALLEY RD.

N

TH
Trailhead

Creek

0   Miles   1

Rockton

Creek

Ride 40

85

RIDE 41
Miles Around the Mill

Location: Mill Bluff State Park between Tomah and Camp Douglas on Highway 12.
Distance: 10.3-mile loop.
Pedaling time: 1–1.25 hours.
Surface: Paved roads.
Terrain: Flat, gently rolling, and one steep hill.
Sweat factor: Low +.
Trailhead: Mill Bluff State Park on U.S. Highway 12 and Funnel Road.

If you want to loosen up before the ride, take a walk (or jog) up the 223 stone steps of Mill Bluff across from the park entrance for some panoramic views of ancient "bluff islands" to the north and high wooded hills of the state park to the south. On the ride, we'll cruise some flats around the bases of some of these bluffs, then grind right into the clutches of a big climb. Look and listen for large military planes zooming overhead on their way in and out of Camp Williams Army National Guard base to the east. The vicinity of I-94 and one of the busiest railroad tracks you'll ever see dim the fun a little on the northern half of the loop, but on the south side the roads are scenic and quiet, with numerous splits and spur roads for added adventure.

We leave the park and head north on Funnel Road, riding right past Mill Bluff. We'll go over and under I-94 and curve into a section crowded by wooded hills. We soon come to a small parking area on the right, with access to a 1.25-mile hiking trail that leads to Camel Bluff (the biggest of the bunch) and unusual rock formations such as Devils Monument and Cleopatra's Needle. Bear Bluff is a bit farther up Funnel Road.

At 1.4 miles, we'll turn left on Gypsum Avenue and head west. Wildcat Bluff is close on our right, so close it is difficult to look up and see the top. Here we pass tall, rounded bluffs poking out of otherwise flat ground like big welts. Those were created during the last Ice Age, when the Wisconsin River was plugged near the Dells area, creating glacial Lake Wisconsin, which covered several counties' worth of land, including these bluffs. They were actually islands at the time, and crashing waves eroded the sides to form these buttes, mesas, and pinnacles. Eventually, sun, wind, and water wore down these mounds to mere hills until they blended back into the plain.

We continue on more flats, passing a farm or two, until the road turns hard right, then changes its mind at 2.6 miles and turns back westbound, cruising a straight and flat stretch to Grover Road at mile 3.2. We'll go left here and enjoy wide-open views of the distant bluffs to the east and the high hills ahead. The road passes over I-94 and arrives at the junction with U.S. Highway 12 at 4.6 miles. We'll go right and left again on the continuation of Grover Road, starting out with a short ride through some dense woods and then past fields of corn. Our road comes to a T intersection at Horizon Avenue at 5.5 miles, and this is where we turn right. A half mile later, we arrive at Hope Road and make another left turn onto a heavenly piece of pavement.

In short order, we begin our one big climb on this ride, about three-quarters of a mile up a steep, curvy path through dense woods. There's time to recover on a long descent on the other side, steadily coasting to County W at 7.8 miles. A left turn here curves around through cropland and pasture among more of these hunchbacked hills, passing County C along the way. By the way, this road leads east to Camp Douglas, where riders can pick up the 15-mile Omaha Bike Trail and cruise south to Elroy, where it hooks up with the Elroy-Sparta Trail (see Ride 42).

On the main route, we return to Highway 12 and Mill Bluff State Park at 10.3 miles.

A stretch of Funnel Road in Mill Bluff State Park.

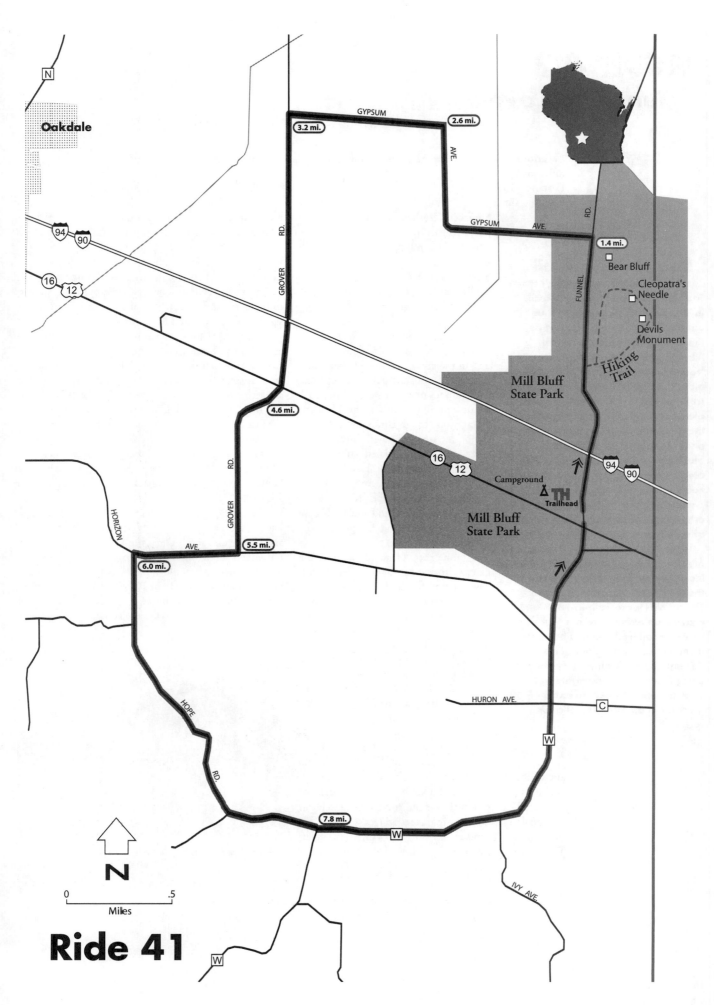

N

Oakdale

94 90

16 12

GYPSUM

3.2 mi.

2.6 mi.

A
V
E
.

GYPSUM   AVE.

1.4 mi.

R
D
.

Bear Bluff

F
U
N
N
E
L

Cleopatra's
Needle

Devils
Monument

Hiking
Trail

Mill Bluff
State Park

G
R
O
V
E
R

R
D
.

4.6 mi.

16 12

94 90

Campground

TH
Trailhead

Mill Bluff
State Park

G
R
O
V
E
R

R
D
.

H
O
R
I
Z
O
N

5.5 mi.

AVE.

6.0 mi.

H
O
P
E

R
D
.

7.8 mi.

W

HURON   AVE.

C

W

W

I
V
Y

A
V
E
.

N

0   .5

Miles

Ride 41

RIDE 42
Tunnel of Love

Elroy-Sparta Trail

The 32-mile-long Elroy-Sparta Trail is the centerpiece of rail trails in Wisconsin and possibly throughout the nation. Originally part of the former 300-mile Wisconsin Bikeway, the trail attracts visitors from all over the United States, more than 60,000 every year. The trail opened in 1965 and is a pleasant departure from run-of-the-mill trails of the same ilk. This one travels through the dramatic bluffs and valleys of the unglaciated region of the state and is heavily wooded through a large portion of its length, blending in other parts with a bucolic tapestry of rolling farmland.

The big attractions of the trail are the three rock tunnels, two being a quarter mile in length and the third three-quarters of a mile. The tunnels were built in 1873 and provide an experience not found on other rail trails. Riders have to dismount and walk their bikes through the dark tunnels, typically using flashlights to navigate to the opposite end. It's like an extra ingredient in an already delicious recipe.

Location: Elroy-Sparta Trail access in Wilton, about 11 miles south of Tomah.
Distance: 15.6-mile loop.
Pedaling time: 1.5–1.75 hours.
Surface: Crushed-limestone trail and paved roads.
Terrain: Flat, rolling, with one steep hill in Norwalk.
Sweat factor: Moderate to high.
Trailhead: In Wilton, on County M just north of State Highway 71/131.

The Elroy-Sparta Trail was the first of Wisconsin's rail trails and one of the first in the country. This ride begins on this popular trail and passes through one of its famous tunnels before exiting onto scenic and hilly county roads. We'll encounter one tough climb and plenty of rolling terrain, along with breathtaking views of the unglaciated countryside. The small towns of Wilton and Norwalk offer quaint restaurants, camping, picnic shelters, and bike rentals. Access to the Omaha, the "400," and the La Crosse River Trails is available in Sparta to the northwest.

From the village of Wilton, the gateway to the Kickapoo Reserve, we'll pay our trail fees and start our ride on the trail heading westbound. As we parallel State Highway 71, the first miles are nearly flat, but we are actually pedaling slightly uphill. The neighboring scenery is heavily wooded, with quick views of both high hills and farmland through the trees. At mile 2.3, we arrive at the entrance to the quarter-mile-long Tunnel 2. If this is your first time on this trail, you're in for a treat. Make sure you or someone in your group brings a flashlight; it's black as night in there—damp and chilly, too. It will take a little time to reach the other end, as it is preferred that bikes be walked through the tunnels. We emerge at the far end at 2.6 miles and begin a gradual downhill, crossing a few bridges, staying close to Highway 71, and rolling into Norwalk at 5.5 miles. The area in town in the vicinity of the trail offers a restaurant, shelters, picnic areas, restrooms, and a convenience store.

We don't need a rest yet, so we'll turn right at County U in town and head north, leaving the main trail for the day. The first 5 miles should have loosened our legs in preparation for a long, steep climb—over a mile's worth—to the top of an open ridge. There are fantastic views in all directions up here, and the terrain relaxes to easy rollers and flats. We ride due east through cornfields to 7.8 miles, where we'll begin a series of stair-step turns to the north and east. At 9.2 miles we turn north at the signs for County U and Keats Road.

Keep on chasing the County U sign at a right turn at 10.4 miles. Kettle Road comes along at mile 11.6, and we will take that to the right. The views are wondrous from up here, the kind that make you slow down or stop altogether to soak it all in. The road makes a hard right and then points downhill in a hurry. This is steeper than the first climb, and the road isn't in the best condition, so use caution on this long flyer. After passing Kerry Road on the right, we enter thick woods and coast to County M at 13.6 miles. We make a right turn and enter the homestretch back to Wilton, arriving at the trailhead at 15.6 miles.

On Sunday mornings from Memorial Day through Labor Day, the Lions Club serves up a pancake breakfast, and bike rentals and bed and breakfasts are available. Do not leave Wilton without stopping in at Gina's Pies Are Square, where the house specialty is (of course) square pies. Gina also owns Wilton's Wienies just down the road. East of Wilton is the Dorset Valley School Restaurant with homemade pies, breads, and cookies.

Taking a break on the Elroy-Sparta State Trail.

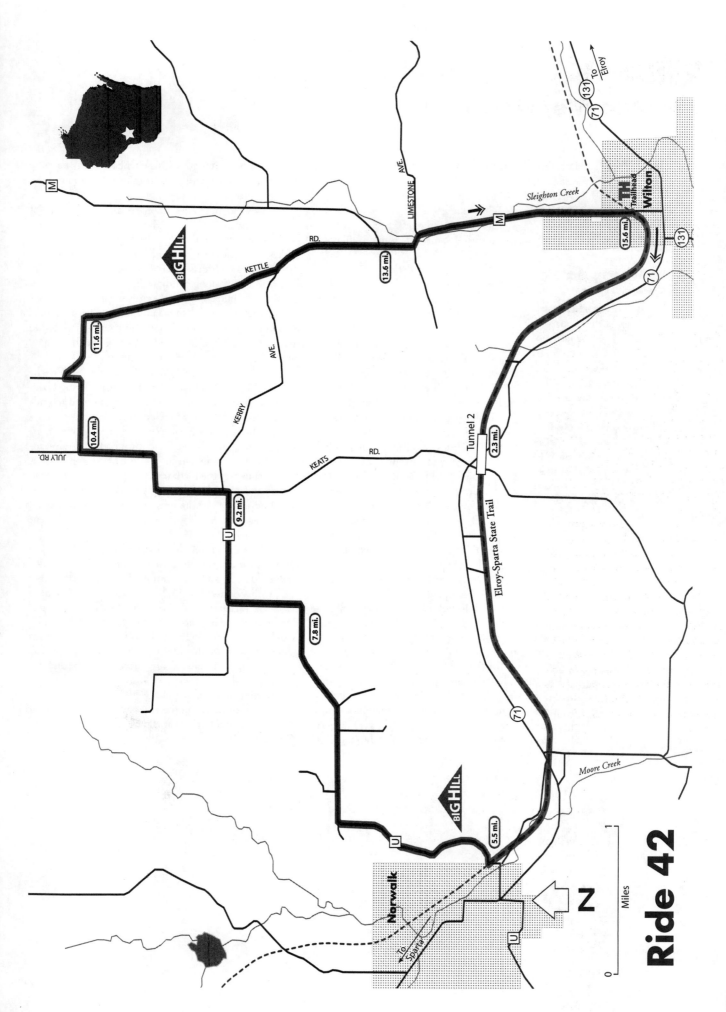

Ride 42

Miles

N

89

RIDE 43
Talk to Me, Goose

Something for Canoeists

A unique attraction of Goose Island County Park is the Goose Island Canoe Trail, a joint project between the Upper Mississippi River National Wildlife Refuge, the U.S. Army Corps of Engineers, the Wisconsin DNR, and the La Crosse County Parks Department. Canoeists can follow a designated route through secluded backwater areas of the river around Goose Island. Trail signs are posted at major "intersections," and reassurance markers are placed at intervals along the route.

Location: Bluffs and ridge tops on county roads southeast of La Crosse.
Distance: 17.5-mile loop.
Pedaling time: 1.5–2 hours.
Surface: Paved roads.
Terrain: Some flat, some rolling, one huge climb.
Sweat factor: Moderate +.
Trailhead: Goose Island County Park on State Highway 35 at County K, south of La Crosse.

This is a fantastic all-around ride, with a couple of impressive climbs, scenic rolling sections, and flat cruising. Starting with a warm-up on Highway 35, we roll onto a Rustic Road that soon serves up a long, difficult climb right up the side of a bluff. It's a beautiful ride, but at almost 2 miles, it will definitely challenge you. Around the midway point of the trip, Brinkman Ridge Road is surely one of the most enjoyable ridgetop roads in the state. Flat or mildly rolling, we are treated to striking views in all directions. Near the end of the ride, we get to coast downhill for almost 5 miles! Goose Island County Park provides an ideal trailhead, complete with superb wildlife viewing, access to the Mississippi, and camping.

We leave Goose Island and head north on State Highway 35, which has a good shoulder, but stay alert for traffic nonetheless. We turn right at U.S. Highway 14/61 at 1.7 miles and a mile later turn right again at 2.7 onto County MM (Rustic Road 26). This stretch starts with an easy roll to the south past a residential area, then heads east at a high bluff. Thus begins another of those maddening segments: a tough, steep climb on a beautiful road that snakes through some gorgeous scenery—in this case, thick woods. There is no relief in the grade, and

it gets steeper as we go, with switchback turns near the top. The hill finally tops out at mile 4.7, making this a 1.8-mile grind.

But we're more than amply rewarded with some of the best views in the state. To the east are rolling farmland and distant bluffs, and to the west is the Mississippi River Valley. After the exertion of the climb and surrounded by the lovely views, riders deserve to stop and take it all in. We then cruise along gently rolling terrain for a while, passing by a buffalo ranch, then easing into flat stretches of open fields. Other than the possibility of battling some wind up here, it's pretty smooth sailing. At 7.7 miles we pass the Coulee Region Model Airplane field, an open area designated for model plane buffs.

A short descent brings us to the junction with Highway 14/61 at 7.9 miles and the end of the Rustic Road. We go right on Highway 61, watching for traffic and riding single file. There is a welcome wayside at 9.4 for anyone needing a quick break. We leave the highway at 10 miles at Brinkman Ridge Road, turning right and heading west, back in the direction of the Mississippi. This is a nice, smooth little road, traveling past homes scattered hither and yon, then curving past cornfields and over small hills. Views of the tops of many distant bluffs are visible, as well. At 12.5 miles we begin a long descent back into the valley.

We pass a gravel pit halfway down, and from here on the road deteriorates a bit, no doubt from the truck traffic, so use a touch of caution. Then comes the junction with County K at 13.2 miles. Turn right here onto K, and, once again, be alert for traffic. We'll fly down this long hill, following the wonderfully named Chipmunk Coulee Creek to our left and passing a few side roads along the way. We should limit our speed in this area so that we can appreciate all of its spectacular beauty, including neat little homes tucked into hillsides and rugged cliffs jutting out from the bluffs.

We coast nearly all the way back to Highway 35 at 17.3 miles. Carefully cross the highway and return to Goose Island.

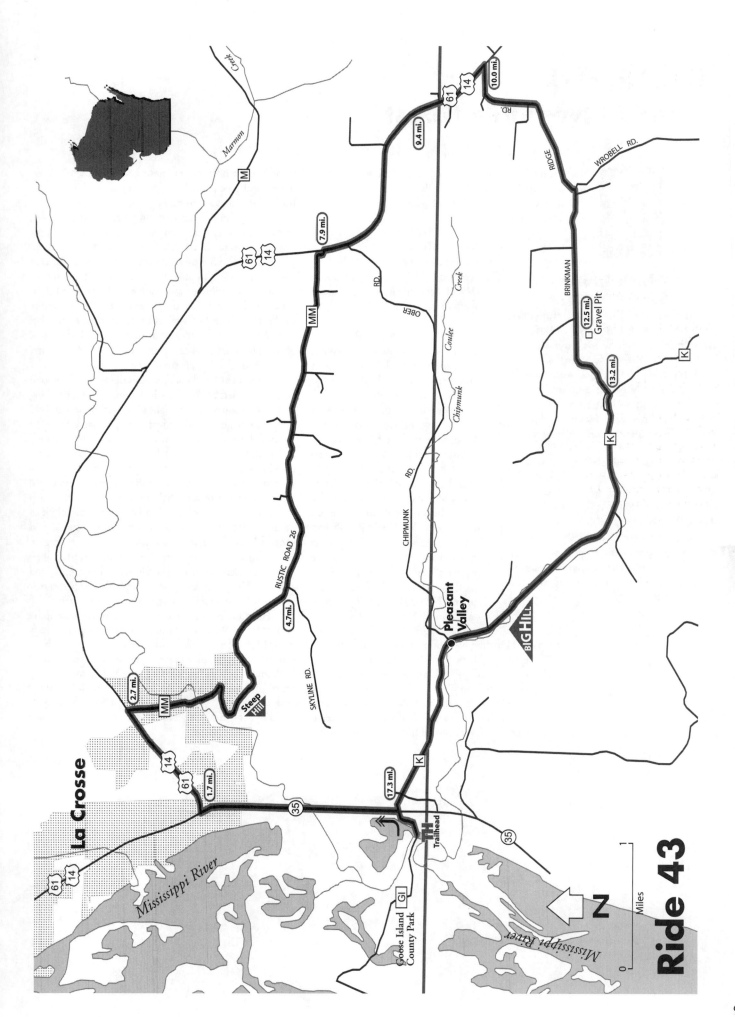

La Crosse

Mississippi River

Mississippi River

Goose Island County Park

Trailhead

Pleasant Valley

Steep Hill

BIG HILL

RUSTIC ROAD 26

SKYLINE RD.

CHIPMUNK RD.

OBER RD.

Coulee Creek

Chipmunk Creek

RIDGE RD.

BRINKMAN RD.

WROBELL RD.

Gravel Pit

Marmon Creek

1.7 mi.
2.7 mi.
4.7 mi.
7.9 mi.
9.4 mi.
10.0 mi.
12.5 mi.
13.2 mi.
17.3 mi.

61 14
61 14
61 14
61
14
M
MM
MM
K
K
K
35
35
GI

N
Miles
0 1

Ride 43

RIDE 44
Black River State Forest

Black River State Forest

The massive Black River State Forest is home to 67,000 acres of flat woodlands, high mounds, ravines, marshes, and boggy lowland. Although the forest has seen extensive logging and ATV traffic, numerous threatened and endangered species rely on it for survival, including the Karner blue butterfly, which is native to this forest.

Recreation is also a big attraction here, with visitors enjoying mountain biking, hiking, camping, hunting, and cross-country skiing. With the wide variety of animal life, wildlife viewing is also popular, especially bird-watching during spring and fall migrations. Routes along the Mississippi Flyway pass over the forest and attract numerous bird species.

Location: Settlement Road in the Black River State Forest, southeast of Black River Falls.
Distance: 24.6 miles out and back.
Pedaling time: 2–2.5 hours.
Surface: Paved roads.
Terrain: Flat.
Sweat factor: Low +.
Trailhead: The junction of County O and Settlement Road, directly north of I-94, near Millston.

Yet another Rustic Road (this time R-54, also known as Settlement Road) is the scene of this ride, which has to rank as one of the quietest and most traffic-free in this guide. We roll along a long path on a road with only a few delicate curves, first through dense forest, then past a sprawling wildlife refuge. The terrain is flat nearly the entire length, with the exception of one moderate hill, and passing vehicles are rare sights. Be prepared for a tranquil ride among local wildlife. Pigeon Creek Campground is situated at the south end of the route and is the perfect place to set up camp for a night or two. Call the forest in advance, (715) 284-1000, if you plan on summer camping—mosquitoes and black flies can send you packing your tent and hurtling back home on the Interstate.

We begin our ride on Settlement Road/Rustic Road 54 where it meets County O. Our northward journey begins on moderately smooth pavement, with dense pine forest whispering along with our tires' steady hum. This is the Black River State Forest, 67,000 acres once covered by an ancient sea. Today the landscape is a mix of flat woodland, sandstone ravines, and marshland. Oak, maple, and pine adorn the high mounds in the area, and the lowland bogs are mostly by white and jack pine.

Pigeon Creek Campground passes by at 1.8 miles, and the road smoothes even more and narrows as it burrows more deeply into thick woods. Look for deer scampering about. At 3.6 miles, on the right, we pass Smrekar Road, which leads to plentiful state-forest hiking, skiing, and mountain-biking trails—some of the best and most varied in the state. The only sizeable hill on this entire road rears up here, but it offers a nice descent on the other side. We reach the trailhead for the Wildcat Trails (more off-road fun) at 4.7 miles. In addition, several ATV routes cross the road along this stretch, so stay alert.

Settlement Road makes a hard right, then very soon afterwards a left at Younkers Road (mile 5). Continuing north, we begin a long, straight stretch with nice views of the area straight ahead and of the 3,700-acre Dike 17 Wildlife Refuge to the west, home to several threatened and endangered species, such as timber wolves, Karner blue butterflies, and a host of other critters. At 9.8 miles we arrive at an access point for the refuge. A stubby observation tower sits in the field a couple of hundred yards to the left, and a quick climb up offers wonderful views of many different varieties of waterfowl, raptors, and songbirds. Look for sandhill cranes, geese, ducks, eagles, cormorants, ruffed grouse, massasauga rattlesnakes, herons, harriers, short-eared owls, deer, otter, mink, and muskrat. This is a special place well worth a stop, so a pair of binoculars would be a fine accessory on this trip.

From the refuge, we continue north through more remote lands. We reach the junction with State Highway 54 at 12.3 miles. This is another wide-open road in both directions, but our plan is to simply do a U-turn and head back south, arriving back at County O, for a total of 24.6 miles, although at times the trip may seem a lot longer than that. At the little town of Millston, just under the I-94 bridge, we can relax and refresh ourselves with some much-needed goodies.

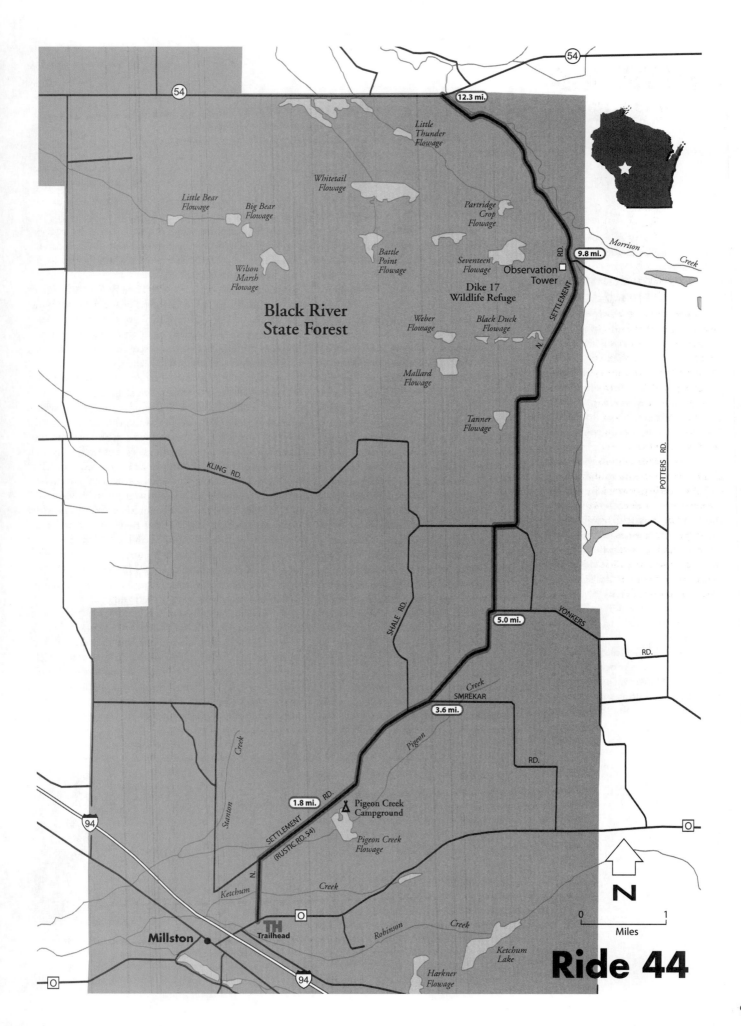

54

54

12.3 mi.

Little
Thunder
Flowage

Whitetail
Flowage

Little Bear
Flowage

Big Bear
Flowage

Partridge
Crop
Flowage

Morrison

Creek

Wilson
Marsh
Flowage

Battle
Point
Flowage

Seventeen
Flowage

9.8 mi.

RD.

Observation
Tower

Black River
State Forest

Dike 17
Wildlife Refuge

Weber
Flowage

Black Duck
Flowage

N. SETTLEMENT

Mallard
Flowage

Tanner
Flowage

POTTERS RD.

KLING RD.

SHALE RD.

YONKERS

5.0 mi.

RD.

Creek

SMREKAR

3.6 mi.

Pigeon

RD.

Creek

1.8 mi.

Pigeon Creek
Campground

SETTLEMENT RD.
(RUSTIC RD. 54)

Stanton

N.

Pigeon Creek
Flowage

O

94

Ketchum

Creek

O

Millston

TH
Trailhead

O

Robinson

Creek

N

Ketchum
Lake

0   1
Miles

Ride 44

94

O

Harkner
Flowage

RIDE 45
An Apple a Day

Trempealeau's Delights

Trempealeau was founded in 1851, just to the south of Perrot State Park, a gem in Wisconsin's park system. It seems that Native Americans and early French explorers regarded the crown of the bluffs along the Mississippi in that area as a "mountain soaking in water," from the original French *la montagne qi trempe à l'eau.* The beautiful "mountain" thus got the name Trempealeau, which it now shares with the tiny town.

The town of Trempealeau sits right alongside the Great River Road, one of the 10 most scenic drives in the nation. In addition to the state park, an expansive prairie spreads to the east, and scenic marshes are nearby, along with two National Wildlife Refuges. You can view a variety of boats, barges, and scenery from the observation tower of Lock and Dam 6, located close to downtown.

Listed on the National Register of Historic Places, the recently renovated Main Street Historic District features gaslight-style lamps and brick walkways to enhance the town's architecture.

Location: County roads between Trempealeau and Galesville.
Distance: 20.8-mile loop.
Pedaling time: 1.75–2.25 hours.
Surface: Paved roads.
Terrain: Flat, with only one big hill.
Sweat factor: Moderate +.
Trailhead: Downtown Trempealeau, where State Highway 35 heads straight east.

This is one of several rides that we take through Wisconsin's gorgeous Coulee Country, amid a string of narrow, hidden valleys that are a delight and a challenge for any rider. This ride is rather tame compared with other coulee excursions, but it provides a glimpse of what the area has to offer. Beginning from the quaint Mississippi River town of Trempealeau, we head north past an apple orchard for some spectacular valley views, although this route takes us on a different series of roads. A spin through the west end of Galesville brings us back through the Caledonia Flats for a splendid trip through diverse terrain. Riders will enjoy plenty of easy, flat riding on this loop, with only one significant climb. Along our route, we'll see just why this area is the place to be for all manner of outdoor recreation; it has been served an extra helping of stunning scenery.

This ride starts by heading east from Trempealeau on State Highway 35 for a half mile to County K. We turn here and follow County K north to a left turn at 1.3 miles on Schubert Road. This is a long, straight, and flat warm-up, passing along cornfields and the town golf course all the way to State Highway 35/54 at 5.1 miles. Watch for traffic on this rather busy highway and turn right; then take a quick left onto Little Tamarack Road, following the sign for Sacia Orchards to the north.

At mile 7.3 the road for the orchards goes off to the left; we continue straight ahead, now in basically an eastern direction, headed for the big bluffs in front of us. The road bends sharply a few times and gently climbs to 8.4 miles and the junction with Sacia Road. A right turn here takes us right through the Sacia Orchards, first passing the large barns and supporting buildings at the base of the hills, then climbing through the orchard's short, gnarly apple trees. This is a long hill, and steep enough to get your attention, but the road surface is sublime and the scenery so pretty the hard work doesn't seem so bad. A sweet descent follows on the opposite side, fast and curvy. Look for the old barn with a cupola on top that makes it look like the Munsters' house.

We reach the junction with County T at 10.7 miles and turn right (south), following a gentle downhill into Galesville at 11.3 miles. A long-ago itinerate preacher, Reverend Van Slyke, claimed, upon seeing this town's heavenly setting, that he had discovered the Garden of Eden. He wasn't far off; the bluffs and rivers here are truly divine. Today the town itself is a collection of historic buildings with loads of small-town charm.

We follow County T as it winds through Galesville to the junction with State Highway 54/93 at 12.3 miles. We hop right across the highway and continue south on County K. There is no shoulder here, but traffic is light. At the junction with County M at 13.6 miles, turn left. Now we start a long haul due south with no curves through cropland and adjacent wetland, with views of distant bluffs along the Mississippi River. Off to our right is the expansive Caledonia Prairie Bottoms, and we keep them in sight all the way to 16.6 miles at 11th Street.

Here we turn right and, on this final westerly stretch, roll over small undulations in the road and pass thick stands of pine in a tree farm. We return to County K at mile 19.6, where we take a left and pedal a little less than 1 mile to Highway 35. After a right, we arrive back at the trailhead at 20.8 miles.

By the way, for an overnight stay in Trempealeau, check out the historic Trempealeau Hotel. The 1871 building was moved to its present location by a team of horses after a fire burned through town. There is a trading post on the property where you can rent bikes and canoes; call (608) 534-6898 for more information.

Sacia Road winding through the apple orchards northeast of Trempealeau.

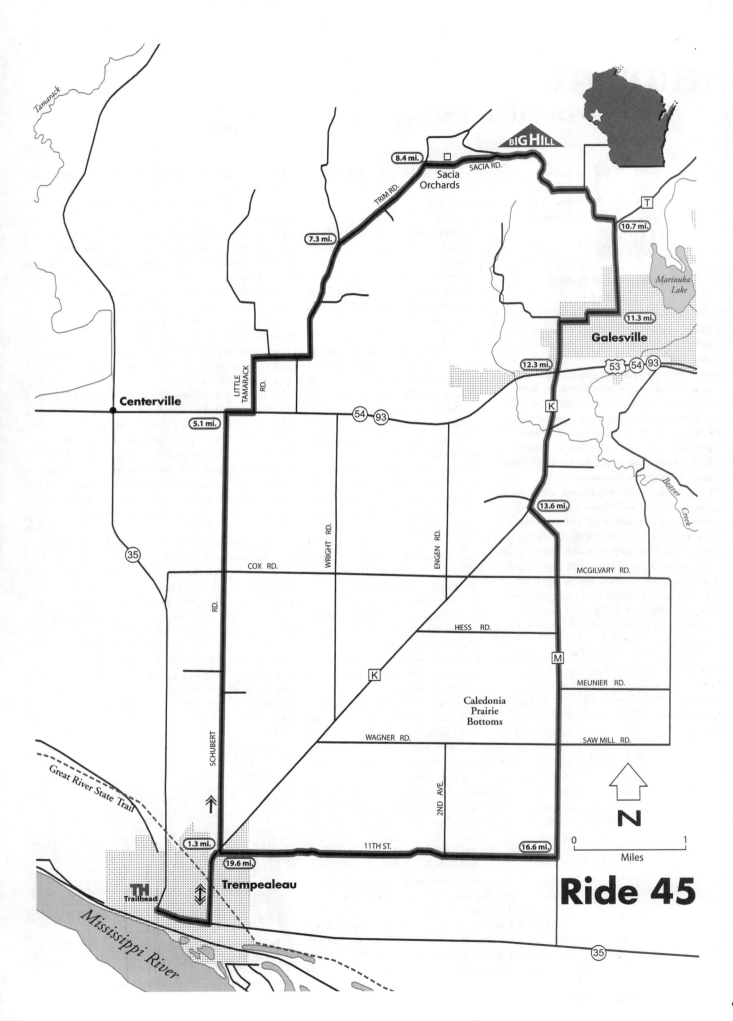

Tamarack

biG**HILL**

8.4 mi.

SACIA RD.

Sacia
Orchards

TRIM RD.

7.3 mi.

T

10.7 mi.

Marinuka
Lake

11.3 mi.

Galesville

LITTLE TAMARACK RD.

Centerville

5.1 mi.

54 93

12.3 mi.

53 54 93

K

35

13.6 mi.

Beaver Creek

COX RD.

WRIGHT RD.

ENGEN RD.

MCGILVARY RD.

HESS RD.

SCHUBERT RD.

K

M

MEUNIER RD.

Caledonia
Prairie
Bottoms

SAW MILL RD.

Great River State Trail

WAGNER RD.

2ND AVE.

N

0   1

Miles

1.3 mi.

11TH ST.

16.6 mi.

19.6 mi.

TH
Trailhead

Trempealeau

Ride 45

Mississippi River

35

RIDE 46
Garden of Eden Excursion

Location: Rural roads between Galesville and Ettrick.
Distance: 23.7-mile loop.
Pedaling time: 2–2.5 hours.
Surface: Paved roads.

Terrain: Hilly, with several long, difficult climbs; some flatter sections near Galesville.
Sweat factor: High.
Trailhead: West end of Galesville at the intersection of West Ridge Road and County T.

Trempealeau County

The Driftless Area. Coulee Country. This is arguably the most stunning area of Wisconsin. When the glaciers were sculpting the land 10,000 years ago, they skipped this part of the state and left behind hills and valleys and rolling countryside that simply radiate with pastoral splendor. Bordered by four rivers—the Mississippi, the Trempealeau, the Black, and the Buffalo—Trempealeau County captivates visitors with picturesque terrain and panoramic views, all shared with an abundance of wildlife like deer, wild turkey, hawks and eagles, fox, songbirds, and a host of others. Cyclists will enjoy flat, valley roads, challenging climbs 2-miles long, flat and rolling ridgetop roads, and thrilling descents down curving roads into the next valley or village.

This is a fantastic ride through some of the most remote lands in Trempealeau County. We'll ride through croplands at first, then into a dense forest with leg-testing climbs. There are several long, flatter stretches along the way that afford some relief. With the exception of a short section of gravel, the roads are in perfect condition for an all-around great ride. The toughest part of the ride may be actually leaving quaint Galesville. This is a gorgeous old town, with many buildings listed on the National Register of Historic Places and impeccably preserved places like the A. A. Arnold farmstead and the Gale College Historic Site. The staggering beauty of the rolling hills and fields, thick forests, clear streams, and rugged cliffs caused an itinerate preacher to think he had discovered the Garden of Eden. Check www.trempealeaucounty tourism.com for additional information.

We begin this ride in Galesville by following County T north out of town for 2.2 miles to a right turn on Zabrowski Lane, a short spur road that leads to U.S. Highway 53. After the mandatory check for traffic, we take a left turn and go a few hundred yards north to Crystal Valley Road. We turn right and follow the road east from the highway past scattered farms and wooded bluffs. At 5 miles and Cory Road on the left, Crystal Valley Road takes a hard right and begins a curvy path toward some high bluffs.

One mile later, we begin our first big climb up Peacock Hill. It's only about a half mile long, but it's steep. On the other side, we are rewarded with a nice descent, which is steeper than the climb, along with some sharp turns for good measure. We coast up to the junction with Skunk Coulee Road at 7.3 miles. Keeping to the left, we immediately start to climb a hill longer than the first. As the road levels near the top, it turns to gravel. This unpleasant stretch is mercifully short, and, besides, there are beautiful views to behold on your right. We reach North

Ridge Road at 8.3 miles, which calls for a left turn to the north.

A long, fast descent on perfect pavement greets us on this road, and we fly to 8.7 miles and the junction with County DD. We take another left turn and are soon greeted by another mile-long climb up tight turns through thick woods. Chances are that you'll meet few other people along here, so enjoy the solitude. Another screaming descent follows the climb and finally levels out as we follow a small stream flowing toward Ettrick. The junction with County D comes along at 12.3 miles, and we take this road to the left (west) for 1 mile to Dopp Road, where we turn left. The town of Ettrick is only another mile north on County D if you're in need of a break or some sustenance.

Heading south, we encounter a fun stretch of road passing by wooded farmland and homes nestled in the big bluffs. Once again we are surrounded by high hills as the road makes its way up another long climb to the 15-mile mark. There are views in all directions up here; be sure to stop a minute and look around. The ensuing descent is such a blast that you might want to turn around and ride back up to do it again. Several sweeping turns are perfect for leaning your bike into them and rocketing back out the other side. We keep flying downhill all the way to Highway 53 at 17.2 miles—a *2-mile* descent.

We turn right on Highway 53 and ride north to 17.5 miles to a left turn on County TT, then another left at County T. We head south back to Galesville on relatively level ground now, passing farms, a wetland area, and cropland. After passing Zabrowski Lane at 21.5 miles, it's an easy spin back to Galesville at 23.7 miles.

For maximum enjoyment, try to arrange your ride close to the first Saturday in October. That's when Galesville holds its Apple Affair, a popular gala celebrating the fall season. A huge, 10-foot apple pie covers the downtown square, and displays from local craftsmen, food stands, and a country market surround the square. There's a bike tour for us and a hearty breakfast and lunch, as well.

A familiar scene in Trempealeau County.

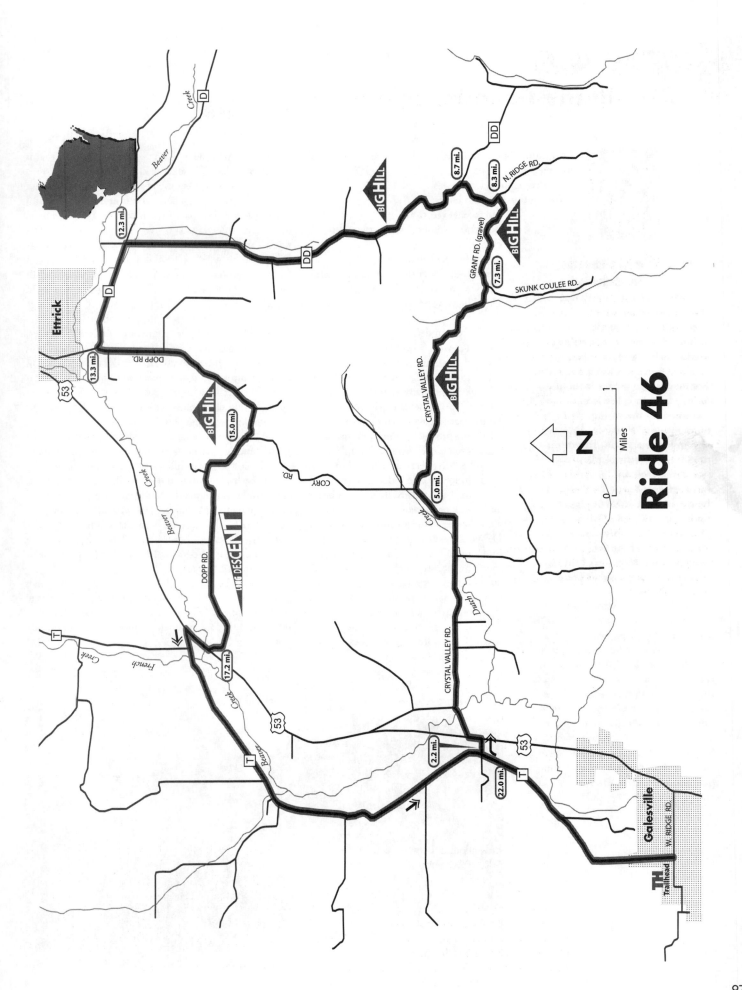

Ride 46

N

Miles

RIDE 47
Oak Ridge Delight

A Bike-Friendly County

Trempealeau County has no fewer than 14 designated bicycle loops within its boundaries. Add to these the nearly 400 miles of paved back roads, and you have a county that's a biker's paradise. One invaluable local resource for finding a route is the ride guide published by the county. The guide includes ride descriptions with maps and hand-drawn pictures by local schoolchildren. Several of the Trempealeau rides in this book are based on those in the guide, with a few detours or modifications. Call (715) 538-2311 for more information and a detailed map of the loops. Also check out the Web site of the Bicycle Club of Trempealeau County (www.ridebctc.com).

Local cyclists want the riding opportunities to be even better. To do so, local groups have organized the Tour de Trempealeau, a one- to three-day bike tour on the county's most scenic roads. It took place for the first time in September 2003 and is planned as an annual event. Proceeds from the event will go toward improving bicycling in the county. The ride is stocked with rest stops, and support vehicles roam the route to aid stragglers.

Location: County and back roads between Ettrick and Arcadia.
Distance: 13-mile loop.
Pedaling time: 1–1.25 hours.
Surface: Paved roads.
Terrain: Rolling, with two difficult climbs.
Sweat factor: Moderate +.
Trailhead: French Creek Lutheran Church on County T, 1.5 miles north of U.S. Highway 53.

After a quiet start, this ride gets interesting, with a scenic cruise through lowland areas and a long, winding climb up and over a ridge. A ride into a postcard-like scene halfway through leads to an exhilarating descent past picturesque farmsteads and a long coast to the finish. The route provides connections to several rides covered elsewhere in this guide.

We leave French Creek Lutheran Church, located on County T, and ride north on T past fields of corn and beans and a local paintball site. Only a half mile along, we reach the junction with County D. We turn left here, then lean left again on County T/D as County I appears on the right. This is a slightly rolling stretch, curving and bending around tall bluffs and rocky cliffs. Lowland areas to the right usually offer glimpses of wildlife. At 3.4 miles, we arrive at the intersection where T splits from D and goes left. We

follow T, a brand-new (2003) piece of pavement that is oh-so velvety, and the road makes all kinds of tight turns to keep us guessing what might be around the next bend.

At 4.3 miles, we encounter our first climb, long but not too steep; there is a fun descent on the other side, offering up some fantastic views of the rolling countryside to the west. At mile 7.2, we arrive at Oak Ridge Drive and turn left. (If we continue to the right on County T for 6 miles, we would end up in Arcadia; with more than 2,000 residents, it's the largest community in Trempealeau County.) The conditions on Oak Ridge Drive are what we came for: silky-smooth pavement, narrow, winding roads both up and down, stunning scenery, and no automobiles. The first stretch of this road winds up a long, tough climb past a deserted farmstead with an old barn and a house that collapsed right on its foundation. The place looks as old as these hills. High bluffs rise up all around us as the scenery changes back to fields of corn and farms along the top of the ridge.

At Linrude Road and 10 miles, we head left down a white-knuckle descent on steep grades and sharp curves. Near the bottom of the hill is a storybook homestead burrowed way back into a fold in the bluff. It's not too much of a stretch to imagine the residents sitting out front on the porch, whittling, maybe, and watching the crazy cyclists whiz by. We leave this idyllic setting and cruise along easy rollers and even some flats past a few more farms and fields of corn to 13 miles and our return to French Creek Church.

Check the map in the Trempealeau County bike guide for more great ride options or additional mileage on this route. Try Oak Ridge Drive farther south, for example, and explore the many coulees and other hidden roads in the area.

Oak Ridge Drive southeast of Arcadia.

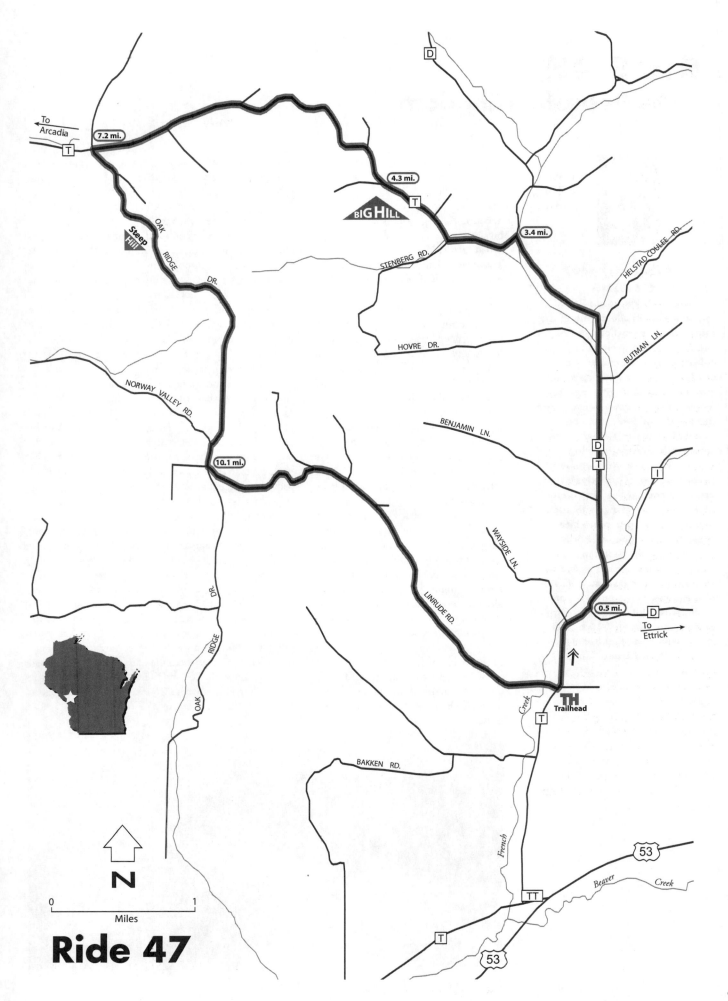

To
Arcadia

7.2 mi.

T

D

4.3 mi.

T

BIG HILL

Steep
Hill

3.4 mi.

OAK RIDGE DR.

STENBERG RD.

HELSTAD COULEE RD.

HOVRE DR.

BUTMAN LN.

NORWAY VALLEY RD.

BENJAMIN LN.

D
T

I

10.1 mi.

WAYSIDE LN.

OAK RIDGE DR.

LINRUDE RD.

0.5 mi.

D

To
Ettrick

Creek

TH
Trailhead

T

BAKKEN RD.

French

53

N

TT

Beaver Creek

0   1
Miles

T

53

Ride 47

RIDE 48
The Peaceful Kingdom

Location: Hilly county roads south of Arcadia.
Distance: 25.7-mile loop.
Pedaling time: 2.25–2.75 hours.
Surface: Paved roads.

Terrain: Rolling, with several medium hills and one very difficult climb.
Sweat factor: High.
Trailhead: Memorial Park in Arcadia, a half mile south of Main Street.

Honoring Our Heroes

Arcadia's Memorial Park is the little-known site of one of the most unique attractions in Wisconsin. The 54-acre park contains a collection of monuments and statues honoring our nation's fighting men and women, with specific memorials dedicated to every conflict the United States has participated in since the middle of the nineteenth century. Running through the park, the Avenue of Heroes walkway provides easy access to each of the memorials. It's laid out in meters, with each one representing a year since Arcadia was founded in 1854.

Many of the monuments contain the names of area residents who served in the wars. There are also tributes to the early accomplishments of area settlers. Other artifacts include an F-16 fighter jet, as well as a steel beam from the 9/11 World Trade Center tragedy.

This is one of the classic loops in Trempealeau County. It's got extraordinary scenery, excellent roads, fun descents, and rolling terrain. It also has one of the most difficult climbs in the entire state. At the end of the loop is a 2-mile downhill to the finish. This is a challenging and rewarding ride, so be prepared to be entertained. With a population of more than 2,000, Arcadia is the largest town in the county and offers plenty of choices for food and other recreational activities, including Memorial Park (see the sidebar).

From Memorial Park on the south edge of town, we ride south on County J, passing Calvary Cemetery and encountering a warm-up climb to 2.3 miles. A long coast on the other side winds through rolling farmland, with steep bluffs to the left and more of them way off to our right. This entire western half of the loop follows rolling terrain to mile 8.2, and here the road takes a sweeping curve up a bluff and up switchbacks into the woods near the top, followed by another exhilarating downhill into the tiny town of Dodge at 12.7 miles. We ride through this one-block-long town and continue on County J to the left, crossing the railroad tracks twice and passing the Dodge Sportsman's Club Park along the way. Just past the park we start a medium-steep climb and break out into open fields again.

We reach the junction with County G at 14.3 miles and turn left, now heading north toward Pine Creek. At 15.7 miles, we roll through this little burg, following the road to a right turn about a third of a mile later onto Pine Creek Ridge Road, as County G angles off to the left. This is an exquisite stretch of pavement that runs north along Pine Creek just off to our left. All around us are steep, wooded bluffs, with a host of trickling streams, a land seemingly populated only by wildlife and cows and horses wandering in the fields.

At this point, we need a little challenge to go with all that beauty, what with the dense forest crowding the road and exquisite glimpses of the valley below. As we pass the front door of a farmhouse at 17.5 miles, the grade of the road increases to about nine percent, without so much as a short, flat stretch to relieve the misery. And it gets steeper: closer to the top the grade reaches a painful 15 percent or so. Then, we finally crawl to the top at 20.2 miles, where at last we can catch our breath and take in big gulps of oxygen.

Soon after, turn right on County G (there might not be a sign), which appears again. Now we're riding along Arcadia Ridge through cornfields. The views are amazing and stretch far into the distance in all directions. This is also a great spot for spying raptors overhead. At 22 miles, we'll turn left onto Meyers Valley Road, where that inevitable long descent occurs. Hold on for a 2-mile downhill run with a few curves providing even more fun. We're dropping 600 feet so we need to be sure to control our speed. Then we coast onto the flats below and roll up to the junction with County J and Calvary Cemetery at 24.9 miles. This is where we take a right turn back to Memorial Park for a total of 25.7 miles.

Meyers Valley Road on the way back to Arcadia.

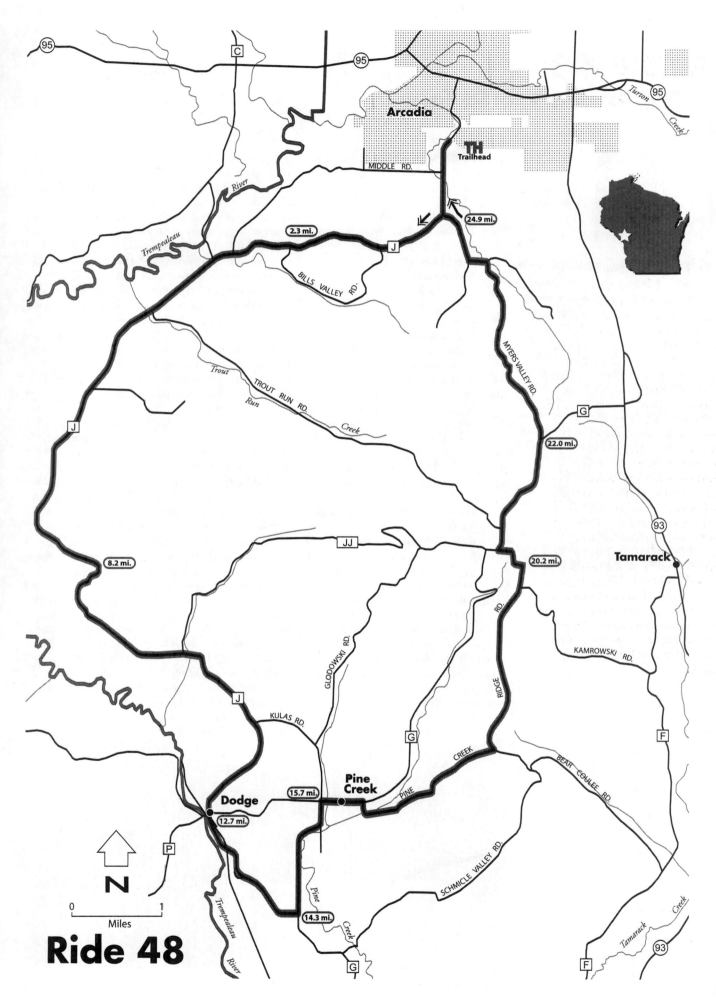

Ride 48

RIDE 49
Top-of-the-World Tour

Location: Hills and dales between Arcadia and Independence.
Distance: 24.7-mile loop.
Pedaling time: 2–2.5 hours.

Surface: Paved roads.
Terrain: Rolling, with one long climb.
Sweat factor: Moderate.
Trailhead: The junction of State Highways 93 and 95 on the northeast edge of Arcadia.

Historic Independence

On the north end of this loop is the town of Independence. Several outstanding historic buildings are here, including the restored 1902 City Hall and Opera House (that's one building, not two), and the handsome architecture of the 1895 Saints Peter and Paul Catholic Church. The clock tower at the top of the city hall has been a proud landmark for the small city for a hundred years. The Wisconsin Historical Society has called it "the most visible outstanding government building in Trempealeau County." The City Hall and Opera House is also at the heart of the town's rich past, and the local government and residents made a commitment to restore this historical landmark, having raised money and donated their time to bring the regal building back to life.

Climbing to the top of Trempealeau County's longest continuous ridge is the centerpiece of this ride. In fact, one biking group has named their tour of the area the Top-of-the-World Tour. True to its name, the ride has views along the way that are among the most stunning in the state. Overall, the terrain is rolling, but the hills (with the exception of the one big climb already noted) are more fun than they are taxing. Prepare to be delighted with the changing terrain, especially the hills, with their exhilarating ups and downs.

From Arcadia, we head east on the wide shoulder of State Highway 95 for eight-tenths of a mile to River Valley Road, where we make a left turn and cruise another eight-tenths of a mile to North Creek Road. We take a right turn and head in the direction of the bluffs up ahead, following North Creek on our left and large hills accompanying us to the right. The scattered homes here are in an area known to locals as Hooterville.

At the junction with Pyka Road at mile 6, we turn right onto silky pavement and climb up from the creek valley to the junction with County N. Here, we turn left and start a long, gradual climb, winding through dense forest, to 9.1 miles and a left on Square Bluff Road. After about 10 feet we are treated to incredible views of the bluffs in the distance and the valleys below. And the best part is that we're going downhill, coasting for quite a stretch and passing an old, vine-covered windmill on a hill over our right shoulders.

Traveling over the longest continuous ridgetop in Trempealeau County, the road offers amazing views of a countryside mixed with small patches of hardwood forest and rolling fields of corn and wheat. A good climb back up takes us to more dreamy views until we come to the junction with Nelson Road on the right at 11.5 miles. We stay left on Square Bluff Road to another fork, this time with Carston Road, at 12, but we continue left on Square Bluff.

At 13.2 miles we come to a confusing intersection with multiple choices. We simply keep on going straight ahead on what is now Kurth Valley Road, dropping down into the scenic terrain we were just recently admiring from up high. This is another fun road, curving and hopping northwest on little rollers through woods at first, then heading back into farmland. We arrive at County Q at mile 15.4 and follow Q to another left at 16.2 at River Valley Road, where we begin cruising south. The road here climbs gently, then travels through more farmland, crossing Plum Creek at 15.8 miles.

From here, it's a roller-coaster jaunt over hills and past farms, forests, and bluffs. On the entire stretch, we are never far from the scenic Trempealeau River flowing to our right. At 22.6 miles, we cross North Creek, followed very soon thereafter on the left by North Creek Road, which we had tackled earlier. We continue south on River Valley Road to Highway 95 at 23.9 miles. We make a right turn and head back to Arcadia, completing a marvelous 24.7-mile loop.

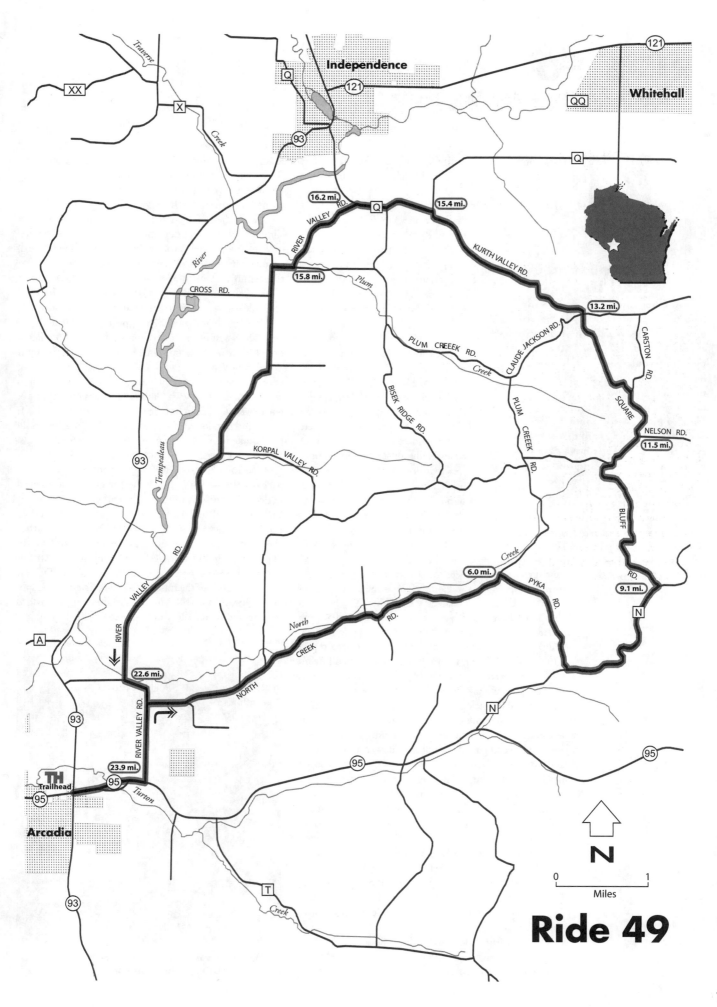

Ride 49

RIDE 50
Fountain of Youth

Trempealeau Trail Help

Another reason for cyclists to love Trempealeau County is the presence of trail stewards on each of the county's 14 loops. Over 250 residents along the routes act as volunteers to lend assistance with directions, repairs, first aid, food, and water. Little blue signs posted along the way identify them. Also, about 130 area businesses offer special discounts to cyclists. These groups have also been instrumental in planning and designing the routes. It is a rare and welcome treat for an area to go the extra mile for our sport.

Location: Rolling county roads near Fountain City, Dodge, and Pine Creek in Buffalo and Trempealeau Counties.

Distance: 35.6-mile loop.

Pedaling time: 3–3.75 hours.

Surface: Paved roads.

Terrain: Rolling, with one very challenging climb.

Sweat factor: High.

Trailhead: The junction of State Highway 35 and County YY in Fountain City.

We chose this loop with a tail for one simple reason: to ride up Glodowski Road. Reputed to be one of the toughest climbs in the state, Glodowski has earned the respect of even the hardiest riders around. Complete with switchback turns, this monster reaches grades of *25 percent!* County G rewards our Herculean effort with a very long descent back to level ground, but there's always the final ascent of Buffalo Ridge Road, no slouch either in dishing out the pain.

To warm up properly for this one, we should probably cruise along State Highway 35 for a spell to get those legs ready, because this ride is tough from the first mile. On County YY, at the south edge of Fountain City, we pedal east and immediately begin climbing a long hill. We eventually reach the top of a hill at 1.8 miles and come to the junction with County M. We go right here and roll on a mildly flat ridgetop past cornfields and farms, then the road hops up and down some exciting rollers to 4.3 miles, where County M turns to the right. We take a left turn here, however, and go down a road that takes us past more cornfields and farms.

Less than 1 mile later, Brandhorst Valley Road turns left and we keep going on what is now Plattes Valley Road. The road goes downhill in a hurry on steep curves and poor pavement into a scenic, wooded valley, so we need to control our speed. We roll onto shiny new pavement toward the bottom of the hill and then enjoy a relaxing cruise from here all the way to County P at 7.7 miles. Let's turn left here and head north along the valley floor between bluffs, past wetlands and lowland crop fields. The little town of Dodge arrives at 9.1 miles, where we cross the railroad tracks and take a right on County J, leaving town almost as soon as we got there. Just past the Dodge Sportsmen's Club Park, we head up a short climb and follow a couple of curves to the junction with County G at 10.6.

After turning left, we follow the arrow for Pine Creek. At 12 miles the main road takes a hard right into this tiny town, but we continue straight ahead on Kulas Road to 12.6 miles, then turn right onto Glodowski Road. This stretch seems benign enough as we roll along the flats between bluffs, eye cows in the pasture, and watch horses frolic in the fields.

Well, the fun's over. At 14 miles, the road starts to climb. After one short downhill section, the road switches back and then ascends with a vengeance. Toiling upward, we pass a house and hit the wall. One consolation is that this climb isn't as long as some of the others in this book—but it's small consolation when our body is screaming to stop. The steepest part is here—so push that gear over, pull on the handlebar, push on the pedal.

The worst of the suffering ends at about 15 miles, a little less than a mile up. Finally, at 15.3 miles, it's over. We turn right on County JJ and get a nice reward for our efforts: a sweet road with a blacktop surface laid down in 2003. The junction with County G comes up at mile 16, where we take a right and begin a joyous descent. This is a long and fast downhill with switchback turns that could be mistaken for those seen in more mountainous areas. Watch your speed on this one.

We roll into Pine Creek at 20, then retrace our route back to the junction with County J at 21.8. Here we need to decide if we want to turn right and go back to Dodge and County P, and face another big climb up Buffalo Ridge, or continue south on G to Highway 35. After choosing the latter, we enjoy a mostly downhill run to Highway 35 at 25.8 miles. After a right turn here, we follow the highway northwest back to County YY near Fountain City and the trailhead at 35.6. The 10-mile spin on Highway 35 isn't the most enjoyable, but the road is smooth and there is an ample shoulder.

Rounding a curve on the Great River Road amidst gorgeous Mississippi River scenery.

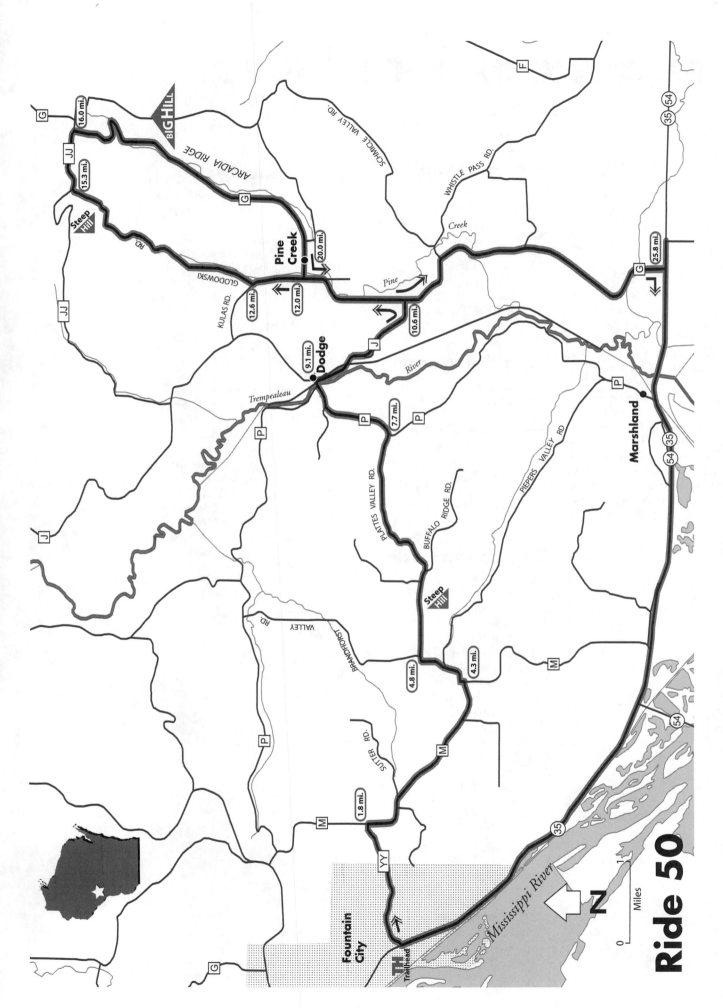

Ride 50

SHORT INDEX OF RIDES

WISCONSIN BIKE SHOPS

Here is a short list of bike shops in the vicinity of many of rides in this book. Remember that bike shops come and go, and a shop you visited yesterday might not be there next time. Call ahead before making a trip.

Northern Wisconsin

Bay City Bicycles
412 West Main Street
Ashland 54806
(715) 682-2091

Marinette Cycle Center
1555 Pierce Avenue
Marinette 54143
(715) 735-5442

Mel's Trading Post
105 South Brown Street
Rhinelander 54501
(800) 236-MELS

Riverbrook Bike and Ski
102 East Maple Street
Spooner 54801
(715) 635-2134

Seeley Hills Ski & Bike
US 63 and County OO
Hayward 54843
(715) 634-3539

Central Wisconsin

Bike Doctor
421 Water Street
Eau Claire 54703
(715) 835-4812

Harbor Bike
112 South Main Street
Waupaca 54981
(715) 258-5404

Hostel Shoppe
929 Main Street
Stevens Point 54481
(800) 233-4340

Red Cedar Outfitters
910 Hudson Road
Menomonie 54751
(715) 235-3866

Spring Street Sports, Inc.
12 West Spring Street
Chippewa Falls 54729
(715) 723-6616

Southeast Wisconsin

The Bikesmiths
2865 North Murray Avenue
Milwaukee 53211
(414) 332-1330

The Fitness Store
1208 South 10th Street
Manitowoc 54221
(920) 684-8808

The Fitness Store
1611 Washington Street
Two Rivers 54241
(920) 794-2245

Quiet Hut Sports
186 West Main
Whitewater 53190
(262) 473-2950

REI
7483 West Towne Way
Madison 53719
(608) 833-6680

Sport Haven
Highways 12 and 33
Baraboo 53913
(608) 356-9218

Spring City Cycle
1314 South West Avenue
Waukesha 53186
(414) 544-5004

Torque Center USA
14666 West National Avenue
New Berlin 53151
(414) 786-4420

Trek Bicycle Store
652 West Washington
Madison 53703
(608) 833-8735

Wheel & Sprocket
6955 North Port Washington Road
Milwaukee 53217
(414) 247-8100

Wheel & Sprocket
1001 Milwaukee Avenue
South Milwaukee 53172
(414) 762-6000

Southwest Wisconsin

Backroad Bicycles
170 Richland Square
Richland Center 53581
(608) 647-4636

Speed's Bicycle Sales
1126 John Street
Sparta 54656
(608) 269-2315

Valley Ski & Bike
321 Main Street
La Crosse 54601
(608) 782-5500

BIKING WEB SITES

Visit these Internet sites for all kinds of great information on bicycling safety, advocacy, places to ride, events listings, and a lot more.

National Sites

Pedestrian and Bicycle Information Center
www.bicyclinginfo.org
Promotes safe places for walking and riding.

League of American Bicyclists
www.bikeleague.org
Promotes riding for fun, fitness, and transportation; also big on advocacy and education.

U.S. Department of Transportation
www.nhtsa.dot.gov
Government site focused on reducing accidents. Includes information on bicycling publications and safety issues.

www.bicycle-rides.com
Type in a state for the latest on organized rides and area bike clubs and shops.

Wisconsin Sites

Bicycle Federation of Wisconsin
www.bfw.org
Much of the same info as the League of American Bicyclists, along with an events calendar and bicycling articles.

www.danenet.wicip.org
Great site devoted to riding in Madison and Dane County. Includes links to hundreds of bicycling-related sites.

www.bikewisconsin.com
Information on Wisconsin's two major cross-state bicycle tours and the Bike Wisconsin Education and Action Coalition.

Miscellaneous

www.peteandedbooks.com
The place to go for books, videos, gifts, and loads of other cycling goodies.

MORE
GREAT TITLES
FROM TRAILS BOOKS & PRAIRIE OAK PRESS

Activity Guides

Great Cross-Country Ski Trails: Wisconsin, Minnesota, Michigan & Ontario,
Wm. Chad McGrath

Great Minnesota Walks: 49 Strolls, Rambles, Hikes, and Treks,
Wm. Chad McGrath

Great Wisconsin Walks: 45 Strolls, Rambles, Hikes, and Treks,
Wm. Chad McGrath

Paddling Illinois: 64 Great Trips by Canoe and Kayak, Mike Svob

Paddling Southern Wisconsin: 82 Great Trips by Canoe and Kayak,
Mike Svob

Paddling Northern Wisconsin: 82 Great Trips by Canoe and Kayak,
Mike Svob

Wisconsin Underground: A Guide to Caves, Mines, and Tunnels in
and around the Badger State, Doris Green

Minnesota Underground & the Best of the Black Hills: A Guide to
Mines, Sinks, Caves, and Disappearing Streams, Doris Green

Travel Guides

Great Little Museums of the Midwest, Christine des Garennes

Great Minnesota Weekend Adventures, Beth Gauper

The Great Wisconsin Touring Book: 30 Spectacular Auto Tours,
Gary Knowles

Tastes of Minnesota: A Food Lover's Tour, Donna Tabbert Long

Wisconsin Lighthouses: A Photographic and Historical Guide,
Ken and Barb Wardius

Wisconsin Waterfalls, Patrick Lisi

Wisconsin Family Weekends: 20 Fun Trips for You and the Kids,
Susan Lampert Smith

County Parks of Wisconsin, Revised Edition, Jeannette and Chet Bell

Up North Wisconsin: A Region for All Seasons, Sharyn Alden

Great Wisconsin Taverns: 101 Distinctive Badger Bars, Dennis Boyer

Great Weekend Adventures, the Editors of Wisconsin Trails

Eating Well in Wisconsin, Jerry Minnich

Acorn Guide to Northwest Wisconsin, Tim Bewer

Nature Essays

Wild Wisconsin Notebook, James Buchholz

Trout Friends, Bill Stokes

Northern Passages: Reflections from Lake Superior Country,
Michael Van Stappen

River Stories: Growing Up on the Wisconsin, Delores Chamberlain

Home & Garden

Wisconsin Country Gourmet, Marge Snyder & Suzanne Breckenridge
Wisconsin Herb Cookbook, Marge Snyder & Suzanne Breckenridge
Creating a Perennial Garden in the Midwest, Joan Severa
Wisconsin Garden Guide, Jerry Minnich
Bountiful Wisconsin: 110 Favorite Recipes, Terese Allen
Wisconsin's Hometown Flavors, Terese Allen

Historical Books

Prairie Whistles: Tales of Midwest Railroading, Dennis Boyer
Barns of Wisconsin, Jerry Apps
Portrait of the Past: A Photographic Journey Through Wisconsin
1865-1920, Howard Mead, Jill Dean, and Susan Smith
Wisconsin: The Story of the Badger State, Norman K. Risjord
Wisconsin At War: 20th Century Conflicts
Through the Eyes of Veterans, Dr. James F. McIntosh

Gift Books

The Spirit of Door County: A Photographic Essay, Darryl R. Beers
Milwaukee, Photography by Todd Dacquisto
Duck Hunting on the Fox: Hunting and
Decoy-Carving Traditions, Stephen M. Miller
Spirit of the North: A Photographic Journey Through Northern
Wisconsin, Richard Hamilton Smith

Ghost Stories

Haunted Wisconsin, Michael Norman and Beth Scott
W-Files: True Reports of Wisconsin's
Unexplained Phenomena, Jay Rath
The Beast of Bray Road: Tailing Wisconsin's
Werewolf, Linda S. Godfrey
Giants in the Land: Folktales and Legends of Wisconsin, Dennis Boyer

For a free catalog, phone, write, or e-mail us.

Trails Books
P.O. Box 317, Black Earth, WI 53515
(800) 236-8088 • e-mail: books@wistrails.com
www.trailsbooks.com